Date Due

Walls Built on Sand

Walls Built on Sand

Migration, Exclusion, and Society in Kuwait

Anh Nga Longva

WestviewPress

A Division of HarperCollins*Publishers*

Copyright © 1997 by Westview Press, A Division of HarperCollins Publishers, Inc.

Published in 1997 in the United States of America by Westview Press, 5500 Central Avenue, Boulder, Colorado 80301-2877, and in the United Kingdom by Westview Press, 12 Hid's Copse Road, Cumnor Hill, Oxford OX2 9JJ

Library of Congress Cataloging-in-Publication Data
Lonva, Anh Nga,
  Walls built on sand : migration, exclusion, and society in Kuwait
/ Anh Nga Longva.
    p. cm.
  Includes bibliographical references and index.
  ISBN 0-8133-2758-X (hc)
  1. Kuwait—Emigration and immigration. 2. Alien labor—Kuwait.
3. Kuwait—Population. 4. Kuwait—Ethnic relations. 5. Kuwait—Social conditions.
I. Title.
JV875.8.A3L66   1997
304.8'5367—dc21   96-49172
                                                                          CIP

The paper used in this publication meets the requirements of the American National Standard for Permanence of Paper for Printed Library Materials Z39.48-1984.

10   9   8   7   6   5   4   3   2   1

Contents

v

Tables and Figure

Tables

Figure

Acknowledgments

Many people have contributed to the making of this study.

In Kuwait, I wish to thank particularly Fatima Ahmed from the *Arab Times*, who shared with me her unique and comprehensive knowledge of migrant conditions and expatriate life, and Bazza Al Batini, who, through her friendship and scholarship, has done more than anyone to help me understand and respect Kuwait and its traditions. I am also grateful to Badria Al Awadi, Shamlan Al Essa, Mohammad Al Haddad, and Suleiman Khalaf from Kuwait University. Jan Braathu and Guri Bergvoll from the Norwegian Embassy went out of their way to help me on my field trip in 1991; Jan and his wife, Iqbal, back in Norway, have assisted me in many more ways. I want to express my deep appreciation to all three for their support and their friendship. Most of all, I am grateful to the many men and women in Kuwait—Kuwaitis and expatriates—who made me feel welcomed, trusted me, and willingly let me inquire into their lives.

Outside Kuwait, my warmest thanks go to Unni Wikan; as the supervisor of my dissertation on which this book is based, she has witnessed its birth and has helped ease its growing pains. I am also indebted to Sharon Stanton Russell, Frederik Barth, Arjun Appadurai, and Axel Sommerfelt, whose constructive criticisms and generous encouragement have been invaluable to me. Finally, Harald Eidheim, Thomas Hylland Eriksen, Randi Kaarhus, Jon Schackt, and Long Litt Woon have taken time from their busy schedules to read and discuss my work and helped to sort out my various analytical and existential puzzlements along the way. Each of the friends and colleagues above has, in her or his own way, helped me better to formulate my thoughts and ground my arguments. None, of course, is to be held accountable for my conclusions.

This book was written while I was affiliated with the Norwegian Institute of International Affairs where I greatly benefited from the interdisciplinary environment. I am also indebted to Eilert Struksnes for his editorial advice, to Liv Høivik who prepared the final typescript, and to Ole Dahl-Gulliksen who drew the maps. The following institutions in Norway have financed the last part of my project: the Research Council of Norway (NFR), the Nansen Fund, the Institute of Comparative Research in Human Culture, and the Royal Ministry of Foreign Affairs.

The NFR and the Institute of Comparative Research in Human Culture have also generously contributed to the publication of this book.

Last but not least, I want to thank my husband, Hans Wilhelm, and our children, Tania and Stian. Kuwait, through peace and war and with all its facets, was our common undertaking. Without their presence by my side and their continuous support, this book could not have been written. It is therefore dedicated to them as a token of my love and gratitude.

Anh Nga Longva
Oslo, Norway

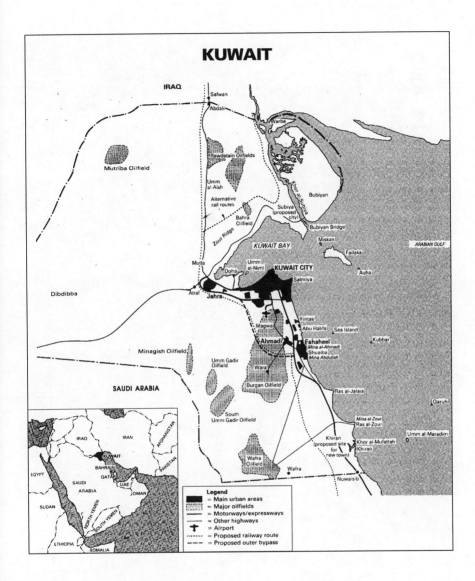

Source: Adapted from Kuwait: A MEED Practical Gudie, pp. viii and ix.

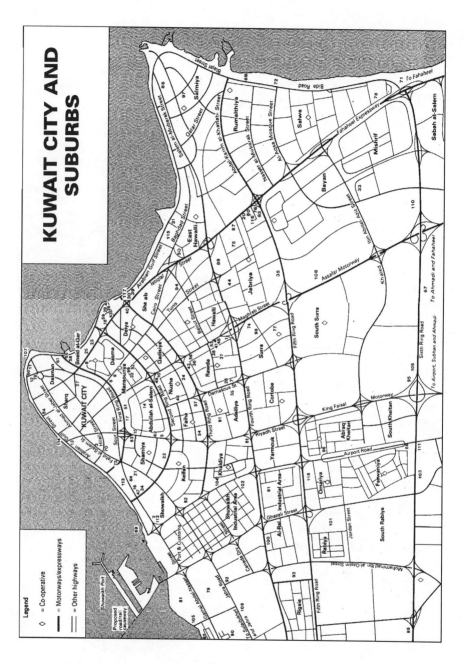

Source: Kuwait Ministry of Information.

1

Introduction

Kuwait in the Literature

When Iraq invaded Kuwait on August 2, 1990, the world reacted with surprise at the sight of tens of thousands of non-Kuwaiti Arabs, Indians, Eastern Asians, and Westerners trapped under the occupation or trying desperately to reach the borders of Jordan and Saudi Arabia. This surprise grew after liberation, when the predicament of approximately four hundred thousand Palestinian residents in Kuwait became a matter of international debate. Suddenly, and in a dramatic way, the world was made aware of the problem that has haunted the Kuwaitis since independence in 1961, namely the imbalanced composition of their population and labor force.

The situation in Kuwait and the whole of the Arabian Peninsula has by now become a classic case of international labor migration (Birks and Sinclair 1980; Sassen-Koob 1981). In nearly all the oil-producing states along the Arabian Gulf, the number of migrant workers is equal to, or higher than, the number of the citizens, and it has been so for an uninterrupted period of several decades. Although migration to the Gulf has been a central concern for workers and governments in the labor-sending and host countries, the subject has aroused rather limited interest in the social scientific community—limited not so much in terms of the number of studies carried out as in terms of the analytical depth and range of approaches. In the case of Kuwait, which is undoubtedly the most studied of all the Gulf countries, migration research focuses almost exclusively on general economic and demographic trends and policies (e.g., Nagi 1982; Sherbiny 1984). A few studies proceed beyond economic patterns and statistical material to investigate the legal framework that regulates labor migration in Kuwait (e.g, Beaugé 1986; Russell 1989a) and to look into migration as the outcome of political concerns (Russell 1989b). To the best of my knowledge, only two studies present

1

substantive accounts of migrants' experience in the Gulf (Nancy 1985; Eelens, Schampers, and Speckmann 1992), and only one monograph has attempted an in-depth study of migration in Kuwait (Al Moosa and McLachlan 1985).

Besides dealing mostly with abstract structural forces and policies rather than concrete human beings, migration research on Kuwait is characteristically restricted to the sphere of the economy and, with a few rare exceptions (e.g., Russell 1989b), does not seriously address the social, cultural, and political impact of the phenomenon on the host society. I do not wish to minimize the importance of macro and quantitative research, without the results of which any other kind of research would be practically impossible. What I suggest is that through the years, these studies have produced a wealth of data that clearly indicate the crucial role migration plays in the local society. These data therefore beg and deserve to be further analyzed and elaborated. In a region of the world where the nationals make up only a tiny minority of the work force, if not of the population, migration is bound to be more than an epiphenomenon of the labor market. If we keep in mind that the Arabian oil-producing countries are newly created states confronted with the enormous task of growing into modern nations, we can begin to glimpse the political and social significance of this massive alien presence for the native populations. An approach that recognizes labor migration as an integral part of social life in the region is therefore urgently needed.

At present two types of research on Kuwait predominate: political and economic studies. With few exceptions (e.g., Crystal 1990), the former tend to concentrate specifically on the formal processes of decision making, from which non-Kuwaitis are entirely excluded. This literature does not bring to the fore the peculiar demographic composition of the emirate and its implications. The fact that migrants do not participate in the political process does not mean that their presence does not affect this process, if only because the native population regards this presence as an opportunity to be exploited or a threat to be thwarted—or as both simultaneously. Although economic studies, on the other hand, devote much attention to labor migration, they unfortunately do so primarily in terms of volumes, trends, and patterns. The subject of social relationships, notably between native employers and migrant employees, is seldom discussed. In the absence of concrete case studies and qualitative data, economic analyses give the impression that Kuwait is a labor camp rather than a society.

The Concept of the Plural Society

I suggest that what many of these studies fail to capture is the fact that Kuwait is a *plural society*.

Some words are more difficult to use than others because they have been appropriated by different disciplines, each of which gives them a meaning that is not only specific to itself but even contradicts the meaning attached to them in another discipline. "Pluralism" is such a word. In the discourse of political scientists, a "pluralistic society" is "a healthily differentiated society" as opposed to "the monolithic structure of totalitarian states" (R. T. Smith 1961:155). In anthropology, on the other hand, pluralism is a societal anomaly, particularly identified with a special type of society found in the European colonies in Southeast Asia before World War II and known, since J. S. Furnivall (1942; 1948), as the "plural society." Furnivall's insights were later taken up by M. G. Smith (1960; 1969a; 1969b), who developed the theory of pluralism that was used in the 1960s in a number of studies of the Caribbean and Africa.

Furnivall defines the plural society as follows:

> It is in the strictest sense a medley, for [people] mix but do not combine. Each group holds by its own religion, its own culture and language, its own ideals and ways. As individuals, they meet, but only in the marketplace, in buying and selling. There is a plural society, with different sections of the community living side by side, but separately, within the same political unit. Even in the economic sphere there is a division of labour along racial lines. (1948:304)

In these plural societies, communal fragmentation and individual atomization are extreme: people experience no sense of belonging to "an organic whole" (1948:306); on the contrary, they identify with a community elsewhere, and "everyone looks forward, more or less eagerly, to returning 'home'" (1942:203). Furnivall sees the plural society as "a business partnership" rather than "a family concern," for the sole common interests the groups share among themselves are "business interests." He looks for some kind of non-material tie but finds none:

> It might seem that common interest should tie them closely, for a dissolution would involve the bankruptcy of all the partners. But the tie is strong only so far as this common interest is recognized . . . In India, caste has a religious sanction, in a plural society the only common deity is Mammon. In general, the plural society is built on caste without the cement of a

religious sanction. In each section the sectional common will is feeble, and
in the society as a whole there is no common social will . . . Few recognize
that, in fact, all the members of all sections have material interests in common, but most see that on many points their material interests are opposed.
The typical plural society is a business partnership in which, to many partners, bankruptcy signifies release rather than disaster. (1948:308)

I have quoted Furnivall at some length because his tropical colonial
societies show striking similarities to contemporary Kuwait. As I will
show, there is the same rationale for migration (demand for and supply
of cheap labor), the same ethnic variation, and the same division of labor
along ethnic lines. In both cases we find the stratified coexistence of
ethnic groups without the integration of formal cultural institutions such
as religion and language ("caste without the cement of a religious sanction"), the predominance of economy as a common denominator ("they
meet in the market-place, in buying and selling"), and the apparently
exclusive concern for profit at the expense of moral considerations
("Mammon is the only deity"). In other words, we seem to have the same
absence of integration between the different ethnic communities and the
same overlap between inter-ethnic relations and labor relations.

However, underneath this surface pattern lie features that sharply
distinguish the case of Kuwait from the "classic" plural societies in the
literature, such as pre-independence Burma, Java, and Uganda, and
present-day Grenada, Trinidad, and Mauritius. These differences include
the following:

1. Kuwait is not a colonial society created in the wake of European
   conquest. It has a history of cultural and, to a large extent, also
   political autonomy.[1] Unlike in the "classic" plural societies, in
   Kuwait political, economic, and social power over the "medley" is
   wielded by the native inhabitants and not by a foreign military or
   commercial oligarchy.
2. Modern labor migration to Kuwait is first and foremost a *voluntary*
   enterprise. Workers come to the Gulf of their own free will and are
   not sent there as slaves or convicts, as was the case with some
   "classic" plural societies in the pre-independence period. As I will
   argue, to speak of "unfree" or "indentured labor" in the case at
   hand—although it may be objectively justified in a number of concrete situations—will result in blurring rather than casting light on
   the analysis. Migration to Kuwait is a costly undertaking, and

migrants generally have to incur heavy debts. Individual agency and the contributing circumstances must therefore be given a significant place in the analysis of the Kuwaiti situation.

3. A third distinction of major importance is Kuwait's use of the politics of citizenship. This dimension, as a key to inclusion and exclusion, played no role, or only a very minor one, in the pre-World War II colonial situation. When Indians migrated to work in Uganda in the early 1900s, for example, they were simply moving from one part of the British Empire to another. The post-independence "classic" plural societies define themselves as countries in which all the ethnic components are equal, in theory and by law, and participate in social life as full-fledged members of the nation-state. Citizenship, in this case, establishes a principle of equality that, even if it is not always respected in daily life, in theory undermines the claim of greater legitimacy by any one group. In Kuwait, this definition encompasses only one ethnic component, the Kuwaitis, and excludes all the others. Here, no one questions the Kuwaitis' claim on land and power. Contemporary pluralism in Kuwait unambiguously arises within the framework of modern contract labor migration from one autonomous national state to another.[2] The fact that the migrant workers are citizens of other states facilitates rather than complicates the task for the Kuwaitis. One example to be studied in detail is the recourse to deportation as a way of punishing migrants found guilty of legal infractions. Deportation is an effective and low-cost method that would be more difficult to wield if the workers were national citizens. The fact that migrants are non-citizens to a large extent legitimates in the migrants' own eyes the politics of exclusion carried out against them. The question of legitimacy is of great complexity. In this study, it will be approached from three angles: that of the Kuwaiti employer's power over the non-Kuwaiti employee, that of identity and perception of self and others, and that of gender relations among Kuwaitis in the light of nation-building concerns.

Alongside Furnivall's "plural society," I would like to juxtapose another model of pluralism: that found in the history of the great empires of the Middle East, most recently the Ottoman Empire, to which Kuwait nominally belonged from its establishment in the early 1700s to the end of World War I. Like the European colonies at the turn of this century, the Safavid Empire, the Byzantine Empire, and especially the Muslim caliphates that resulted from successive waves of conquests and Islamization included within their borders a wide range of peoples with different languages, customs, and religions. The rulers of these empires seldom tried to homogenize the population. The Ottomans, for instance, were content with levying heavier taxes on those who stood farthest from the official orthodoxy (Inalcik and Quataert 1994; Zubaida 1989).

Unlike in Furnivall's model of pluralism, the criteria according to which the various components of the Ottoman Empire were classified were not racial but confessional. The main categories were Muslims and *dhimmis* (or Peoples of the Book, i.e., Christians, Jews, and Zoroastrians). Although Ottoman laws regulated in detail the public life of the empire, non-Muslims were free to observe the rules dictated by their religious creeds and to have their own courts of law presided over by their community leaders. Social identification of self and others in terms of religious affiliation was thus strengthened through this confessional classification of the constitutive elements of the population and the use of religion as an organizational social device. The "coexistence of autonomous agglomerates" (Carré 1993) is a recognized characteristic of Islam. This is by no means the same as saying that ethnic identity based on language and common origin was entirely absent. Because the Ottoman Empire was a theocratic empire—a caliphate—with Islam as its official ideology, Muslim Arabs always enjoyed a privileged moral, and often also political, position within it. It was an organization based on undeniable discrimination and a clear *de facto* as well as *de jure* inequality between the communities, with the Muslims at the top of the hierarchy. Yet, this discrimination was seldom accompanied by violent persecution (Carré 1993). Though ethnically, religiously, and institutionally differentiated, the various populations interacted in the economy and, as Zubaida (1989) argues, they partook of a common popular culture facilitated by the spread of Arabic, the language of the Quran. Thus, throughout the Middle East, until World War I put a definitive end to the era of large empires in the region and inaugurated the age of the nation-state, the plural society was the universal rule rather than the exception.

In more than one way, the organization of Kuwaiti society today could be viewed as a continuation of the Ottoman tradition of pluralism. Again, as with Furnivall's plural society model, there are substantial differences that cannot be overlooked, especially those introduced through the politics of citizenship in the context of the modern nation-state. I will show, however, that characteristic features of "Ottoman pluralism" can be found in today's Kuwait, not so much at the level of policy and regulations as at the level of the conceptualization and expression of ethnic identities.

Migration and the Nation-State

The central role of citizenship emphasizes the underlying tension between migration and the nation-state. International migration in the late twentieth century differs from similar population movements in previous centuries because of the current division of the entire world into nation-states with boundaries, a centralized governing apparatus, and explicit rules for membership. No matter how liberal a country may be in opening its borders to migration, the very existence of the state by definition requires that criteria be set up to define and differentiate between citizens and non-citizens. Far from being an archaic feature of closed societies of the past, this discrimination is particularly salient in modern societies characterized by an advanced system of social welfare since, to be genuinely meaningful, these social goods are necessarily limited, and their enjoyment is therefore contingent on proof of national membership. Kuwaiti citizenship entails substantial material and social advantages. The parallel existence of these privileges and the particularly aggravating population imbalance means that the native minority experiences and assesses migration in terms of a cultural zero-sum game: the larger the presence of non-Kuwaiti migrants, the more threatened the position of the Kuwaitis and, eventually, their cultural identity. As a result, the principle and practice of exclusion are particularly compelling. As with all politics, the maintenance and reproduction of the politics of exclusion require an administrative, legal, and ideological apparatus. In Kuwait, the creation of this apparatus was intricately linked to the start of oil production, modernization, and labor migration. In other words, it was an event that touched upon the very social fabric of the pre-oil system of relationships between all the main components of society: town-dwellers and Bedouins, Sunni merchants and Shia laborers, and, most important, men and women. The structure of dominance established and maintained by Kuwaitis over non-Kuwaitis cannot, therefore, be studied apart from the question of change and continuity within Kuwaiti society proper.

The concept of the plural society has been controversial since the term was coined by Furnivall, and many authors have explicitly denied that its use can be justified empirically or analytically (e.g., Benedict 1962; Braithwaite 1960; Eriksen 1992). Its weakness is that it was born from the *a priori* assumption that societies are homogeneous and cohesive entities. In the past twenty years at least, this view has lost much ground in social theory, and there is a general recognition that societies are imperfectly integrated and that there are inconsistencies between the ideas on which societies are built and social practice. Far from being an anomaly, pluralism is acknowledged to be a normal property of social reality. It is, therefore, no longer a form of socio-cultural deviance to be accounted for by a special analytical approach, as Furnivall and the proponents of the theory of pluralism contended.

All modern societies are complexly differentiated; to speak of societies is, by definition, to assume an underlying plural situation. Heterogeneity of social composition is a matter of degree. What interests us is how societies represent opportunity structures and how actors make choices in plural contexts. Why do they choose, for example, to emphasize and reproduce differences, instead of ignoring or underplaying them? I suggest that instead of rejecting it, we could fruitfully make use of the concept of the plural society to describe *situations where ethnic differentiation is sustained by a complex relationship between social practice and official political ideology*. In this study, the term is used to bring into focus the generalized practice by the state and its citizens of politics aimed at emphasizing and maintaining ethnic differences. It is in this sense that Kuwait must be understood to be a plural society.

Pluralism and Integration: A Research Program

The puzzle confronting all students of sharply differentiated societies is what holds these societies together. Furnivall, for one, is convinced that economic considerations alone accounted for the existence of the colonial plural societies, hence their inherently vitiated ("uncivilized") nature (1948:310). For M. G. Smith it is force rather than economic activity that keeps the plural society together, most particularly when the dominant section is also a minority (1960). Both Furnivall and Smith focus on the structural aspects of pluralism and the genesis of the plural society. Zubaida's (1989) interest lies elsewhere. Taking the structure of Ottoman society as a historical given, he seeks to illuminate the social life that unfolded under pluralism and to assess its cultural outcome. In other words, unlike Furnivall and Smith, Zubaida is not concerned only with the structural technicalities of the plural society but also with the actual way of life of its people. Thus he notices that, despite the separateness of cultural identities prevailing under the plural system of the Muslim empires, an astonishing number of "common cultural themes" recur throughout the Middle East. His examples range from the spontaneous spread of the Arabic language to magic beliefs and practices, to the use of the tomato in Middle Eastern cuisine—all components in what was the remarkably resilient popular culture of the region. Zubaida concludes that interaction across communal boundaries and through the division of labor inevitably gives rise to a degree of "communality of culture" (1989:101).

Plural societies inevitably present the anthropologist with the following questions: How can we identify an organization that we call a society in the face of such a wide range of diversity? Is there any commonality between the various ethnic groups and, if so, what is its source and how is it reproduced? What is it that makes possible the flow of interaction and communication across the many divides? How is the "medley" held together? Implicit in these questions is an invitation to explore how the case of Kuwait can help us think about society and culture. These topics will be addressed in the last chapter, after an exhaustive presentation of the organizational characteristics of societal life in Kuwait.

The present study, which takes into consideration developments in Kuwait prior to the Iraqi invasion, is not concerned with labor migration *per se* but with labor migration as a major component in the dynamics of social life under conditions of pluralism. Concretely, this study is concerned with the relations between two sharply differentiated social categories, the Kuwaitis and the non-Kuwaitis, each of which had its own preoccupations and projects in which the other was used as a means to their achievement. For the non-Kuwaitis the major preoccupations and projects were centered around *life improvement,* while for the Kuwaitis they were centered around *nation-building.* My purpose is to show that the two projects closely impinged on each other: the non-Kuwaitis migrated and worked under circumstances peculiar to a country in the throes of material and identity change, while the Kuwaitis modernized and built their national consciousness against a background of substantial labor importation.

My approach to pluralism comes closer to Zubaida's than to Furnivall's and Smith's. Although I will show that economic motivations and use of force were indeed crucial and pervasive elements in Kuwait's plural society, I wish to go beyond the analysis of structural relations. I will look into how structural forces conditioned the actors' life-strategies and perception of self and others, *and* how the outcome of these strategies and perception in turn led them to redefine an objective system of exclusion, dominance, and economic exchange into a cultural world of meaningful experience. I do not claim that the same kind of cultural commonality exists in contemporary Kuwait as did in the Ottoman Empire. We find in the case at hand no cogent cultural commonality such as the sharing of a language or items of belief, if only because the current situation in Kuwait has been in existence for less than fifty years. What we find at most is disparate evidence of awkward and hesitant attempts in this direction. The parallel between the two cases is thus neither one of substance nor even of forms, but a parallel of processes that can be subsumed under the term "integration." I will argue that the question of integration in plural societies should be approached not only from the angle of structural inclusion/exclusion but also from the angle of the actors' experience. The case of Kuwait seems to indicate that this type of subjective integration obtains even in the face of the most stringent segregating constraints. The question of what mechanisms lie behind this paradox is the central guiding concern in this study.

How to Study Unbounded Worlds?

One implication of migration is the extreme unboundedness of the social networks and universes of discourse and relationship encountered, especially among the migrants. A topic of important theoretical and epistemological character, societal unboundedness gives rise to serious difficulties of method. Because I have had to deal concretely with the problem in the field, and because it hovers in the background of the material and the analysis presented in this study, it is appropriate that it should be made explicit from the very start.

The nature of societal unboundedness has recently been granted much attention by scholars from diverse schools of thought (e.g., Barth 1992; Hannerz 1992a; Ingold 1990; Tilly 1984; Wallerstein 1988; Wolf 1988). Arguing that societies are essentially systems of relations, these authors reject the conventional postulate of orderly societal boundedness; societies, as Barth (1992:21) puts it, are more or less "disordered systems characterized by an absence of closure." While common to all social aggregates, these features are particularly salient in contexts where migration is a predominant characteristic.

By definition, migration refers to the fact that people move across geographical space and settle for shorter or longer periods in places away from home. The spatial dimension that is such a crucial part of the phenomenon of migration emphasizes the difficulty of delimiting the social world in which migrants live. Migration inevitably entails that people are engaged in social universes that are far apart in space, yet are inextricably joined since they all converge in the person of the migrant. Nowhere is the truth of societal unboundedness better illustrated than here. Systemic disorder and absence of closure entail methodological problems that cannot be ignored by students of migrant life.

To take the notion of societal unboundedness or absence of closure seriously, I should have pursued the networks of relationships spun between Kuwait and the migrants' homelands. "Following the loops" (Bateson 1972, in Barth 1992:25), I should have started from Kuwait and extended my inquiries much further afield, wherever the expatriates had their significant cultural and emotional points of attachment. By limiting my observations to what took place *here* and *now* between actors whom I could follow and to the immediate structures that framed their daily existence, I gained insights into only a fragment of my non-Kuwaiti informants' lives and social universes. Investigating the socio-material circumstances in the migrants' hometowns, who their kin, friends, and neighbors were and what positions they held among them, the abstract forces of world economy, etc., could have led me to a better understanding of the circumstances influencing their decisions in Kuwait. Such a project, however, is obviously too vast to handle. As it was, I had to limit my field in terms of topic (society and culture in Kuwait), space (only Kuwait, and mostly Kuwait City), time (only the period from 1987 to 1989), and personnel (only some groups of expatriates and Kuwaitis). As a result, the "society" I observed centered around a circumscribed universe of social relationships and cultural representations and discourses associated with Kuwait. This was in spite of the fact that many of my non-Kuwaiti informants made it perfectly clear to me that what counted most for them was what happened thousands of miles away from Kuwait.

The notion of *circumscription* is explored by Devons and Gluckman (1964) in their reflections on the practical feasibility of social research and the difficulties of studying a topic as fluctuating and complex as social reality. The authors' conclusion is that the only procedure available to us is circumscription, by which they mean that

> the anthropologist . . . cuts off a manageable field of reality from the total flow of events, by putting boundaries round it both in terms of what is relevant to his problems and in terms of how and where he can apply his techniques of observation and analysis . . . [In doing so] he ceases to follow real connexions, and from them abstracts a set of such connexions as he thinks he can study profitably. He assumes they form a system. (1964:162–3)

The danger is, of course, that circumscription is carried out in such an implicit way that we find ourselves trapped in an epistemological mirage of our own making: in other words, we mistake a methodological device adopted for purposes of observation and analysis—circumscription—for the essence of what it is that we try to observe and analyze. Put in another way, our circumscribing becomes society's boundedness. It is by making our methodology explicit that we can guard ourselves (and our readers) against this serious pitfall. As I see it, the alternative to circumscription is to approach society from the world-systems perspective, that is, to tackle the subject at the macro level of "big structures and large processes" (Tilly 1984). But if, on the other hand, we identify our study objects as "real people doing real things" (Ortner 1984), as I do, we need to revert to the concrete actors and circumscribe the field.

Fieldwork and Problems Encountered

The research on which this study is based took place between 1987 and 1989, while I lived in Kuwait with my husband, a Norwegian diplomat, and our two children. I arrived in the emirate in September 1984 and left it for good in December 1991, ten months after its liberation from Iraqi occupation. Between January 1990 and December 1991 I lived in Norway, but returned to Kuwait on three occasions, once before and twice after the invasion of August 2, 1990.

My research was preceded by a period of three years, during which my anthropological exertions were concentrated not on Kuwait but on the writing of a *magister* dissertation about Vietnamese refugees in Norway, a project initiated in Oslo before I moved to the Middle East. From 1984 to 1987 I was, therefore, simply a resident in the emirate, discovering as a "lay" person life in a country that was previously unknown to me. For three years I "soaked" myself in Kuwaiti life without any clear ulterior motives. I learned to understand the society not through goal-oriented participant observation but through spontaneous "participant living," if I may use such an awkward phrase. My acquaintance with Kuwait was not governed by theoretical concerns. I had the privilege of gathering a stock of knowledge based on daily, prosaic experience, the usefulness of which I did not fully appreciate until I started systematic research in 1987.

Kuwaiti society is strictly stratified in terms of ethnicity and class. As I shall elaborate in detail in the book, the most obvious dividing line is drawn between Kuwaitis and expatriates.[3] The bridge linking the two categories is the employer–employee relationship, a central feature of the social organization of the emirate. On the margin of this dual constellation we find the diplomatic community, a tiny population, which, within the Kuwaiti context, represents a structural anomaly: ethnically, they are "expatriate," while in terms of class status, they are "Kuwaiti." In Kuwait, I moved in and out of various social worlds. I met and interacted with Kuwaitis and non-Kuwaitis, some of whom saw me as a member of the diplomatic community, an employer, a customer, etc.; others, as a Vietnamese-born woman, a mother, a housewife; others again had a more complete picture. In my various roles and statuses, I elicited various reactions, and I reacted to these reactions. Like everyone else, I was positioned in terms of gender, ethnicity, and class, and was part of a microcosm where signals, impressions, actions, and reactions heaped upon each other and blended into vivid images.

If participant observation is a problematic base on which to build an analysis because of the pervasive fusion of objective and subjective practices (Clifford 1986), "participant living" is even more so. The crux of the problem is that it is extremely difficult to step back from the latter experience and sort things out when it is over, because one does not enter into it in an organized, scientific frame of mind. Participation, in this case, mobilizes the person *in toto*; it is pervaded with subjectivity, and there is little time or room for reflection. The "participant living" that I went through from 1984 to 1987 undoubtedly provided me with my most vivid impressions about life in Kuwait and remains for me an important fund of background knowledge of this society. It was during those three years that I had my first direct observations of the rigid ethnic and class segregation between Kuwaitis and non-Kuwaitis and, above all, of the harsh regime to which some categories of migrant workers, in particular the unskilled laborers from Asia, were submitted. But the information I acquired before 1987 was acquired neither systematically nor purposefully. Moreover, I tended to react to what I saw around me with moral indignation, which considerably impaired my ability to approach life in Kuwait in those years with an analytic frame of mind.

Just as the years of "participant living" inevitably shaped the actual research, the period between August 1990 and December 1991, when Kuwait was invaded, occupied, and then liberated and rebuilt, is bound to leave its imprint on the analysis. Those sixteen months of, among other things, intense anguish for friends and acquaintances, provided me with the unexpected opportunity to check the strengths and weaknesses of my hypotheses about the Kuwaiti–expatriate relationship and the importance of the expatriates for Kuwait's existence as a society and as a nation. Events during this period threw into relief the ambivalent implications of migration and led me to question more and more the conceptualization and use of the notion of integration in the social sciences. The war and its aftermath also allowed me to understand how infinitely complex were the views and feelings of both Kuwaitis and expatriates about their lives in the emirate—much more so than I had thought previously.

Methodology

The main period of research itself, from 1987 to 1989, stands in contrast to the experience in living before and after it. It was not long before I realized the problems of initiating research with clear-cut assumptions about the basic data, especially when these assumptions are strongly colored by an emotional bias of a moral nature. It became clear to me that the knowledge I had been gathering spontaneously since 1984 was ambivalent: it provided me with a *feel* for Kuwaiti society rather similar to that a native has for his or her society; but it also carried with it the inevitable burden of myopic subjectivity and personal prejudice. Since 1984, my sympathies had been predominantly for the expatriate workers. Although I met with Kuwaitis and had friendly relations with many of them, these relations had often remained superficial. I could not identify myself with them, or perhaps I did not wish to. Since my intention was to study the relations between Kuwaitis and expatriates, I became increasingly worried that this moral bias prevented me from really hearing the Kuwaitis' voices in the interactional dialogue betweeen the two parties.[4]

Subjectivity, I felt, was my worst enemy. As a result, my research program was aimed at gathering the kind of data that would allow me to ascertain that my information and knowledge were genuinely and generally valid, and that my theories about Kuwaiti society did not arise from my biased views. In other words, I was looking for data of a general, public, and discursive ("objective") nature that either confirmed or falsified what I thought I already knew.

Observation (rather than participation) from a distance, as it were, characterized my research. From 1987 I deliberately stepped out of the ordinary stream of "participant living" in order to scrutinize life in Kuwait better. I was no longer content with observing and listening to private persons. I interviewed Kuwaiti policymakers and officials from the Ministry of Social Affairs and Labor, the Ministry of Interior (responsible for immigration and residence), the Ministry of Planning, the head of private education (responsible for non-Kuwaiti education), the Zakat House (a state institution responsible for charity to the needy), and similar institutions. I also sought information from doctors, teachers, priests and ministers from the Catholic and Protestant churches, organizers of expatriate clubs and associations, labor attachés from the labor-sending countries, local journalists, and social scientists. I spoke to labor-recruiting agents, trade unionists, ordinary employers, and employees. With the kind assistance of a Kuwaiti judge, I was allowed to attend trials at the labor courts; I also discussed aspects of the labor law with lawmakers and with lawyers who specialized in the defense of migrant workers. To learn about the labor conditions in the early period of Kuwait's development, the 1950s and 1960s, I spoke with Palestinian and other Arab expatriates, some of whom had become Kuwaiti citizens since then, who participated in building this city-state almost from scratch. To learn about pre-oil Kuwait in general, I spent many days listening to elderly Kuwaiti women and men; I dug into censuses and statistics, historical and legal documentation, news reports, and theoretical literature. What I read, heard, and was told by experts, I checked with ordinary people who lived what the others studied. I also checked these data against my own personal experience. In this way, I learned to listen more attentively to all my informants.

As in the other Gulf Cooperation Council (GCC) countries, entry to Kuwait by a foreigner is subject to visa and sponsorship requirements. A researcher, for instance, must, in principle, be sponsored by the Ministry of Higher Education through Kuwait University, the Institute of

Scientific Research, or other national institutions. I owed my presence in the country to my status as a diplomatic dependent. This status placed me in the privileged position of not depending on any Kuwaiti sponsorship and of being free to study whatever I felt like without needing a formal research permit as long as the objects of my interest were simply the people around me. The fact that I was free vis-à-vis the authorities did not mean, however, that I was free from the obligation to enlighten my informants as to the purpose of my activities. Considering the ethnic and class stratification prevalent in Kuwait, this required that I explained my own status ("anthropologist-cum-diplomatic dependent," or vice versa). This information was particularly necessary in the case of the Kuwaitis, in whose country I was present by virtue of my diplomatic status. I could not take advantage of this status and of the hospitality I was being granted to obtain information from private Kuwaiti citizens without their knowing consent, especially on the delicate matter of Kuwaiti–expatriate relations.[5] Although the majority of the people I approached were minimally interested in my research explanation, their knowing about it did define me as observer rather than participant. A typical feature of the migrant communities in Kuwait is everyone's natural curiosity about others who might be in the same situation as themselves. Thus my interest in the workers whom I approached was paralleled by their interest in me, so that I always ended up informing them about myself. Such information inevitably shaped the premises of our interaction.

The insights I gained into my informants' lives do not strictly answer to the conventional standards of social anthropology: they do not result from my having shared my informants' daily routines from dawn to dusk as I did not live in their homes but in my own; nor did I try to have them adopt me as one of them. I always met, interviewed, befriended, and discussed with Kuwaitis and non-Kuwaitis in my real capacity, with my own social and ethnic background clearly stated. Not having shared their routines, I was able to observe only those aspects of my informants' lives in which they allowed me to take part. I derived my knowledge about their situations partly from their testimony and partly from my "double-positioned" observation—both through "participant living" and through ethnographic inquiry—of the patterns of public behavior. If I seem at times to give much room in the study to hard facts and empirical data, it is because I have the feeling that my ambition to depict and explain the relationship between expatriates and Kuwaitis and the overall context in which this relationship took place calls for the presentation of an exhaustive body of background information. I hope that my analysis will justify this point of view.

Notes

1. As will be seen in Chapter 2, Kuwait had been under the formal authority of the Ottomans and the British. But in practice, and as far as internal policy was concerned, it can by no means be claimed that Kuwait had been ruled or administered by either of the two powers.

2. Here, Kuwait's dealings with the Palestinians who did not carry a Jordanian passport were an exception. Until the Iraqi invasion and its devastating consequences for the Palestinians, this community was granted special treatment by the Kuwaitis, which implicitly acknowledged the stateless Palestinians' status as refugees rather than migrant workers.

3. "Expatriates" is the common designation of migrant workers in the Gulf countries.

4. As it turned out, I did not hear the voices of *all* the expatriates either. And what I heard I tended to interpret in the light of my moral indignation. I only really understood this later, when I returned to Kuwait after the war and listened to accounts by Kuwaitis and expatriates of how they had survived *together* under Iraqi occupation.

5. In the late 1980s, the question was critically related to that of Kuwait's internal security, especially after the bombing of the French embassy, an attempt on the Amir's life, and the hijacking of a Kuwait Airways plane—and as the Iran–Iraq war dragged on on Kuwait's very doorstep. That the local authorities were not eager, generally speaking, to see it treated by outsiders is reflected in the fact that social scientists on contract assignment in Kuwait systematically avoided writing about the situation of migrant workers.

2

Kuwait Through History: A Tradition of Migration and Open Networks

Pearl Diving, Sea Trade, and Caravans

In the past, Kuwait was associated with the dual tradition of trade and nomadism that had characterized Eastern Arabia up to the advent of the oil industry in the twentieth century. Trade and nomadism imply migration.

The creation of the town of Kuwait itself in the early eighteenth century was the result of the migration of the Bani Utub, a group of families from the Adnani[1] tribe of Anaza, which inhabited Najd and Northern Arabia (Abu Hakima 1982; Lorimer 1970). The Utub[2] left their original homeland during a protracted spell of severe drought that caused a large population movement among the Anaza away from Central Arabia toward the outlying and coastal areas. After several years of tribulations that took them to Hasa and Qatar, where they learned seafaring, and possibly to the Persian littoral and Southern Iraq (Abu Hakima 1982), the Utub finally settled down in a tiny fishing village known first as Qorain[3] and later renamed Kuwait. According to documents from the East India Company, this happened around 1716.

Kuwait lies in the northeastern corner of the Arabian Peninsula, on a gently undulating plain of arid sand and gravel that forms part of the Arabian desert. With no surface water, almost no rainfall, and extreme climatic conditions, Kuwait's physical environment was scarcely amenable to animal and vegetal life. But it had an excellent natural harbor, one of the best in the Gulf, and it was situated immediately south of the mouth of the Shatt al Arab River, which was the crucial supply line for the city of Basra and the southern region of Ottoman Iraq. Given its physical characteristics, the little town depended on the sea for its livelihood. The Utub Bedouins gave up their pastoral way of life and became fishermen, sailors, and traders. Kuwait grew rapidly into a politically stable center for both maritime and desert trade, serving as a port for the sea-going vessels and as a depot for goods carried by caravans to the hinterland (in particular Najd). The town became yet another center along the coast, through which passed the sailors, merchants, and nomads of the region, forever on the move in search of work.

The trade network was relatively dense and extensive. It is reported that in 1758 large caravans of five thousand camels and a thousand men passed through Kuwait (Abu Hakima 1982). In the nineteenth and early twentieth centuries, the Kuwaitis were known throughout the Gulf for their merchant fleet. Most of it consisted of small boats, used for pearling and the local carrying trade (Rihani 1983). The pride of Kuwait rested, meanwhile, in its *booms*, the larger deep-sea vessels that plied between Kuwait in the north and Oman, India, and East Africa in the south. The cargo of the *booms* that set sail for the south in November each year was mainly Iraqi dates, ghee, and Arabian horses; they returned in the spring, loaded with spices, rice, sugar, manufactured goods, and wood for boat-building from India, coffee from Yemen, tobacco and dried fruits from Persia, and mangrove poles for house-building from East Africa (Abu Hakima 1982; Lorimer 1970; Villiers 1940). From June to October, the *booms* remained in the harbor while the sailors went diving for pearls that were sold to Indian merchants from Bombay.

Although the Kuwaiti boats were owned by Kuwaiti merchants and were under the command of Kuwaiti captains, they were built by boat-builders from Bahrain and manned by crews of Kuwaiti, Persian, Omani, and Yemeni sailors. In 1904, according to Lorimer, Kuwait had a population of 35,000. The largest group was the Arabs: among them were the Kuwaitis proper (i.e., the original settlers from Central Arabia and the local tribes of Kuwait), and tribes and families from the Lower Gulf and Southern Iraq. Lorimer also mentions a rather large population of assimilated slaves and ex-slaves of African origin (4,000). The most numerous non-Arab group, meanwhile, consisted of Persians from the Iranian littoral. With the exception of a tiny Jewish population from the Basra area, pre-oil Kuwait was uniformly Muslim. The Kuwaitis proper and most other Arabs were Sunni, while the Persians were mainly Shia.

If one were to map Kuwaiti society before World War II, one would encounter, even by then, the difficulty of circumscribing a complex social reality. The Kuwaitis could be said to participate in three inter-related cultural spheres. The first was the *Northern Gulf* sphere that linked Kuwait to Southern Iraq; with the old city of Basra as its administrative and commercial capital, and the holy towns of Najaf and Kerbala as centers of religious pilgrimage, Southern Iraq was the heartland of Shia Islam, a rich cultural area where Arab, Turkish, and Persian traditions met and fused together. While the culture of Southern Iraq was substantially sedentary, that of *Central Arabia*, the second cultural sphere to which Kuwait belonged, was unambiguously nomadic. Having been founded by Najdi families from the powerful Central Arabian Anaza tribe, Kuwait maintained close kinship and tribal relationships with the Bedouin tribes of Arabia. It was, therefore, an actor in desert politics, all the more so since the town traded actively with the hinterland. Finally, Kuwait owed its survival to sea trade, which meant that it actively participated in the world of mercantile exchange organized around the *Indian Ocean*, with ramifications all the way to Ceylon in the east and Zanzibar in the south.

Although the majority of Kuwait's inhabitants came from a rather limited geographical area conveniently known today as "the Gulf," as traders and nomads they were tuned to events and related to people existing far beyond their immediate vicinity. The networks of trade partners and occasional acquaintances included Arabs, Persians, Indians, and Africans. Although each ethnic group had its own language and customs, there was, in the case of the Indian Ocean, a common pool of "creolized" culture that allowed the traders to communicate with one another: according to elderly Kuwaitis who had taken part in sea trade before the 1950s, Arabic was commonly understood by all, but it was an Arabic heavily infused with Persian, Urdu, Hindi, and African words and phrases. Information about commodity prices and the situation of the markets and the political upheavals that affected them, and news about marriage alliances, family feuds, extraordinary feats, and foul treachery traveled far and fast aboard the ships and along the caravans. More stable contacts were also inevitably created, as, for instance, when the wealthy merchants sent their sons to train in the trade business in Basra, India, or Aden, some of whom came to live there permanently as the company's local representatives (Field 1984; Villiers 1940). Even ordinary merchants and sailors sometimes maintained households in both Kuwait and the towns along the trade route. Basra, Karachi, Calicut, Sur, Aden, Lamu, Mombassa, and Zanzibar were the nodal points through which pre-oil Kuwaiti society connected with the other participants in the sea-trade network centered around the Indian Ocean.[4]

Politics and Society in Pre-Oil Kuwait

Ever since it came into existence, Kuwait was identified with the Utub migrants from Najd who founded it, in particular with the Al Sabah. The prominent status of the Sabahs is of recent date, however. Originally, they were simply chosen by the other Utub families to administer the affairs of the town while these families themselves took care of trade, the most profitable and prestigious activity. Until the late 1800s, real power and social ascendency rested with the merchant families, whose work generated the income on which Kuwait critically depended for its existence. The Al Sabah shaikh was at best *primus inter pares*; he was never their overlord. This historical division of tasks between the merchants and the Sabahs is known in Kuwait and throughout the Gulf as the "pact" that accounts for Kuwait's unique political stability in an area prone to violent feuds and tribal warfare. Many see in it the reason why, alone among the Gulf states, Kuwait had a tradition of check-and-balance between the ruler and the mercantile elite long before the Western notion of democracy was introduced into the region, and as the reason why the idea of parliamentary politics has survived there in spite of the odds. Barred from sea-trading activities,[5] the Al Sabah partly depended on the merchants for their incomes. Economic dependence made them accountable; hence the well-anchored tradition of political consultations between the shaikh and the merchants; hence also the latter's view of political participation as a natural process to which they were entitled—a perception that deeply contrasted with the situation in the neighboring emirates; hence, finally, the relative political cohesion among the Kuwaitis—a cohesion that has, at times, been subjected to some difficult tests (Crystal 1990) but has, on the whole, proved to be remarkably resilient.[6]

Officially, Kuwait was part of the Ottoman Empire until the end of World War I. In reality, the farther one moved from Istanbul, the weaker its authority became. Already tenuous in Basra, Ottoman rule was hardly felt in the Arabian Peninsula (Abu Hakima 1982). In practice, Eastern Arabia was ruled by a number of powerful tribes, the largest being the Bani Khaled, whose fiefdom since the seventeenth century had run from Kuwait in the north to Al Hasa in the south and bordered with Najd to the west. The Utub had settled in Kuwait with the permission of the Bani Khaled, with whom they maintained friendly relations throughout the eighteenth century. In the nineteenth century, the rule of the Bani Khaled was contested by the Wahhabis from Central Arabia. Under the military leadership of the house of Saud, this religious revival movement from

Najd spread by force over Eastern Arabia, eventually overunning the Bani Khaled.

For much of the nineteenth century, Kuwait retained its *de facto* autonomy. Its leaders, uninterested in power politics and eager only to develop their trading activities, skillfully navigated the maze of alliances and counter-alliances between the rival tribes, careful not to provoke any one of them. But by the end of the 1800s events in the region made it increasingly clear that, in order for this small emirate to survive, it would sooner or later have to align itself more closely either with Britain (which had gained a permanent naval presence in the Lower Gulf through its treaty with the Trucial States and Bahrain) or the Ottomans in Iraq for protection. In 1899 Mubarak, the only emir (or ruler) in Kuwait's history who came to power by force,[7] signed a secret Exclusive Agreement with Britain whereby the latter would assist Kuwait in case of aggression; in return, Mubarak pledged not to cede, sell, or lease any of his territory to any power without Britain's consent (Crystal 1990).

Pre-oil Kuwait was not a homogeneous socio-cultural system, if only because of the coexistence of the sedentary and the nomadic cultures. The Arabians have traditionally conceptualized the difference between the two as being intrinsic and involving fundamental values. Among the most basic divergences was each group's perception of trade activities. While the economic and social existence of the settled communities revolved around these activities, the Bedouins looked upon trade with contempt and stooped to selling and buying for a livelihood only in the most dire situations (Al Essa 1981). For Bedouins, it was the desert raid, elevated to the rank of a national institution, that lay at the base of the economic structure (Hitti 1970), and the settled communities of Arabia lived in constant fear of such raids. In Kuwait the townspeople had always been familiar with the money economy through trading across the Indian Ocean. But with the Bedouins the exchanges were made on a barter basis, with the nomads coming to town during their *musabila* (seasonal visits) with their pastoral products to pay for the manufactured goods they had acquired the previous season and to acquire new ones (Dickson 1951). Another major difference between the sedentary merchants and petty traders and the nomads was the former's attachment to the town of Kuwait. To the nomads, the town had its pragmatic utility as a market place, but it was the desert that was vested with expressive and symbolic significance. To the sedentary community, on the other hand, the town of Kuwait was not only an important source of livelihood but also the very locus where communal life arose and unfolded. The town also provided its inhabitants with a much needed physical security in a permanently hostile environment.

Much of the mutual identification among the town-dwellers, therefore, derived from the need to protect themselves against common dangers. One such danger—the memory of which is inscribed in the Kuwaitis' history books and occupies a central place in their collective remembrance—occurred in 1920, when Ibn Saud unleashed his Ikhwaan troops against Kuwait. For two months, the population of Kuwait worked round the clock to build a wall to protect their town. The Ikhwaan were stopped in Jahra, some thirty miles northwest of Kuwait, thanks to the British, who, in compliance with the terms of the Exclusive Agreement, lent their support to the Kuwaitis. Even so, the wall and the collective efforts that went into its erection remained the symbol of Kuwaiti unity against external threats. The battle of Jahra in 1920 created a special bond between the town-dwellers who had taken part in it and invested them with an unshakable claim to membership of the Kuwaiti community. This event, it is often said, saw the birth of an explicit Kuwaiti "national" awareness by creating a nucleus of hard-core citizenry encompassing those who had taken part in the events and their descendants. Until the Iraqi invasion in 1990, 1920 was the most significant year in Kuwait's history. As we will see in Chapter 3, today it plays a critical role in the way the state adjudges Kuwaiti citizenship.

Although united against outside enemies, pre-oil Kuwait was also a stratified society: among the people of *al hadhar* (the sedentary), asymmetric power relations separated the mainly Sunni, Najdi merchant elite and the predominantly Shia laborers (Ismael 1982). Likewise, the hierarchical structure of the tribal world clearly distinguished the noble (*shareef*) camel-herding tribes from the semi-sedentary, sheep-breeding ones (Dickson 1951; Ismael 1982). There was a formal prohibition of marriage between the elites and their subordinates. Yet they all lived in economic symbiosis and were interlocked in a complementary division of labor: most Shias served as crews for the predominantly Sunni merchants and captains; the inferior tribes supplied the townspeople with products from agriculture and fishing, but they also worked as shepherds for the noble tribes and as pearl divers for the merchants. Between the noble tribes and the merchants, there was an exchange of food and woollen clothing for tobacco, coffee, weapons, and other manufactured goods (Ismael 1982).

Oil: Prosperity and Its Implications

Oil was discovered in 1938, at a time when Kuwait was in the midst of a profound economic crisis. The stock of pearl oysters in the Gulf had been dwindling rapidly during the 1920s and 1930s; moreover, the merchants had to face the growing competition of the Japanese cultured pearl industry. Besides, in 1923 Ibn Saud had declared a long-drawn economic war on Kuwait by forbidding his subjects to trade with the town. Combined with the world depression throughout the 1930s and the pearl crisis, the blockade, which lasted fourteen years, debilitated Kuwait's economy and threatened its very existence. The 1920s and 1930s were the darkest period in Kuwait's history, marred by economic strangulation, loss of territory to Ibn Saud,[8] and internal disputes. The twilight of the Indian Ocean sea trade also spelled the decline of the merchants' role and the end of the power balance between merchants and ruler. The political emasculation of the former and the rise of the latter were to increase dramatically with the advent of the oil economy. The discovery of oil raised many hopes, but World War II delayed its exploitation, and the first shipment of crude oil did not take place until 1946. From then on, however, Kuwait's economic situation was secured, and the problems that the emirate had to face were of an altogether different character.

Among these, inadequate human resources loomed largest. To carry out the modernization projects financed by their new oil revenues, the Kuwaitis needed a kind of expertise that the sailors, fishermen, and Bedouins of the Gulf region could not provide. The British-owned Kuwait Oil Company, for instance, had to turn to India and Pakistan for many of its first oil workers (Crystal 1990; Seccombe 1986). It seems that few Arabs from outside the peninsula were eager to migrate to Kuwait in those days. Even the prospect of high wages could not tempt qualified workers from the Middle East to come and work in a part of the world traditionally viewed by sedentary Arabs as the heartland of "uncivilized nomadism" (Ibn Khaldun 1967).[9] The creation of the State of Israel in 1948 which uprooted and dispersed over half a million Palestinians, provided a solution to the Kuwaitis' manpower problem. For the male Palestinian refugees living a precarious life in crammed camps in Egypt, Jordan, and Lebanon, Kuwait was "the opportunity in exile" (Brand 1988). Unlike the other Arabs, their circumstances made them willing to enroll for work in the desert emirate. Their appearance there from 1948 onwards was to be of crucial significance for Kuwait's development.

Palestinian migrants have contributed importantly to the building of modern Kuwait. They created its new infrastructure and set up its institutions, which they staffed, ran, and developed (Brand 1988; Ghabra 1987). In the process, many built themselves a livelihood and found in Kuwait, for several decades, a more or less safe haven in their exile. Meanwhile, more Iraqi and Iranian workers converged on Kuwait (Table 2.1). With these three groups, Kuwait's needs for manpower during the 1950s could be said to be adequately met.

After Kuwait achieved independence in 1961, the influx of migrant workers from the entire Middle East increased substantially. In addition, a large number of Bedouin nomads in the area between Kuwait and Saudi Arabia applied for permission to settle on its territory. By now, Kuwait's oil revenues had reached a level that allowed the government to create a generous welfare system: although most of it applied only to Kuwait's own citizens, there were advantageous fallouts for the expatriates as well (such as subsidies for food, water, and electricity, and free healthcare). With its rapid growth, the small country offered numerous opportunities to all and was therefore becoming most attractive to the neighboring populations.

In 1973, in the wake of the October War, the Arab oil-producing countries declared the export restrictions and production cutbacks that made it possible for OPEC to carry out substantial increases in oil price. Kuwait's oil revenues jumped from US$1,795 million in 1973 to US$7,094 million in 1974 (Table 2.2). From being the land of opportunity for migrants from neighboring countries, Kuwait now became the magnet that irresistibly drew professionals and laborers from East and West. As the country's development strategies shifted from relatively modest infrastructural construction in the 1950s and 1960s to ambitious projects of industrial development and extensive social services in the 1970s, it needed all the manpower it could get. Kuwait opened its doors to new migrants, including the second wave of Palestinian refugees following the Arab debacle of June 1967, Lebanese fleeing the civil war in their country, and other Arabs and Asians from the subcontinent and the Far East. Between 1975 and 1985, the non-Kuwaiti population increased by 256 percent, while the Kuwaiti population increased by 194 percent (mainly through the integration of local nomadic tribes, but also through a very high birthrate). By 1988, Kuwait had a population of almost two million, compared to slightly more than 200,000 in 1957— the last year the Kuwaitis were a majority in their own country (Table 2.3). Of these two million, less than 27 percent were Kuwaiti citizens. The road to this predicament had not been traveled without misgivings.

TABLE 2.1 Population of Major Non-Kuwaiti Nationalities in 1957

Gender	Iraqi	Iranian	Palestinian	Egyptian
Male	18,728	18,378	11,616	858
Female	7,307	1,541	3,557	876
Total	26,035	19,919	15,173	1,734

Source: Kuwait, Annual Statistical Abstract, 1989.

TABLE 2.2 Fluctuations in Government Crude Oil Revenues for Selected Years

Year	Government Oil Revenues (in thousand KD)
1946	200
1951	7,500
1956	103,921
1961	164,702
1966-7	292,100
1971-2	500,900
1972-3	537,500
1973-4	584,000
1974-5	2,534,800
1980	3,819,161
1982	1,238,318
1985	746,345

Source: Kuwait, Annual Statistical Abstract, 1989.

TABLE 2.3 Enumerated Total Population with Percentage of Kuwaitis and Non-Kuwaitis, 1957–1995

Year	% Kuwaiti	% Non-Kuwaiti	Total
1957	55.0	45.0	206,473
1965	36.1	63.9	467,339
1975	30.9	69.1	994,837
1980	28.5	71.5	1,357,952
1985	27.7	72.3	1,697,301
1990	26.5	73.5	2,125,053
1995	37.2	62.8	1,830,000

Source: Kuwait, Annual Statistical Abstract, 1989.

The 1950s and 1960s were Kuwait's formative years, during which it did its apprenticeship as a rich, modern, autonomous state. It also learned to become a full-fledged Middle Eastern country.[10] With the advent of oil production and the end of sea trade, Kuwait definitely turned its back on its Indian Ocean past. As the presence of the Palestinians, Egyptians, Syrians, and other Arabs increased, it was more and more drawn into the sphere of cultural and political life centered around Cairo, Beirut, Baghdad, and Damascus. This was hardly surprising, since the migrants brought with them their political ideologies and conflicts: the Egyptians, Nasserite socialism and pan-Arabism; the Palestinians, the Arab–Israeli conflict; the Syrians and the Iraqis, their own versions of Ba`ath ideology. Pan-Arabism and Ba`athism were modern, left-leaning ideologies hostile to the hereditary emirate system of Kuwait. In the immediate post-World War II decades, they had a strong appeal for the first generation of young Kuwaitis sent on state scholarships to universities in Cairo, Beirut, Great Britain, and America. Back in Kuwait, these intellectuals felt a stronger political affinity with the educated Arab migrants than with their more conservative countrymen. They formed the backbone of the liberal opposition to the government. The most disturbing regional political event, meanwhile, occurred in the late 1970s, with Khomeini's revolution in Iran and the ensuing Iran–Iraq war. These involved the sizable Shia minority in Kuwait[11] and touched on a raw nerve of the entire Gulf region, namely, the problem of Sunni–Shia relations.[12]

Since migrants were employed in key areas (education, information, business, and the state bureaucracy), each of these political ideas spread like wildfire, transmitted through the medium of the common Arabic language and favored by Kuwait's relatively liberal social policy. As Kuwait's role within OPEC and OAPEC and its involvement in Middle Eastern politics grew, the government became increasingly uneasy about the vocal presence of Arab expatriates. The second half of the 1960s witnessed a period of political turbulence. The liberal opposition was increasingly critical of government policies. The general tendency among the decision-makers was to link political radicalization of the Kuwaiti urban elite to the large presence of Arab migrant workers (Russell 1989a). In 1965 the government adopted a series of laws aimed at reinforcing internal security. Two groups were targeted: the local press and foreign workers. A number of newspapers were suspended and many migrants were rounded up and deported (Crystal 1992). Repeated political confrontations between the government and its critics led to the decision by the emir to dismiss the National Assembly altogether in 1976. By then, the need to restrict Arab labor immigration seemed more pressing than ever to the government, but everyone was aware of the negative impact this would have on the labor market. The merchant oligarchy, concerned with profitability, was resolutely opposed to it. The solution to this dilemma materialized in the form of migrant workers from Asia, who appeared *en masse* in the Gulf after the 1973 oil boycott was declared (Table 2.4).

One should be careful not to exaggerate the role of the oil boycott in explaining the remarkable shift in the ethnic composition of the migrant workers in Kuwait from the mid-1970s onwards. It may be that Kuwait would have had to seek out Asian migrants in any case, since the number of Arab workers available for migration to the Gulf began to decrease.[13] It may also be that Indians and others from the subcontinent were bound to become more interested in migrating to Kuwait, considering the long history of trade relationships between the subcontinent and the Gulf (Adleton 1992). A more plausible explanation, meanwhile, is that the post-1973 shift in the pattern of migration in Kuwait was the combined effect of an aggressive policy by some Asian countries to promote the export of labor and Kuwait's readiness, for a number of reasons,[14] to accept this offer.

TABLE 2.4 Composition of the Non-Kuwaiti Population by Regional Origin, 1975–1985

Regional Origin	*1975*		*1980*		*1985*	
	Number	*%*	*Number*	*%*	*Number*	*%*
Arab	419,187	80.2	574,495	72.5	642,814	63.3
Asian	97,813	18.7	204,104	25.8	355,947	35
African	440	0.1	1,601	0.2	2.039	0.2
European	4,280	0.8	9,984	1.3	11,908	1.2
American	814	0.2	1,997	0.2	3,142	0.3
Others	47	-	158	-	163	-
Not stated	168	-	-	-	-	-
Total	522,749	100	792,339	100	1,016,013	100

Source: Kuwait, *Research Studies on Population,* No. 3, 1987.

The 1973 oil boycott created serious economic problems for the world at large but in particular for the developing countries. For the densely populated countries of Asia that depended entirely on imported oil for their incipient industrialization, it meant either economic stagnation with catastrophic social and political consequences or the incurring of huge debts. Often the quickest alternative was to export the only asset these countries had in abundance, namely, their human resources. As an illustration, India registered a ninefold increase in its oil budget between 1971 and 1976. What literally saved the country was the sixfold increase during the same period in the total remittances sent home by Indian expatriates (Pant 1987). The strategy of oil in exchange for human resources was viewed as the only viable solution by India, Pakistan, Korea, and the Philippines. They were soon followed by Sri Lanka, Bangladesh, and Thailand (Table 2.5).

TABLE 2.5 Non-Kuwaiti Population by Nationality in 1990
           (by thousands)

Country	Total Population	Active in the Labor Force	Families
Jordan/Palestine	510	110	400
Egypt	215	180	35
India	172	130	42
Pakistan	90	77	13
Bangladesh	75	65	10
Sri Lanka	100	79	21
Philippines	45	38	7
Thailand	8	7	1
Other Arab countries	175	100	75
Other Asian countries	62	50	12
Other countries	15	11	4
Total	1.467	847	620

Source: ILO, *Rapport informel sur les travailleurs migrants du Koweït touchés par la crise du Golfe,* 1991.

Widening the Networks: The New Labor Migration

The post-oil boom labor market was divided into an "Arab" and an "Asian" sector, with the Iranians in a category of their own. As the organization of the labor market will be treated in detail in the next two chapters, suffice it to mention here that the allocation of the various ethnic groups in this market had been clear from the beginning. Arabs were found in all types of occupation, except that of domestic servant, and usually at a level superior to Asians. The latter were concentrated mainly in low-paid jobs in the private sector. Straddling the two groups, ethnically speaking, the Iranians worked mostly as merchants and laborers, but never in the government and the domestic spheres.

There were several ways in which Arab and Asian migrants differed from each other. The first difference was in the mechanism of recruitment. In the private sector, with the exception of large construction projects, labor migration from the Arab countries to Kuwait was often an individual enterprise: the prospective worker found an employer through direct personal contacts either with Kuwaitis or with expatriates already settled in the emirate. The personal network of friendship, kinship, and acquaintances that existed between people in Kuwait and the Arab countries played an important role in providing the Arab migrants with employment. In the public sector, the recruitment took place through bilateral agreements between a Kuwaiti public institution (e.g., the ministries of Health, Education, Justice, Religious Affairs) and its Arab counterpart, especially in Egypt and Jordan. Such agreements provided the Kuwaitis with an annual quota of experts (such as doctors, teachers, judges, preachers) to be employed in Kuwait for a limited contract period.

Unlike Arabs, Asians were seldom recruited directly by their employers. The majority had to pass through intermediate recruitment agencies. These agencies played a crucial role in taking stock of, informing about, matching, and manipulating the supply of, and demand for, labor at both ends of the line. In doing so, they usually made handsome profits. The presence of agencies was necessary since there were, as a rule, no direct contacts between Kuwaiti employers and Asian employees. It also made the whole process of migration more costly for Asian migrants in comparison to Arabs (Eelens et al. 1992). Besides, although all the Asian governments tried to regulate by law the level of fees chargeable by the agencies for their services, few were able to control the actual implementation of these laws. In 1989, for instance, Sri Lankans who sought work in Kuwait paid an average of 27,000 rupees (*ca* US$1,000) to their local agencies for the processing of their applications and travel documents. In principle, the fee was fixed at 2,700 rupees (US$100) (Eelens et al. 1992). According to a study by the International Labor Organization (ILO 1991) carried out on the eve of the Iraqi invasion, the debt incurred by an Indian worker in order to finance his or her out-migration to Kuwait averaged US$1,700.

Arabs and Asians also differed in their duration of residence in Kuwait. In 1985 the average residence period for all the migrants was 9 years (Table 2.6). Arabs had a longer average length of stay (median: 9.2 years) than Asians (median: 3.7 years). Among the Arab migrants, nearly 46 percent had lived in Kuwait for more than 10 years, the majority of them being Palestinians/Jordanians and Egyptians (Research Studies on Population [RSP] No. 3). As for the Asians, less than one-fifth (18 percent) had had the same length of stay. The fact that the turnover was greater among the latter was supported by the larger percentage of those who stayed for less than one year (16.1 percent versus 5 percent for the Arabs).

TABLE 2.6 Duration of Stay for Arab, Asian, and European Populations in Kuwait, 1985

Duration of Stay	Arabs (%)	Asians (%)	Europeans (%)
Less than one year	9.3	16.1	33.7
One year	5.2	13.8	18.0
Two years	6.1	13.7	13.0
Three years	5.9	9.6	7.7
Four years	5.4	6.4	6.3
Five–nine years	26.6	22.4	15.0
Ten–fourteen years	17.5	9.1	2.8
Fifteen+	28.3	8.9	3.5

Source: Kuwait, *Research Studies on Population*, No. 3, 1987.

TABLE 2.7 Arab and Asian Female Population and Labor Force Participation Rates Before the Oil Boycott, 1965–1970

	1965		1970	
Regional Origin	Total female population	Crude female lfp (%)	Total female population	Crude female lfp(%)
Arab	61,559	10%	128,120	9%
Asian	9,908	10%	15,863	16%

Source: Abridged from Russell 1990. Female population over age 15 is not
available by groups of countries; therefore only crude labor force participation
rates can be calculated.

TABLE 2.8 Arab and Asian Female Population and Labor Force Participation Rates After the Oil Boycott, 1975–1985

	1975		1980		1985	
Regional Origin	Total female population	Crude female lfp (%)	Total female population	Crude female lfp (%)	Total female population	Crude female lfp(%)
Arab	181,76	10%	234,289	12%	264,110	12%
Asian	31,179	30%	56,148	35%	118,035	61%

Source: Abridged from Russel 1990. Female population over age 15 is not available by groups of countries; therefore only crude labor force participation rates
can be calculated.

Unfortunately, data on reasons for residence are not available for the
year 1985. They are, however, available for the year 1980 (RSP No. 3).
To the question of why they were in Kuwait, 51.4 percent of the expatriates replied "to accompany relatives," while 47.9 percent gave "work" as
the reason. Work was the main reason given by non-Arabs (69.7 percent)
but not by Arabs (39.6 percent). Work was also the main reason for male
immigration (66.9 percent), while "accompanying the head of the household" was the main reason for female immigration (83.3 percent). In this
respect, there was a clear difference between Arab and Asian women:
while the former came to Kuwait mostly as dependents, the latter came
as migrant workers. Between 1960 and 1985 the crude percentage of
workers among Asian women jumped from 10 to 61 percent, while the
equivalent percentage among Arab women increased from 10 to 12 percent (tables 2.7 and 2.8). Among Arabs, "accompaniment" was most

widespread in the Palestinian community, as it was here that the highest expatriate dependency ratio[15] had been registered (Shah and Al Qudsi 1989).

The large presence of dependents among Arabs indicated that the sex ratio was more balanced in this group than among Asians. Sex ratio and the possibility of normal family life are two important factors for the stability of any migrant community. Whereas men and women in the Arab population were mostly related through marriage, men and women in the Asian population were not. To the extent that Asian workers were married, they were usually not accompanied by their spouses and did not live in Kuwait as family units. This influenced both their duration of stay (making it shorter) and the local stereotypical perceptions of their moral and sexual behavior (see Chapter 5).

On the whole, and as we will see in greater detail in Chapter 6, Arab migrants felt more at home in Kuwait than Asian migrants. In most cases, it did not take long before the Arabs reconstituted their social universe in the emirate. More often than not, the individual migrated to an already established circle of relatives and acquaintances from his or her native village or neighborhood. Moreover, linguistic and cultural commonality played a central role in the Arabs' fast adaptation. Their privileged position in the labor market as compared to Asians was another important factor.

A Multi-Ethnic, Multi-Cultural Society

The succinct data on expatriates' duration of residence in the emirate given above indicate that Kuwait was not merely a work camp for transient laborers, as one might easily assume from statistics about mass labor migration. Here it is appropriate to point out that in 1985, 30 percent of the 1.02 million non-Kuwaitis registered by the census were born in Kuwait (RSP No. 3). For the population—both the Kuwaitis and the long-time resident expatriates—there was a definite pattern of continuity in which the migratory flux itself constituted a constant feature of social life.

With the "Asianization" of its labor market, Kuwaiti society underwent important transformations. The most obvious change was the growing use of English as a common language: most street signs and all shop signs were now in both Arabic and English; Kuwait Television had two channels, KTV 1 with programs in Arabic and KTV 2 with programs in

English; Radio Kuwait had an exclusively English-language FM station, in addition to the various Arabic stations; to the *Kuwait Times*, established in 1961, was added in 1977 the *Arab Times*, and both dailies carried pages in Urdu and Hindi twice a week; most pieces of legislation, official decrees, and statistics were available in English translation; everywhere—in shops, government offices, hospitals, hotels—English was becoming as common as Arabic, and sometimes even more so.[16] The choice of English as an alternative working language can be traced back to Kuwait's past connection with Britain and the British-dominated Indian Ocean. But it was also a natural choice, considering the nationalities of the new migrants from the Indian subcontinent and the Philippines. Within each community, however, there existed a whole range of languages and dialects,[17] the sounds of which were becoming nearly as familiar as Arabic in the streets of Kuwait.

Post-oil Kuwait did not only adopt English as a language. In a way rather similar to other city-states of trade in the world—for instance Hong Kong and Singapore in the Far East and, of course, the other oil emirates of the Lower Gulf (e.g., Dubai)—Kuwait had a strikingly Western outlook, most typically expressed in its modern infrastructure and its pattern of consumption. Apart from oil and oil-related products, the country produced little. The Kuwaitis imported practically everything they consumed, from foodstuffs and clothing to raw materials and equipment, to plants, and livestock. Although an important amount of goods came from neighboring Middle Eastern countries, the emirate's major trade partners were Europe, the United States, and Japan. The shelves of Kuwaiti supermarkets were filled with French yogurt, German sausages, Belgian salad dressing, Dutch lettuce, Swiss cheese, and American peanut butter. Flowers in the flower shops were flown in from the Netherlands, Cyprus, and Colombia, clothes were imported from Paris as well as Beirut and Taiwan, while cars and all electric and electronic equipment came from Japan and Korea.

The Western strain in Kuwaiti life was mixed with pervasive Arab and Asian features. Thus a shopping tour on Friday (the Muslim holy day) could start at the open market on the Fourth Ring Road, a typical Bedouin event, lead on to Ikea, the Swedish furniture shop, where courteous Indian salesmen offered Swedish *pepperkakor* to the customers at Christmas time, and continue to the gold souk, where Italian and Indian jewelry hung in sparkling rows in the shop windows. In between, one might drop in at the Mishrif Fair Center, where young computer enthusiasts of all nationalities explored the latest Western and Japanese computer technology. In each neighborhood shopping center one found in a row a Pizza Hut, a chicken tikka restaurant, and a Lebanese-style *shawarma* stand, squeezed between the cooperative supermarket, the barber shop, and the vegetable shop. The emirate was criss-crossed by a highway network that neatly divided the city into residential neighborhoods. Both the roads and the neighborhood systems were evocative of California and its middle-class suburbs, while the white Kuwaiti mansions were vaguely reminiscent of the American *ante bellum* South. The daily consumption of Western and Japanese technology was not restricted to a few well-to-do people but was spread throughout the population, admittedly in varying degrees of sophistication: for instance, the migrants recorded messages to their families on cassette and video tapes almost as frequently as they wrote letters, while cellular phones, fax machines, and satellite dishes were as common as the car or the telephone to most Kuwaitis long before they became popular in the West.

In all aspects of life, the market catered to the tastes of all ethnic groups. In music shops, Egyptian stars like the late Umm Kulthum and Abdel Halim Hafez competed with Lebanese Fairouz, Kuwaiti Nabil Shuail, and a host of Indian, American, and Filipino pop singers. The video shops offered pirate copies of Hindi dramas and Egyptian comedies as well as the latest Hollywood films. The Kuwaitis had their own theaters, where the satirical comedies of Abdel Husein Abdel Ridha attracted large crowds, while the English-speaking middle-class expatriates watched roving British theater companies perform Shakespeare plays in the ballrooms of the five-star hotels.

As far as religion was concerned, the post-oil boom migration introduced much variation. Although many migrants from the subcontinent were Muslims (especially Pakistanis and Bangladeshis), one found among the new migrants Sikhs, Hindus, and Buddhists. Meanwhile, the largest "organized" religious communities (i.e., those with a church where collective rites were performed at regular intervals) were the Christians. According to the official statistics, the presence of Christians had increased from 1 percent in 1957 to 6.4 percent in 1980 (Annual Statistical Abstract 1989).[18] The percentage increase in 1985 (the last census taken before the war) was not made public, which might indicate a growth large enough to be considered worrisome for some segments of the indigenous population. The first Christians appeared in Kuwait with the Iraqis and Western Arabs. After 1975 the Christian population grew substantially due to migration from Kerala, Goa, Sri Lanka, and the Philippines. Traditionally, the Kuwaitis' attitude toward Christians was one of sympathetic tolerance, concretely expressed by the presence in downtown Kuwait of a large Catholic church donated by the emir.[19] The Protestant Church had also a compound a stone's throw away from the Church of the Holy Family. Both Protestants and Catholics had churches in Ahmadi, the oil town south of Kuwait. These two communities obviously enjoyed a special status in the emirate. The other religious communities were not equally privileged and had to be content with a more subdued existence, holding their services in anonymous-looking houses and flats spread over the town.

The Catholic Church was, as an exception, allowed to run a couple of schools, attended mostly by non-Kuwaiti Christian children. In the field of education, the line of division was officially between Kuwaitis and non-Kuwaitis, with the former attending the free public schools and the latter attending the private "community" schools. In reality, approximately half of the students in the Kuwaiti public schools were non-Kuwaitis, the majority being Palestinians/Jordanians, while the rest were nationals from the Gulf countries (Social Statistics 1988). Most non-Kuwaiti children, meanwhile, attended community schools. The presence of a community school was a sign of the relative stability and prosperity of a community, and indicated that its composition in terms of gender and age was close to normal. There were, for instance, no Sri Lankan, Filipino, or Bangladeshi schools, while there were Palestinian, Iranian, Egyptian, Pakistani, and Indian schools,[20] and a series of US, British, and French schools. The Western schools were usually not considered to be community schools since they were attended by children of various nationalities; the common denominator here was not ethnic origin but class, since the children attending these schools came from well-to-do families who could afford to pay the high tuition fees.

The geographical pattern of residence also reflected the ethnic diversity of the population. Kuwait had residential areas identified as "Kuwaiti," "mixed," and "rural" (i.e., populated by settled nomads). The "Kuwaiti" areas were inhabited by wealthy urban Kuwaitis. Only a handful of foreigners were found here, most of them upper middle-class Westerners and Arabs. As their name indicates, the "mixed" areas were mostly populated by urban Kuwaitis and expatriates of all nationalities. Some areas were identified with one particular expatriate group; largest and most homogeneous were the Palestinian neighborhoods of Nugra and Hawally, while smaller areas were known to be inhabited predominantly by Iranians, Indians, and others. Except for the segregation between "Kuwaiti" and "mixed" areas, however, one cannot claim that residential patterns were drawn along ethnic lines. Rather they followed class lines.[21] Thus the central and eastern parts of Kuwait were considered wealthier than the western and outlying neighborhoods; these were the so-called "rural" areas, Bedouin territory *par excellence*, where many unskilled expatriates also lived. As will be seen in the next chapter, not all the settled nomads were Kuwaiti citizens, since among the "rural" population there were people who fitted in neither the "Kuwaiti" nor the "expatriate" categories.

In the late 1980s, cultural and ethnic heterogeneity was well established as one of the most characteristic features of life in Kuwait. At the level of work and economic production, one had the distinct impression that the population, with all its diversity, formed an interdependent unit. At the same time, each ethnic group was engrossed in matters occurring in Kuwait or elsewhere that affected it alone and that the other groups were hardly aware of, or interested in. And there was a clear ethnic segregation when it came to friendships and other informal relationships. Yet again there were events, such as the Iran–Iraq war, that engaged the attention of all the ethnic communities because of the impact on security, trade, and the employment market in Kuwait, or, at an entirely different level, the opening of the giant round-the-clock Sultan Center supermarket. Finally there were situations, institutions, and concepts that most residents in the emirate, regardless of their nationality and cultural background, could immediately relate to.

Most prominent among these commonalities was the framework within which the relations between natives and migrants unfolded and which reflected the way the Kuwaitis organized the society in order to protect themselves against the migrant majority. Let me first introduce the politics of exclusion.

Notes

1. Historically, the Arabs are divided in two groups, the Adnani, or Northern, Arabs and the Qahtani, or Southern, Arabs. On a contemporary map, the line between Adnani and Qahtani runs roughly from the northern tip of the Republic of Yemen in the west to the United Arab Emirates in the east.

2. *Bani Utub* could be translated as the House of Utub. The meaning of *Utub* is not quite clear. According to Abu Hakima, it may derive from the root verb

ataba which means to move, to travel from place to place; the Al Sabah themselves seem to be of this opinion (Abu Hakima 1982:3). In this case the name of the founding tribe of Kuwait would be literally "the House of the Migrants."

3. Usually spelled as *Grane* in English sources.

4. The fact that the Gulf was in those days an integral part of this commercial sphere was clearly shown by the generalized use of the Indian rupee as the common currency. The Gulf states switched to the dinar in the 1960s.

5. On the other hand, the Al Sabah owned date plantations in Southern Iraq that gave them a substantial income. They were also engaged in caravan trade and levied taxes on the nomads who traded with Kuwait (Lorimer 1970; Abu Hakima 1982; Crystal 1990). However, these could not compare with the income generated by sea trade, which remained the main source of wealth for the whole of Kuwait.

6. The best proof of this cohesion occured when Iraq invaded Kuwait in 1990. The Iraqis tried in vain to find a Kuwaiti who would challenge the rule of the Al Sabah and step into their place. They found no one. The Kuwaitis surprised foreign observers by unanimously closing rank behind the emir. For a detailed study of Kuwait's political history, see Crystal 1992 and Ismail 1982.

7. In 1896, Mubarak killed his two brothers, Muhammad I and Jarrah, who he thought were leaning too much toward Ottoman Iraq.

8. This took place at the Conference of Uqair held in 1922 to discuss the borders between Kuwait, Iraq, and Ibn Saud's Sultanate of Najd, under the auspices of Great Britain which had both the mandate over Iraq and the authority to manage the foreign affairs of Kuwait in accordance with the 1889 Exclusive Agreement between the British and Mubarak. In this capacity, His Majesty's representative, Sir Percy Cox, handed over to Ibn Saud nearly two-thirds of Kuwait's territory.

9. This is the sedentary-nomadic antinomy writ large. Ibn Khaldoun wrote in the fourteenth century:

> Places that succumb to the Bedouins are quickly ruined. The reason for this is that the Bedouins are a savage nation, fully accustomed to savagery and the things that cause it. Savagery has become their character and nature. They enjoy it, because it means freedom from authority and no subservience to leadership. Such a disposition is the negation and antithesis of civilization . . . Under the rule of the Bedouins, their subjects live as in a state of anarchy, without law. Anarchy destroys mankind and ruins civilization. (*The Muqaddimah* 1967:118-119)

Although written in 1377, Ibn Khaldoun's analysis of Bedouin character and customs as seen through the eyes of urban Arabs can still be quoted to describe the view that many ordinary Arab men and women from the cities of Cairo, Damascus, Beirut, etc. have of the inhabitants of the Peninsula today. In his recent book, writing about the oil resources of the Arabian states, the Egyptian political writer

Mohammad Heikal had this revealing sentence: "A prize of unimaginable proportions had been handed to desert people who lacked the history or the culture to absorb it, while Egypt, the centre of Arab experience and culture, received only small change." (*Illusions of Triumph*, 1992)

The cultural gap between Eastern Arabians and the rest of the Arab world was long maintained by the presence of the desert. Only with the advent of commercial aviation and the building of the desert highway did the physical barrier break down, and the Kuwaitis could start tending to their Middle Eastern relations at the expense of their previous Indian Ocean connections.

10. Besides being a source of remittances on which the Arab labor-sending countries became increasingly dependent, Kuwait played an important role as an aid donor to the Arab world: in 1961, the same year it became independent, the country set up the Kuwait Fund for Arab Economic Development; in 1968 it joined the Arab Fund for Economic and Social Development newly established by the Economic Council of the League of Arab States. From 1973 to 1981 Kuwait's official development assistance amounted to nearly US$1 billion (Gerner 1985). Among the major recipients were Egypt, Sudan, the former People's Democratic Republic of Yemen, and the Palestinians in the occupied territories.

11. It is estimated that the Shia represented ca. 30 percent of the native Kuwaiti population.

12. For an overview of the question, see Cole and Keddie, eds. 1986; Momen 1985; and Robin Wright 1986.

13. It has been suggested that the oil-induced prosperity of the mid-1970s benefited the whole Middle East and allowed the traditional Arab labor-sending countries to initiate their own development programs. This led to a decrease of interest in Gulf migration among their populations (Birks and Sinclair 1980).

14. There is a persistent theory among experts on labor migration to the Gulf that the local governments deliberately switched from hiring Arab workers to hiring Asian workers when they realized what a political danger Egyptian, Palestinian, Syrian, and other Arab expatriates could represent for their stability. While this argument makes eminent sense, it has never been adequately proved. My contention is that there is not one specific reason for the switch. Rather, what made the prospect of hiring Asian workers attractive to the Kuwaitis and other Gulf employers was a combination of economic, political, and social factors, as will be demonstrated in the following chapters.

15. Defined as the ratio of persons aged less than 15 and more than 65 to persons aged 15-65 multiplied by 100.

16. In hospitals, restaurants, and hotels, where staff tended to be overwhelmingly Asian, a patient/customer who spoke only Arabic often had to have an interpreter.

17. Among the largest non-Arabic languages were Hindi, Malayalee, Konkani (spoken by Indians), Punjabi, Urdu (Indians and Pakistanis), Bengali (Bangla-

deshis), Sinhala and Tamil (Sri Lankans and Indians), Farsi (Iranians), and Tagalog (Filipinos).

18. Similar statistics do not exist for other religions, which, according to Islam, do not qualify as such. By religion, the Kuwaitis meant only the "religions of the Book," i.e., Islam, Christianity, and Judaism.

19. The church was built on a prime location, at the very heart of Kuwait City, on a piece of land that Abdullah al Salem, emir of Kuwait between 1950 and 1965, offered to the Catholic community in 1954. Abdullah even granted the bishop a loan without interest to cover the costs of construction. When, after its independence, Kuwait adopted a law forbidding non-Kuwaitis to own real estate properties in the country, the Church was asked to pay a symbolic yearly rent of KD 1 (SanMiguel 1978).

20. With its ten branches, nearly 10,000 students, and 500 teachers by 1990, the Indian School in Kuwait was among the largest overseas Indian schools in the world.

21. The distinction between ethnicity and class as principles of social organization and classification in Kuwait is a complex topic that will be discussed in Chapter 5.

3

The Politics of Exclusion

*Voilà donc une première définition
du héros tragique: il est l'enfermé,
celui qui ne peut sortir sans
mourir: sa limite est son privilège,
la captivité sa distinction.*
Roland Barthes, *Sur Racine*

Putting Exclusion in Place

In the early years of oil development (the 1940s and 1950s), Kuwait
did all it could to attract and facilitate the immigration of foreign workers who, at the time, were first and foremost Palestinian refugees. While
most Arab countries were less than enthusiastic in welcoming these
exiles into their territories, some of them simply and systematically
arresting anyone born in Palestine and interning them in camps without
further ado (Ghabra 1987), Kuwait opened its doors to practically everyone, whether they were teachers, doctors, administrators, engineers, or
peasants, and gave them work. All the testimonies I have gathered concurred on one fact: the Palestinian intelligentsia was, in those days,
admired, respected, and emulated by the Kuwaiti merchant class. At the
time, nationality was not yet an issue and, although Kuwait adopted its
first Nationality Law in 1948, people, on the whole, were still using the
age-old custom of classifying self and others according to their birth-
places and not according to their formal subjection to a state. This seems
to indicate that Kuwait's strategy toward its migrants has not always
been based on exclusion. In order for a politics of exclusion to evolve
successfully, three conditions are required: first, there must be an acute
sense of *external* threat, which presupposes that there is a sense of *internal* identification; second, there must be a central apparatus with the
capacity to provide both the ideological and the administrative means to

implement and reproduce exclusion, the best candidate for this role being the state; and third, there must be a cultural tradition favorable to the idea of exclusion, which, I suggest, can be found in Kuwait's tribal ideology.[2] Although these conditions had existed right from the beginning of the oil age, it was only in the aftermath of the oil boom, from the mid-1970s onwards, that they were fused together into a powerful dynamic that not only characterized the policy of the state but also pervaded general practice in everyday life. Prior to this period tensions and conflicts had existed and measures had been taken to exclude foreigners. But it was only after the oil boom that exclusion really became a coordinated system of ideology and practice with a strategic target and a coherent mode of procedure.

From the mid-1970s onwards, with the enormous increase in Kuwait's oil revenue, it gradually became clear that the purpose of the Kuwaiti migration policy was to maintain the transient character of labor immigration in order to ensure that the migrants did not settle down permanently in the country. Given their numerical superiority, this would inevitably have changed the character of Kuwaiti society. It was this concern for their own cultural survival, rather than the fear of the migrants' encroaching upon their newly gained material benefits, that has guided the Kuwaitis' treatment of the question of labor migration throughout the years. As a result *non-integration*, rather than integration, was viewed as the basis of social stability. In carrying out this politics of exclusion the Kuwaitis consistently played on the diacritical differences between the migrants and themselves, maintaining, reinforcing, and, when necessary, inventing such differences. The politics of exclusion was mediated through various measures aimed at countering the integrative effect of time and interactive habitualization. It ranged from formal categorization and legislation to informal customs and practices in everyday life and the manipulation of cultural values and symbols. Leaving the latter aspects to be treated in chapters 5 and 7, I will focus here on the structural features of exclusion.

The Delineation of Ethnic and Social Categories

In order to carry out a politics of exclusion, one must be able to distinguish between the various groups and classify them according to whether they qualify as an in-group or as an out-group with reference to a central set of criteria. To state that the overarching dividing line in

Kuwait was that between natives and migrants is correct but not particularly illuminating. The organization of Kuwaiti society is perhaps best conceptualized in terms of concentric circles, with the nuclear circle consisting of an aggregate of features that one can gather under the general designation of "Kuwaitiness." The other ethnic communities were positioned around this nucleus and at various distances from it according to the degree of compatibility they shared with the Kuwaiti standard. The greater the compatibility, the closer to the center; the lesser, the farther away from it. This positioning, meanwhile, was never static; it shifted according to whether we assess compatibility in terms of cultural isomorphism (for example: does a given group speak the same language, have the same religion, the same customs, as the Kuwaitis?) or in terms of types, actual frequency, and closeness of social interaction. I will contend, for instance, that the Palestinians shared many common cultural features with the Kuwaitis but that, in some respects, they did not necessarily entertain closer contacts with them than did, say, the Indians. Distance and compatibility, hence exclusion and inclusion, were thus both categorical and situational, a contention I will explain in more detail presently.

In Kuwait, we find three overarching categorical dichotomies in terms of which persons were identified and classified: Kuwaiti–non-Kuwaiti, Arab–non-Arab, and Muslim–non-Muslim. These are categories that were officially acknowledged in the public discourse of social life, universally understood, and, in principle, purely descriptive and value-neutral. In reality, given the Kuwaiti context, they were loaded with a wide range of connotations, and the definition of at least one of them ("Kuwaiti") was hotly disputed among the Kuwaitis themselves. As dichotomies for inclusion and exclusion worked out by the Kuwaitis, they naturally had native characteristics as their basic terms of reference. The more inclusive a category was, seen from this viewpoint, the less useful it was to the Kuwaitis, hence the less weight it carried in the general social context of Kuwait.

The First Dichotomy: Kuwaitis–Non-Kuwaitis

Undoubtedly the most outstanding among the three, this dichotomy was based on the critical criterion of *citizenship*. Citizenship was a novel concept in Kuwait and the other nations of Arabia, which were never lands of immigration in the sense that this phrase is used about America and Australia. As we saw in the previous chapter, there had always been an intense pattern of migration and exchange in the Arabian Peninsula before the advent of oil. In the absence of agriculture, people were compelled to migrate regularly in search of work and livelihood. Wherever they could find both, they settled down temporarily or permanently but always retained their ethnic identity. Thus sailors and laborers from Bahrain, Oman, and Persia worked and lived in Kuwait for years, but they remained known as Bahrainis, Omanis, and Persians. They did not "become" Kuwaitis. The same was true for Kuwaitis who moved to other towns in Arabia, where they remained known as Kuwaitis, sometimes generations after they had become an integral part of the local community.

Traditionally, most people in the region were identified according to their membership of a tribe (or its sub-divisions, the clan and the extended family), or according to the locality from which they originated. Such family names as *Al Yamani* (the Yemeni), *Al Najdi* (from the Najd), *Al Hijazi* (from the Hijaz) are common throughout the Gulf region. In contemporary Kuwait, for instance, *Al Hasawi* (from the Hasa region), *Behbehani*, and *Dashti* are the names of well-known families (Behbehan and Dasht are two areas in Western Iran). They allow the immediate identification of their bearers in terms of ethnic origin (Iranians in the case of Behbehani and Dashti), religion (Shia), and social status (urban merchants).

The Politics of Citizenship

It was only after World War II, with the emergence of nation-states in the region, that attempts were made to bring about a formal recognition of the incorporation of new members into the state within a relatively short time span. Citizenship became a blanket designation that overlooked tribal and geographic origins, although, as we have just seen, underneath the blanket the old distinctions lived on. Seen from the viewpoint of the local population, citizenship was a classificatory principle alien to their way of conceptualizing social relations. The most meaningful social categories, for marriage purposes for example, were still drawn up along other lines—extended families for urban Kuwaitis and tribes for settled nomads. Tribal ties, especially, spread across the modern borders, mostly over to Saudi Arabia but also to Iraq and the Lower Gulf. As an actual social structure, tribes may have lost some of their previous significance; as a referent for social identity and loyalty, however, they still played an important role (Al Haddad 1985). Citizenship, one of the fore-most characteristics of the modern nation-state, and tribal ideology have, in many cases, cohabited uneasily under a regime that has been described as the "simultaneity of the unsimultaneous" (Tibi 1990). As a result, the conceptualization of citizenship in Kuwait and, I daresay, throughout the Gulf region is a topic that still needs a great deal of investigation.

It is common to hear that what gave citizenship its crucial significance in Kuwait today were the social privileges and material benefits it implied. Although correct, this statement requires further explanation. Kuwaiti citizens did enjoy welfare and social benefits that were extensive by any standards. Yet the majority did not apprehend them as privileges but as dues. If the citizens had any perception of being privileged at all, it was because they compared themselves with the non-Kuwaiti majority to whom these same privileges were denied. For example, if the right to own land seemed such a coveted prerogative, it was because it was denied to the non-Kuwaiti majority, not because it was granted the Kuwaiti minority. Likewise, the comfortable and leisurely life associated with Kuwaitis acquired its full meaning only when compared with the circumstances under which many of these migrant workers lived. One can thus claim that, even more than the privileges it imparted, what really gave citizenship its significance was the presence of the disproportionately large *non-citizen* population. Not only would the privileges have been concretely fewer without this presence, but also their enjoyment and appreciation would not have been the same for lack of contradistinction.

In the context of this multinational society, Kuwaiti identity was the identity to which the fewest people could make claim. Because it was based on citizenship, the social category "Kuwaiti" was the most closed and exclusive category, just as its opposite, the category "non-Kuwaiti," was the most open and inclusive one. The distinction between Kuwaiti and non-Kuwaiti was a fundamental feature of daily life in the emirate, and it was actively used by everyone and in every conceivable situation. There were indeed few public situations in Kuwait where Kuwaiti identity was not automatically granted preeminence over non-Kuwaiti identity, a point which will be amply illustrated in Chapter 5. Let us take a closer look at the development of Kuwaiti citizenship, this most crucial of all diacritical features.

Two decrees adopted in 1948 defined as "originally Kuwaiti" "members of the ruling family, those permanently residing in Kuwait since

1899, children of Kuwaiti men and children of Arab or Muslim fathers also born in Kuwait" (Crystal 1990). Naturalization was possible for people who had lived in Kuwait at least ten years, were employed, and spoke Arabic; it could also be granted "by special order for valuable services." On the other hand, citizenship could be revoked within five years as a penalty for diverse crimes, among them "propagating anti-Islamic ideas" (Crystal 1990). In this original legislation, the *jus soli* principle was acknowledged, since permanent residency and birth on Kuwaiti territory automatically gave access to Kuwaiti nationality. This is a noticeably modern innovation, which contrasted sharply with the tradition of classifying people according to the birthplace of their identifiable ancestors, not their own, which is the same as aligning citizenship with blood or the *jus sanguinis* principle. By espousing the *jus soli* principle, Kuwait's 1948 legislation was inclusive rather than exclusive.[3]

Eleven years later, in the new Nationality Law of 1959, which is the one in effect today, the category "originally Kuwaiti" was widened to include descendants of those settled in Kuwait since 1920 instead of 1899, but the category "children of Arab or Muslim fathers also born in Kuwait" was dropped. The *jus sanguinis* principle reasserted its preponderance: only sons of Kuwaiti fathers can claim citizenship. Naturalization was still possible for the others, but it was severely constrained. Within less than thirty years, the law was amended seven times: in 1960, 1966, 1972, 1978, 1980, 1981, and 1987. Two amendments were of major importance: the 1960 amendment, which restricted the annual number of cases of naturalization to fifty—but this seems to have been meant for non-Gulf cases only;[4] and the 1981 amendment, which restricted the granting of Kuwaiti nationality only to Muslim candidates.

It is worth noting that, in Kuwait, citizenship is understood primarily in terms of access to social rights. The political dimension of citizenship is somewhat underplayed because the exercise of one of the most basic political rights, participation in parliamentary elections, has been granted to Kuwaiti citizens only sporadically since independence. Although Kuwait officially adopted a constitutional regime after independence in 1961, the elected National Assembly has been suspended twice, once in 1976 and again in 1986. The first suspension lasted five years and the second six years. Besides, suffrage was the privilege of only male citizens twenty-one years old or over, who belonged among the so-called "original" or "first category" Kuwaitis—i.e., those whose forefathers were residents in Kuwait in 1920, the year of the Battle of Jahra. This event, it is often claimed, saw the birth of an explicit Kuwaiti "national" awareness by creating a nucleus of hard-core citizenry encompassing those who had taken part in the events and their descendants. These people qualified as full-fledged "first category" Kuwaitis. Suffrage was thus denied to the majority of the Kuwaiti nationals—all the women, the naturalized Kuwaiti males, and their sons. Before the Iraqi invasion, the proportion of men with full political rights was estimated at less than 5 percent of the total population (Crystal 1992). The question of granting suffrage to all adult male citizens has been recurrent since Kuwait achieved independence. According to a law passed in July 1966, naturalized citizens could exercise their political rights twenty years from the date of the adoption of the law, that is, by July 1986. In 1986, however, the law was amended shortly before the dissolution of the National Assembly, extending this period to thirty years from July 1966.[5]

Since the difference between Kuwaiti citizens and expatriates, who all carried national passports from other countries, was unambiguous, there was never a "citizenship controversy" between these two categories. Both Kuwaitis and migrant workers knew their own and the others' national status and the rights and limitations deriving from these statuses. It was among the local population itself that controversy existed, and it was inevitably linked to access to benefits and privileges attached to citizenship.

I suggested earlier that Kuwaitis took the social and material benefits they enjoyed for granted. It was often argued that since oil was the country's natural resource, "given to the Kuwaiti people by Allah," it was only natural that the revenues from its exploitation should be used for the benefit of the people. That Kuwait was a "welfare state" should not be a surprise for anyone, said the Kuwaitis. In fact, many were convinced that the welfare system could have been more developed; in their view, the state, as the administrator of oil wealth, fulfilled badly its most important function, that of distributing this wealth among the people. Many felt that they were being cheated. The rich (i.e., the ruling family and the merchants), they said, got all the money, while the rest of the population, who were state employees and lived on their wages, received only the leftovers. The main bone of contention among the native population was a definition of Kuwaitiness that arbitrarily regulated access to political power and, consequently, to material benefits. At stake, however, was not the demand for greater *inclusion*; rather it was the demand for a more fair *distribution* among those who were already included, that is, those already defined as Kuwaitis.

But the citizenship controversy in Kuwait was a complex and intricate problem that touched upon more than just the matter of distribution of privileges. It lay at the heart of the question of how to balance the population so as to guarantee the state a degree of viability while not infringing too brutally on the cultural fabric of the society. In any country, there are basic functions that need to be fulfilled, and not all of them can be entrusted to foreign workers. There are, for example, the tasks related to internal security and the armed forces. Very few Kuwaiti citizens were interested in having a career in the police and the army, except at the level of officers and administrators. For the rank and file the state had to look to recruit elsewhere. From independence until August 1990, Kuwait had found a solution in the presence of the so-called "stateless," popularly known in Kuwait as the *bidoons* (from *bidoon jinsiyya*, literally "without nationality").[6] The *bidoons* fell neither under the category of Kuwaitis nor under that of non-Kuwaitis in the sense of expatriates (i.e., nationals of other countries with temporary residence in Kuwait). They consisted of two main types of people: the nomads and the mercenaries.

The stateless nomads did not register with the authorities at the time the 1959 Nationality Law came into force, due to a combination of failure to understand the importance of the newly introduced concept of citizenship and an attempt to hold on as long as they could to their traditional pattern of cyclical migration. Also, initially, the young state of Kuwait went a long way to permit and facilitate the survival of this tradition by leaving its borders open to the nomads' comings and goings.[7] In the 1960s they were allowed to settle permanently in Kuwait without, however, being formally granted the status of citizens. Until 1986 they could enjoy the free health and educational services offered by the state on a par with the Kuwaitis. In return they were expected to provide the country with its rank and file recruits for the army and the police under the command of officers who were Kuwaiti nationals. With their background as fighters and marauders from the desert, most nomads, unlike the urban Kuwaitis, willingly entered the armed forces, all the more so as this occupation was generally considered as the best way of gaining access to nationality. Service in the armed forces also allowed them to benefit from the free housing scheme that was otherwise an exclusive privilege of the citizens. Since they benefited from the free education offered to the Kuwaitis but were excluded from ownership rights (hence from owning a trade business in the private sector), most of the educated *bidoon* nomads who did not opt for a career in the army or the police chose to enter the technical professions (e.g., engineers, medical workers) and academia. Similar to the Kuwaitis in outlook, dialect, and tradition, their status as stateless was often apparent only to the informed natives. Before the war, many expatriate residents in Kuwait were unaware of their existence as a separate social category, especially as the official census regularly counted them as Kuwaitis, a fact to bear in mind when we read the population and labor statistics. Besides, the boundary between "Kuwaiti" and "*bidoon*" was porous in the case of the nomads due to naturalization and intermarriage.[8]

The second category of *bidoons* were the mercenaries. Unlike the nomads, who had never had any formal citizenship previously, the mercenaries were citizens from the surrounding Arab states (mainly Iraq, Syria and Jordan). Although officially Kuwait has a system of universal conscription, the lack of enthusiasm for things military among the native male population at the crucial period of independence, when an army had to be created, made it necessary for the authorities to turn to the services of non-citizen soldiers. But, as a self-ironical Kuwaiti has explained to me, "no states like to admit to having a mercenary army." So in order to avoid the embarrassment of such an admission, the Ministry of Defense listed the men as stateless, in this way lumping together two different groups of people who served the same national purpose.

In the *bidoons* the Kuwaitis thought they had found a solution to their predicament: they had at their disposal a population part of which (the nomads) were, for all practical purposes, native, yet, through lack of citizenship, were willing to perform the necessary tasks in the armed forces. Moreover, the *bidoons* helped to inflate the demographic data but without, at the same time, having full access to all the socio-economic benefits. This curious situation lasted until the mid-1980s. When Khomeini's revolution swept across Iran and war broke out between Iran and Iraq, much of the Kuwaitis' concern for the country's internal security found its concrete expression in the existence of the *bidoons*: their ambiguous status as an unacknowledged population provided a human pool into which Iraqi refugees, draft dodgers, and infiltrators as well as absconding workers and illegal aliens could easily blend after getting rid of their identity papers.

In 1986, the authorities abruptly changed their policy: the *bidoons* lost access to education and health services. From that time on they were to be viewed and treated in the same way as the non-Kuwaiti expatriates. Gradually it became more difficult for them to get jobs. By late 1988, if convicted of a crime, the mercenary *bidoons* were deported back to their original countries, to the extent it was possible to establish the identity of these countries. In 1989 the Ministry of Planning acknowledged publicly that the *bidoons* had so far been counted as Kuwaitis in the censuses and statistics, and it released the real percentage of the Kuwaitis in the population (28 percent instead of 40 percent) and labor force (14 percent instead of 20 percent).[9] In 1989, I was told that the *bidoon* population was approximately 200,000.[10]

We thus have the paradoxical situation where citizenship as a classificatory principle was at one and the same time *insignificant*, because it arbitrarily cut across older and more deep-seated patterns of identification along the lines of tribes and extended families, and *crucial*, because of its vast instrumentality in bringing about social differences measurable in terms of material and, particularly, political and social advantages. Those in power made use of citizenship not only to exclude the expatriates but also to organize and define the internal power relationships. The clearest illustration was the distinction made between the enfranchised "first category," or "original Kuwaitis" (whose forefathers were settled in Kuwait since 1920), and the disfranchised "second category," or naturalized Kuwaitis. Kuwaiti women of both categories did not have the franchise. As a result of these electoral practices, most Kuwaitis, prior to the 1990 Iraqi invasion, did not construe citizenship in terms of the exercise of political rights. What citizenship meant for the Kuwaiti masses, as opposed to the privileged enfranchised upper class, was access to the welfare benefits which extended beyond free education, healthcare and housing, as will be seen presently.

Citizenship and the Social Rights

Before the war, all residents in Kuwait, irrespective of their nationalities and ethnic origins, enjoyed substantial general social benefits. These ranged from free health services, free telephone, generously subsidized electricity, water, gasoline, and basic food stuffs (such as oil, rice, sugar, milk, lentils, and tomato paste). In 1982–1983, 10 percent of GDP went to the payment of all subsidies, including those toward water and electricity. In addition to these universal benefits, there were others to which only Kuwaiti citizens had access.

Education, from primary school to university, was entirely free, as was healthcare. There were in addition a number of allowances which only Kuwaiti citizens were entitled to, such as family allowances, marriage allowances,[11] living allowances for students, and others. Of considerably greater importance, however, was the benefit of free housing. By most standards, the Kuwaiti housing system was exceptional and therefore merits some attention. All married Kuwaiti men were entitled to their own private house. Originally, they had the choice between receiving a ready-built house or, if they earned a monthly income over KD 600, a plot of land and a loan of KD 56,000 to build the house of their choice. This loan was interest-free; the borrower was expected to repay KD 85 per month and, after seventy years, the debt was cancelled. This second alternative did not work out satisfactorily as many citizens squandered the money instead of using it to build the house and had to apply for new loans. For a while, the government suspended this system and the Kuwaitis had to accept ready-built, so-called "middle-class" houses. These were houses of a standard size of 500 sq.m and came in six different models. The architecture was "modern" and "Western"— rooms, for instance, were not built around an interior courtyard. Yet care was taken to retain some of the main traditional Kuwaiti features, such as the *diwaniyya*, a reception room with direct access to the street where the men of the household receive their male guests without disturbing the female members of the family. However, few owners were happy with the ready-built houses, and soon the National Housing Authority was flooded with applications for loans in order to make changes to the buildings. Such changes sometimes had disastrous consequences—in many cases amateurish enlargements caused whole buildings to collapse. The plot-and-loan system was reinstated as a parallel alternative. One rule remained unchanged: during the first ten years of his ownership of a government house, the citizen was not allowed to rent or sell it, since it was still considered state property. Houses and plots were distributed on the basis of seniority of application; tribal, social, and religious affiliations were, in principle, irrelevant. This egalitarian policy led to the mixing of a population that had traditionally followed such affiliations as principles of residence. In the short term, it created considerable social tensions; consequences in the long run are more difficult to predict.

Another social benefit attached to Kuwaiti citizenship was guaranteed employment. Since this topic will be covered in detail in the next section of this chapter, it suffices here to quote Article 41 of the Constitution, whereby the Kuwaiti State pledges to provide all its citizens with a job appropriate to their level of skills.

Every Kuwaiti has the right to work and to choose the type of his work. Work is a duty of every citizen necessitated by personal dignity and public good. The State shall endeavour to make it available to citizens and to make its terms equitable.
(The Constitution of the State of Kuwait 1962, official translation)

In addition to these substantial social benefits, Kuwaitis enjoyed special rights that allowed them to expand and develop their sources of income if they so wished and if their abilities permitted them to. These were the right to sponsorship and the right to own real estate properties. I will not elaborate on the subject of sponsorship since it will be the central topic of the next chapter. As for ownership of real estate, before the invasion it provided citizens with a solid source of income. Many Kuwaitis made fortunes from renting accommodations to the 1.2 million-strong expatriate population, either directly or through the non-Kuwaitis' employers.[12] Since non-citizens were forbidden by law to own real estate in Kuwait, they were at the mercy of the Kuwaiti landlords and the latter's willingness to abide by the Rent Law.[13] A crucial requirement for the exercise of both rights to sponsorship and real estate ownership was the continued presence of a large expatriate population.[14]

The Second Dichotomy: Arabs–Non-Arabs

This distinction was much less restrictive than the Kuwaiti–non-Kuwaiti dichotomy, since "Arabs" included Kuwaitis and the majority of the non-Kuwaiti population. Besides, this category was inclusive, not only in terms of ethnic origin but also in terms of class, since the richest Kuwaiti employer and the poorest Egyptian employee equally qualified as Arabs.

As compared with non-Arabs, Arab identity in Kuwait implied, first and foremost, the objective advantage of relative cultural and linguistic familiarity. I say relative because, as already pointed out, there could be important differences, both objective and subjective, between Western Arabs and Gulf Arabs. The fact that non-Kuwaiti Arabs were by no means a homogeneous group further complicates any general statements about Arabism in Kuwait. Before the war, Kuwait was perhaps the country in the Gulf where the official rhetoric about Arab unity came closest to being a reality, at least when this unity was measured in terms of Arab presence in the country and Arab influence on the local society. This was closely related to the presence of a large, stable, and prosperous Palestinian community, active in both the public and private sectors.[15]

Unlike non-Arabs, Arabs were not considered by Kuwaitis as foreigners (*ajaanib*), simply as non-Kuwaitis (*ghair kuwaitiyyin*). The Labor Law, for example, speaks of "Kuwaiti laborer," "Arab laborer," and "foreign laborer." Describing a colleague to me, a Kuwaiti had said: "She is not a foreigner, she is Egyptian" (*hiyya mu ajnabiyya, hiyya masriyya*). The discernible sense of mutual identification based on the common use of the Arabic language was reinforced by the absence of unambiguous income disparity: some Arabs, in particular Palestinians/Jordanians but also Lebanese, Syrians, and Iraqis, were wealthier than many Kuwaitis themselves. As a rule, Arabs were better employed and better paid than non-Arabs (Table 3.1): practically everywhere Arabs were the immediate superiors of non-Arabs and served as the representatives of the Kuwaiti head or owner in companies, factories, and offices. They generally enjoyed a more elevated social status than non-Arabs, which brought them into closer contact with the natives in the areas of work and business. When we spoke English together and I asked my Kuwaiti informants whether they had many "expatriate" friends, their answers, whenever positive, always referred to people of various Arab nationalities, never to non-Arabs.

TABLE 3.1 Variations in Monthly Salary (KD) and Working Hours per Week Among Some Major Nationality Groups in Kuwait (males), 1983

Nationality	Monthly salary (KD)	Working hours per week
Kuwaitis	424	40.9
Palestinians/Jordanians	358	43.5
Egyptians	251	46.3
Iraqis	307	43.5
Indians	192	49.0
Pakistanis & Bangladeshis	201	47.6
Syrians & Lebanese	448	46.7
European, Americans	362	47.7

Source: Abridged from Shah and Al Qudsi 1989.

Nevertheless, this does not mean that the interaction between Kuwaitis and Arabs was close in absolute terms. Most of the time it was limited to formal encounters in the public sphere, such as the office, the school, the shop and the mosque. In the private sphere, on the other hand, the Kuwaitis seemed to have opted for a policy of keeping Arab migrants at arm's length. Many Arab expatriates had never been invited to a Kuwaiti home, no matter how long they had been living in the country. Likewise, Arabs seldom established ties of informal friendship with Kuwaitis. Although there was a growing tendency for men among the lower middle class, in particular settled nomads, to marry non-Kuwaiti Arab women (especially Egyptians) as their second or third wives, such marriages were construed as misalliances by most Kuwaiti families. This was particularly true for the urban middle class. Here, marriage was often monogamous and the partners' family backgrounds, not only their nationalities, were of critical importance. Marriages between Kuwaiti women and non-Kuwaiti Arab men were a relatively rare occurrence, because women stood to lose rather than gain from such unions, as I will show in greater detail in Chapter 7.

Despite this lack of close informal interaction between Kuwaitis and Arab expatriates, and the pronounced tendency to national endogamy, it remains true that the Arabs shared a closer affinity with the Kuwaitis than the rest of the expatriate population. They were included in the Kuwaitis' definition of social humanity in a way that non-Arabs, in particular the Asians, were not. In their interaction with the Arabs, Kuwaitis showed a great concern for the judgments the Arabs passed on them, judgments that they knew were embedded in a value system comparable to their own. Consequently, they also felt a greater need for impression management than in their interaction with the non-Arabs; hence the paradoxical feature of cultural closeness and social distance that characterized Kuwaiti–Arab relations and the absolute absence of Arab workers in certain occupations, as will be shown presently.

The Third Dichotomy: Muslims–Non-Muslims

This was the least explicitly articulated dichotomy. Not only was the category "Muslims" the least exclusive of all, embracing as it did Kuwaitis, Arabs, *and* a good many non-Arabs as well, but it was also an open category: while it was practically impossible to become a Kuwaiti or an Arab, anyone could at any time convert to Islam. As a result, this dichotomy was much less instrumental than the two preceding ones. As a marker of identity, Islam was generally submerged by the more salient criteria of ethnic origin and citizenship.

On the level of discourse, the Muslim–non-Muslim dichotomy appeared to have a mainly abstract and rhetorical value, to be used on special political and religious occasions and for specific and limited purposes. In a society where, according to official statistics, Muslims represented over 90 percent of the population, Islam was a uniting rather than an excluding factor. Therefore the dichotomy was seldom explicitly used by Kuwaitis. In practice, however, there was a clear and widespread positive bias toward Muslims and all things Islamic, in particular Islamic behavior and the overt subscription to Islamic values. This was not so much because of their religious meaning as because of their close association with Kuwaiti cultural identity. In this sense, there was a similarity between Muslim status and Arab identity: since Arabs and Muslims shared a common language and, to a certain extent, a common socio-religious discourse with the Kuwaitis, Arabism and Islam dispensed to these men and women a recognizable humanity, as seen from the native population's viewpoint. Translated into practice, this "humanity" did not necessarily mean closer social relationships, rather the opposite, as already suggested. Yet, in many cases, it did provide a degree of protection against the harshest treatment in employment situations. This argument may be used to explain why the 90,000-strong Pakistani community in Kuwait differed from Indians and Sri Lankans. Like these other subcontinental nationals, the majority of Pakistani migrants to the Middle East were production workers (Shah 1983). There were more unskilled than skilled workers among them, with the skilled workers being concentrated in occupations such as drivers, carpenters, masons, and tailors (Shah 1983). Yet, as was the case with Arabs, one did not find Pakistanis in the lowest paid jobs, for instance, cleaners. However, Muslim identity alone is obviously an insufficient explanation, since another national group, the Bangladeshis, was also uniformly Muslim but was strongly represented in the cleaning sector, which was, as we will see, one of the least paid and most vulnerable.[16] This difference emphasizes the role played by factors such as skills and the historical links existing between the migrant communities and Kuwait in determining the occupational and social niche occupied by these communities in the local system of ethnic and labor stratification. It also shows that relatively little importance was attached to the Muslim–non-Muslim dichotomy in social life in Kuwait when compared to the other two dichotomies.

What sets the category "Muslim" apart from the categories "Kuwaiti" and "Arab" was the fact that it was indiscriminately open. As a potential channel for "category crossing" it represented a weak link that could threaten to defeat the Kuwaiti politics of exclusion. It is from this perspective that one has to understand the absence of religious proselytizing in the emirate. "Category crossing" did occur, nevertheless. According to figures released by the Ministry of Awqaf (endowments) and Islamic Affairs, there was a steady trickle of conversions to Islam each year (for instance, 347 in 1988). Most of the converts were male migrants from the subcontinent. I have no data on the possible consequences of conversion for the social/occupational status of the new Muslims. Materially speaking, a needy Muslim benefited from the financial assistance of the House of Zakat[17] and, during the month of Ramadan and the religious festivities, could partake of the free meals served at the mosques. The meals were not insignificant for many of the semi- and low-skilled male migrants who did not have their families with them in Kuwait, lived in cramped quarters shared with other laborers, and had no opportunity to cook a proper meal after a long day's work.

With regard to the occupational advantages, I have been able to find only one area in which Muslim identity could make a difference: in the category of domestic servants, a Muslim woman from Sri Lanka was more expensive to hire than a Christian one (KD 120 versus KD 80). This seems to indicate that religion did make a difference in the way some Kuwaitis evaluated the migrants, especially when they were to be employed in positions of trust, such as in private homes. In other words, it was not in every situation that the differentiation between Muslims and non-Muslims was operationalized, nor was it used by everyone. Kuwaiti women in particular tended to place emphasis on this aspect, which could explain why the only concrete instance I have come across where this dichotomy was actively and explicitly used was precisely in the area of recruitment of servants. Yet, this evidence is not altogether conclusive: indeed, it must be observed that if some Kuwaiti employers insisted on hiring Muslim Sri Lankans or Muslim Filipinas as maids, they never recruited Arab women to do this job, even though, statistically speaking, there were many more Muslims in the Middle East than in Sri Lanka or the Philippines. This was all the more striking as Kuwaitis commonly lamented that their children learned to speak bad Arabic when brought up by foreign nannies. Hiring Muslim and Arabic-speaking domestic personnel would logically have been a better solution, but it was one that, as far as my observations indicated, Kuwaitis never resorted to.

Exclusion and the Conceptualization of Work

Since the 1950s the flow of migrant workers to Kuwait had been continuous. If its source in the labor-sending countries seemed inexhaustible, so did the demand in the host country. The scope of the need for manpower widened as oil income grew and as the projects of infra-structure-building became more ambitious. By the 1980s, as the phase of construction neared its end, the phase of maintenance and service took over. By then, also, the native population had settled down to a way of life in which the migrant workers' presence had become one of the principal mainstays. Factories, offices, hospitals, schools, shops, and the large private houses had to be manned and kept up. Inevitably, the migrants' presence itself created further demands, further markets, and further opportunities. The Kuwaitis' dependence on the migrant population grew at an exponential rate. With it grew the politics of exclusion under the aegis of the state. It was in the area of work that exclusion gained its clearest expression, most of all in the distinction between Kuwaiti *employment* and non-Kuwaiti *labor*.

Although *employment*, *labor*, and *work* are terms that are often used interchangeably, many scholars, in particular the sociologists of work, have drawn attention to the important difference between them, not least in the way actors themselves perceive their activity (Arendt 1958; Berger 1964; Blauner 1964; Parker 1983). Of the three terms, only *employment* implies a social relationship and the idea of remuneration for activity performed during set hours. The terms *work* and *labor* refer to the activity itself. *Work* has the broadest meaning of "activity" as opposed to "rest;" it does not necessarily imply remuneration as in employment, nor does it always lead to production: work can be productive or unproductive. What it does imply, however, is the exertion of effort. *Labor*, on the other hand, has a more specific meaning. It is commonly understood in the sense proposed by Arendt of a necessary activity "for the sake of making a living" (1958:127). It is often a synonym for fatigue, travail, and burden, as Parker (1983) remarks. It was in the sense of labor that work has been, at different times and in different places, looked upon as a curse, a drudgery, or an undignified thing to do. The distinction drawn here between Kuwaiti employment and non-Kuwaiti labor reflects the situation in the actual labor market as well as the discourse and attitude of both natives and migrants which associated the concept of work (*shughul*) as labor exclusively with the migrants. In the following pages, I will show that this distinction came to prevail through a process that turned what was essentially an objective weakness, namely, Kuwait's acute shortage of resources and skills, into an exclusive social privilege, namely the Kuwaitis' radical discrimination between their own activities and the work of the non-Kuwaiti migrants.

The Division of Labor According to the Logic of Exclusion

The only reason why the migrant workers were in Kuwait was to work. The overwhelming majority of those migrants who were not workers were workers' dependents. With a few exceptions, the migrants were spread over the whole spectrum of the labor market, at all levels except the highest. It was thus in the labor market—rather than the market place, as Furnivall suggests for his tropical plural societies—that Kuwaitis and non-Kuwaitis met in the first place, and it was the logic of the labor market that primarily fashioned their relationships. Labor, as an aspect of social organization and a social activity, and the labor market were of utmost importance in the context of the Kuwaiti plural society. As elsewhere, employment in Kuwait was primarily a function of demographic factors, skills, and opportunity.

As far as demography is concerned, Kuwait's problem was not only the small size of the native population but also its young age (Table 3.2). With almost half of its citizens aged under 15 and the majority of those between 15 and 19 being in education, by the late 1980s Kuwait had a clearly inadequate supply of human resources. By comparison, the non-Kuwaiti population pyramid was unmistakably one of active workers: here the largest age group consisted of males between 25 and 45 and, while the 0–15 group was rather substantial, the category aged 65+ was extremely small.

In the area of education, the Kuwaitis were proud of their achievements in the eradication of illiteracy. They liked to remind the population that upon independence in 1961, nearly half (48.7 percent) of the Kuwaitis were illiterate; by 1985, this percentage had been brought down to 17% (ASA 1989). Among the GCC countries, Kuwait alone made not only primary but also intermediary education compulsory for both boys

TABLE 3.2 Population Pyramids for Kuwaitis and Non-Kuwaitis, 1988

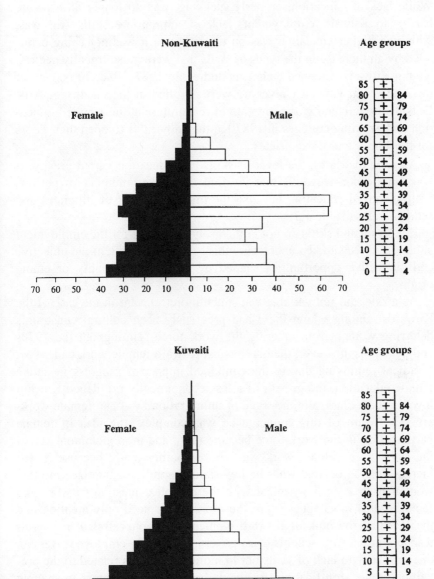

Source: Kuwait, *Annual Statistical Abstract*, 1989.

and girls. In 1989, education took up 9.4 percent of the national budget. While lack of education, properly speaking, was no longer an absolute barrier to Kuwaiti employment, lack of appropriate skills still was. Although higher education was on the increase, it was not being paralleled by an increase in the types of skills that were most urgently needed. Young Kuwaitis shunned technical studies. In 1987–1988, 70 percent of the students at Kuwait University were enrolled in the Faculty of Arts. Outside the university, the low rate of registration at the Applied Education and Training colleges in 1987 led the authorities to open their doors for the admission of expatriates.

As for expatriates, the level of skills and education varied greatly. It was among non-Kuwaitis that we find the highest number of persons with advanced education but also the highest number of illiterates and semi-literates (Table 3.3).

Education and skills do not in themselves account for the employment situation in Kuwait. To understand this, we need to look at the objective and subjective opportunities shaped by sex and nationality or ethnic origin.

As a rule, the sex variable was much more relevant in the case of the Kuwaitis, among whom there had previously been cultural constraints deterring women from entering the work force. Throughout the 1970s and the 1980s, however, the bias against Kuwaiti female work underwent a radical rethinking due to the combined impact of progress in native female education, the growth of a less economically privileged Kuwaiti lower middle class, and the wave of immigration by Asian female workers. The result of this convergence was complex: the idea of female participation in the work force became more and more common, yet, at the same time, female work was viewed ambivalently because it was increasingly associated with the low-status, morally stigmatized migrant women from Asia. I will deal with the complex question of work and female status in Chapter 7. For the moment we need only mention that the fact that the bulk of Kuwaiti women were concentrated in jobs as teachers in Kuwaiti schools or as government sector employees was not due primarily to lack of skills but to moral constraints related to the prevailing ethnic stratification. As for the role of ethnic factors in shaping work opportunities, it is best understood through a review of the three sectors in the Kuwaiti economy.

TABLE 3.3 Percentage Distribution of Labor Force in Kuwait According to Educational Status, 1985

Educational status	Kuwaiti		Non-Kuwaiti	
	Male	Female	Male	Female
Illiterate	17.0	2.5	24.8	24.4
Read and write	12.6	1.9	26.4	33.1
Primary	15.3	4.4	7.7	2.6
Intermediate	25.8	21.1	11.2	4.3
Secondary & post secondary	19.5	44.8	18.1	21.7
University	9.8	25.3	11.8	13.9
Total	100.0		100.0	

Source: Kuwait, Research Studies on Population, No. 3, 1987.

TABLE 3.4 Percentage Distribution of the Economically Active Population by Sex, Nationality Group, and Major Occupational Groups, 1985

Occupation	Kuwaiti			Non-Kuwaiti			% of non-national workers in each occupation
	M	F	M+F	M	F	M+F	
Professional & technical work	13.4	52.1	21.0	13.7	22.4	15.4	76.2
Administrative & managerial work	3.8	0.9	3.2	1.5	0.2	1.2	62.3
Clerical & related work	24.8	38.8	27.6	8.9	9.6	9.0	58.8
Sales	5.9	0.4	4.8	7.1	0.9	5.9	84.3
Services	39.2	7.1	32.9	18.0	66.6	27.6	78.5
Agricultural & husbandry	2.6	0.2	2.1	2.4	Neg.	1.9	79.6
Production work & other manual labour	10.3	0.5	8.4	48.4	0.3	39.0	95.3
Total	100.0	100.0	100.0	100.0	100.0	100.0	81.4

Source: Kuwait, Research Studies on Population, No.3, 1987.

The Public Sector

In 1985, Kuwaitis and *bidouns* accounted for 18.9 percent of the total work force (RSP No. 2). Taken alone, the Kuwaitis represented only 14 percent. From independence in 1961 until the 1980s, the state had kept its pledge to provide citizens with employment in the public sector if they wished to work. It was here, therefore, that the majority of Kuwaiti workers were concentrated, especially in services, clerical, and professional occupations (Table 3.4). "Services," decidedly the largest category, was a mixture of diverse jobs ranging from guards of official buildings, such as ministries and schools, to *farash* (lower-level employees without clearly defined tasks) and drivers for visiting dignitaries.[18] Most of the jobs in this category did not require formal education. Kuwaitis with secondary education and especially those with a university degree were automatically employed in leading positions. Throughout the years, this system had engendered a large bureaucracy, where the citizens occupied more or less symbolic functions while an army of expatriate employees was needed to perform tasks that, in many cases, were related to the maintenance of the bureaucracy itself. In 1989, 92.3 percent of the native work force was employed in the public sector, the overwhelming majority by the government.[19]

Non-Kuwaitis employed in the public sector had lower wages than their Kuwaiti colleagues and, not being citizens, were not included in the national scheme of retirement and social benefits. On the other hand, both Kuwaitis and non-Kuwaitis benefited from the absence of income tax. Compared to workers in the private sector, non-Kuwaiti employees in the public sector were in an advantageous position. They enjoyed greater freedom vis-à-vis their employer, which, as an official institution, was often merely an abstract entity; their work situation was more secure, since they were not at the mercy of the personal whims of a private employer; their working conditions were usually adequate, their travel expenses were covered by the employer, and so, generally, were their housing expenses. Besides, it was relatively easy for an expatriate employed in the public sector to bring along his family. The condition was that he earned a monthly salary of no less than KD 450,[20] whereas expatriates in the private sector had to earn at least KD 600[21] per month to be granted the same right.

One can argue that the main function of the public sector was to serve as a channel through which the state redistributed the oil income to its citizens. By providing them with jobs in this sector, the government was not so much fulfilling its pledge to employ the citizens in a meaningful productive activity as its pledge to use the revenue from its unique natural resource for the benefit of the Kuwaiti people. Except for a few key positions, a job in the public sector meant first and foremost that a citizen was entitled to a salary on the state's payroll; only secondarily did it mean that he or she was expected to perform a precise function. This contention can be checked against the fact that Kuwaiti male employees were entitled to retirement with full benefits after merely twenty years of service; for national female employees the minimum period was fifteen years. In both cases, retirement comes at a time when the employees are reaching the most productive stage in their careers, rich with enough accumulated experience yet still years away from biological old age. That the quality of the citizens' work performance was of secondary importance was also supported by the pattern of promotion: Kuwait University, for instance, gave deanships and professorships to all the newly-produced Ph.D.-holders of Kuwaiti nationality, bypassing in the process older and more experienced foreign lecturers, who were never granted tenure but were hired on a two-to-three years' contract.

An important argument in support of this appointment policy, here as elsewhere in the public sector, was the need for the country to "Kuwaitize" its labor force. After three decades of intense investments in education, the Kuwaitis felt they were ready to take over the running of their own country. Kuwaitization was likely to lower productivity and work quality in its initial phase, but these were drawbacks that were inevitable and, it was hoped, would be overcome. The only problem was that Kuwaitization took place only at the top level. By the mid-1980s, Kuwaitis occupied all the higher echelons in the public sector: ministries and other governmental institutions, schools and the university, the hospitals, official mass media, sporting clubs, etc. With the increase in education, it was expected that the younger nationals would also enter the next highest levels, entrusted until then to the Arab expatriates. While the talk about Kuwaitizing the public sector created much anxiety among the high-waged educated Arabs and their few Asian colleagues, there had been few signs so far that the policy was being effectively implemented, even in the face of a growing number of young Kuwaitis graduating from schools. Many Kuwaitis, both male and female, still conceptualized work in terms of public employment, that is, a relationship established between themselves and the public sector as a formal way of gaining access to yet another distributive network of welfare services that were essentially a due to all citizens. On the other hand, work as labor, that is to say a necessary activity for the purpose of making a living, was a thing mainly associated with the migrants. The House of Zakat reported helping a large number of nationals living below the level of minimum monthly income recognized by the state (KD 400).[22] Yet it had not occurred to most of these citizens in need to apply for jobs usually performed by foreigners. For a Kuwaiti, to do so would have been to blur the Kuwaiti–non-Kuwaiti dichotomy, mix categories, and confuse identities. The concentration of Kuwaiti workers in certain occupations within the public sector could thus be seen as both the expression for a preference for types of work activity and a way of stating their ethnic identity and distancing themselves from the rest of the population.

The Private Sector

Although the majority of Kuwaiti workers was employed in the public sector, even here expatriates were more numerous than natives. But it was in the private sector that non-Kuwaitis were really predominant. According to Kuwaiti labor law for the private sector, Arabs shall be given priority over non-Arabs:

> Priority of employment shall be made in the following manner:
> 1. A Kuwaiti labourer
> 2. An Arab labourer, holding a work permit, or being registered with the Ministry of Social Affairs and Labour
> 3. A foreign labourer, holding a work permit, or being registered with the Ministry of Social Affairs and Labour.
> (Article 10 of the private sector Labor Law 1964, offical translation)

In practice, the Kuwaitis' recruitment policy followed only one principle, that which Furnivall (1942) identifies in the tropical colonies as "the survival of the cheapest." Everywhere, Arab labor was more expensive than Asian labor (Table 3.3). In some occupations, however, the Kuwaitis had no choice but to employ Arabs, for example in jobs that required fluent knowledge of Arabic. From 1975 onwards, labor migration from Asia had no doubt impinged upon the Arabs' work opportunities in Kuwait. But, for two reasons, it had not always played the constraining role one might expect: after the oil boycott, the rate of economic activity was such that there was to a certain extent room for both Arab and Asian migrants.[23] More important still, Arabs and Asians filled different functions in Kuwaiti society and performed different jobs.

The majority of non-Kuwaitis were employed in the private sector. This sector included everything from small grocery stores, tailor shops, and car repair workshops to cleaning companies, trading companies, private schools, private hospitals and banks, hotels, and so on. Private business was owned by the Kuwaitis, but its employees were almost exclusively expatriates (98.4 percent). In 1989, 68 percent of the total migrant labor force worked in the private sector.[24]

There was a significant difference between the public and the private sectors: while the public sector stood for security and social benefits for its employees, the private sector stood for efficiency and competition. But because of Kuwait's special situation, both sectors had a common purpose: the indirect redistribution of the benefits created by the oil economy to the citizens involved in them. Trading activities, the very core of the private sector, were meant to be an easy source of income for the Kuwaiti nationals just as jobs in the public sector were. Therefore, not only were the private companies and their owners exempted from most forms of taxation, but they also benefited from substantial support by the state.

The principle behind this policy was clear: to allow the sector to make the highest possible profit. Since the employers in the sector were exclusively Kuwaitis and the employees overwhelmingly non-Kuwaitis, the best strategy was to reduce all costs related to labor to the minimum. The state's most important contribution consisted of creating a labor market that was pliant to the demands of the private sector employers. As long as the labor supply was maintained at the same level, the state's non-interventionist policy was indeed the cheapest and, in the short term, the most profitable. It also reinforced the separation between Kuwaitis and non-Kuwaitis by channeling the former into the public sector and the role of private sector employers, while locking most of the non-Kuwaitis into the category of private sector employees. Indeed, the Kuwaitis shunned employment in the private sector, where the salaries were low and unregulated and the employers could flout, without much risk, the provisions of the labor laws. Nor were the Kuwaiti employers eager to employ Kuwaiti workers owing to their generally acknowledged low productivity. In 1989, however, as the government was preparing the five-year plan for the period 1990–1995, the growth of the public sector had reached such proportions that technocrats in the government were considering the possibility of encouraging citizens to move over to the private sector. One suggestion was to offer financial incentives to private companies willing to employ citizens.[25] Outside the small circle of government technocrats, however, the idea was considered far-fetched and the proposal was never actually implemented. These occasional declarations of intent to reverse the politics of exclusion, which became more frequent by the late 1980s, did not even begin to undermine the formidable habit of dichotomous thinking among the population. The base of this thinking had rapidly sedimented within less than two decades of intense practice, supported most of the time by the state and all the other actors.

It did, indeed, seem meaningless for a Kuwaiti citizen to work as an employee for a poor salary when he or she could at any time start a private business and employ foreigners to run it at a low cost, especially since many expatriate businessmen, eager to gain a foothold in the Kuwaiti market, were willing to enter into a business partnership with the nationals. The Commercial Law of 1980, which regulated business activities in Kuwait, stated that non-Kuwaitis were not allowed to undertake any commercial activity in the emirate unless they had a local partner whose share in the business was at least 51 percent (Kassim 1986). These partnerships could take various forms but the most prevalent one was the small-scale business association between a Kuwaiti and an expatriate trader. A common formula was the one in which both partners contributed their share of the capital and divided the annual profits between themselves. It was, however, not uncommon for the non-Kuwaiti to provide the entire capital—51 percent of which was declared owned by the Kuwaiti partner—the expertise, and the labor, and to manage the business, while the Kuwaiti provided his or her sponsorship. By law, the Kuwaiti partner's signature was the only one valid in all legal and banking and business deals; premises could be rented and employees recruited only in his or her name. In return for this sponsorship, the Kuwaiti got a share of the profits. This share and the modalities of payment were negotiated between the partners. The percentage collected by the sponsor did not necessarily remain fixed. After the 1982 crash of the Souq al Manakh parallel stock exchange (Darwiche 1986),[26] in which many Kuwaitis lost considerable amounts of money, there was a trend among business sponsors to raise their share of profits in the joint ventures. Most Kuwaitis were involved in this type of private business. In principle, employees of the government sector were not allowed to do so, but they deftly dodged the law by signing their wives' or their sons' names in the partnership (Nancy 1985).

The Kuwaiti citizens' right of access to expatriate capital and profit in the private sector was viewed as perfectly legitimate because the amount claimed by the Kuwaiti sponsor/partner was perceived as a tax collected on the foreigners' profit-making activities carried out on Kuwaiti territory. What makes the situation singular here was that these "taxes" were not paid into the state's coffers but directly into the bank accounts of private citizens. This illustrates my above suggestion that the state lent much support to the private sector by laying down the conditions necessary to make it an easy source of income for practically all Kuwaiti nationals. Because of these advantages, most Kuwaitis owned a business of some sort. Even those who worked in the public sector, including the top civil servants, dabbled in trade as a side activity, almost a hobby—except that, in many cases, this hobby was financially more rewarding than the job in the public sector. One reason Kuwaiti employees retired early from public service was to dedicate themselves full-time to their activities in the private sector while enjoying their retirement benefits.

The "Domestic Sector"

In the shadow of the public and private sectors we find the grey area of the economy that, for lack of a better designation, I will refer to as the "domestic sector." This comprised gardeners, drivers, cooks, nannies, servants, and all other migrants employed in private homes. In terms of the concentric configuration proposed at the beginning of the chapter, this sector was the circle that stood farthest from the Kuwaiti nuclear circle: it consisted entirely of non-Kuwaitis who were, in the main, non-Arabs and, in most cases, non-Muslims as well. In other words, the workers in the domestic sector shared few common cultural features with their employers. At the same time, these aliens were the migrant group that penetrated most deeply into the private spheres of Kuwaiti life (the home and the family). The presence of salaried workers, who were predominantly female, at the very center of a universe traditionally consisting of blood relatives, affines and, until the 1950s, slaves,[27] gave rise to much confusion in the local pattern of gender interaction, which was minutely regulated by Islam.

Unlike the public and private sectors, each of which had its own code of labor laws, the domestic sector was unregulated. Among its most striking features were its socio-demographic profile and its ethnic particularities.

Data about the size of the population of domestic workers were unclear. Estimates for 1989 ranged from 100,000 to 130,000. The sector employed mainly Asian workers from India, Sri Lanka, and the Philippines. The majority of the workers were female, which explained why Pakistanis and Bangladeshis were practically absent in this occupational group, since these two countries did not allow their female nationals to work as domestic helpers abroad. The workers' educational level was low: this group accounted for the large number of illiterate and semi-literate female expatriates (Table 3.5). Lack of legal protection, the predominance of women, and low educational background combined to make domestic workers the most vulnerable to exploitation and abuse, a situation of which the labor-sending countries were acutely aware. In January 1988, Manila imposed a ban prohibiting Filipino women from working as maids abroad; in September of the same year, New Delhi issued a similar ban, particularly aimed at three countries in the Middle East, including Kuwait. But no one heeded the prohibitions: they were violated by the receiving countries and by the recruiting agencies, as well as by the female migrant workers themselves. The Philippine and Indian governments issued the bans half-heartedly, knowing fully well that tens of thousands of families could not make ends meet without the remittances from this group of migrant workers.

Arab women have never been employed as domestic helpers in Kuwait. As far as I know, neither have Arab men, except as gardeners. Obviously, it was easier for Kuwaitis to introduce a non-Arab Asian than an Arab into the core of their domestic sphere. Part of the reason lay in the paradox of cultural closeness and social distance described earlier, and the fact that few Arabs would be ready to submit to the harsh working conditions; besides, many Kuwaitis do heed the Quranic injunctions against inhumane treatment of other Muslims. Another reason lay in the steady decline of wages in this sector. In the 1970s and even early 1980s, a domestic worker could hope to earn an average of KD 80 a month. With board and lodging included, this was a good salary for any unskilled worker from India, Sri Lanka, the Philippines, or the Middle East. Even then, however, no Arabs were recruited to work as servants. In the 1980s, with the general recession, there was a drop in salaries in most occupations. The domestic helpers and other unskilled workers were the most affected. Between 1987 and 1990, most employers fixed the servants' wages at KD 30. As we will see further on, some did not even pay the sum regularly.

Not all employers in the domestic sector were Kuwaitis. In fact, this was one area where natives and expatriates enjoyed pretty much the same services, provided the latter were part of the middle class. Admittedly, expatriates were not allowed to hire domestic servants unless the head of the family belonged to the professional class (e.g., medical doctors, professors, lawyers), or both spouses worked. Further, unlike the

Kuwaitis, each expatriate family was allowed only one servant. But implementation of the law in this area was so lax that practically anyone who could afford it (and even those who could not) had an Asian domestic worker at their service.

Similar to domestic workers in terms of low skills and high vulnerability were the employees of the cleaning companies. Kuwait employed armies of Asian laborers to keep its buildings and streets clean. One can grasp the immensity of the workers' task only if one has experienced the omnipresence of sand and dust in this part of Arabia. Every day, at dawn, the companies' buses dropped thousands of Indian, Sri Lankan, Bangladeshi, and Thai cleaners and sweepers in ministry offices, hospitals, and schools, on the streets, and even on the highways. The cleaners' salaries were among the lowest of all: in 1989, they had fallen to KD 20–40 a month. Here again, low wages and deplorable working conditions meant that the sector specialized in employing Asians only.

The rapid growth of the domestic sector and its equivalents in the private sector during the 1980s aggravated the ethnic character of the organization of labor and ethnic stratification in Kuwait. As we will see later on, it contributed to accelerating the processes of perception, definition, and evaluation of self and others in terms of ethnic attributions and occupations.

In this chapter, I have attempted to identify the rationales behind, and the social parameters of, the Kuwaiti politics of exclusion. I have suggested that *citizenship* and the *organization of work* were the two most crucial elements used not only to define and classify individuals and groups but also, by immobilizing them in the relevant categories, to ensure the reproduction of the structure of exclusion. Building social walls in the form of classification and labor-related differentiations, however, is only part of the business of living in a plural society. The other part, and the most important one, is how to interact *through* the walls. Indeed walls are not built to shut off interactions but to regulate them. The question is, then, what openings, large and small, official and unofficial, were there in Kuwait that allowed people to meet and deal with each other? Once objective exclusion was secured through immigration and occupational policies, what mechanisms and devices were mobilized to secure subjective exclusion, which consisted in defining the out-group as radically *other*, while at the same time allowing for smooth functional interaction?

Notes

1. "So here is a first definition of the tragic hero: he is the prisoner who cannot break free without dying: his limit is his privilege, captivity his distinction." (my translation)

2. There is an extensive literature on tribalism in the Arabian peninsula. For a critical assessment of the existing analyses, see al-Naqeeb 1990.

3. For a detailed comparative study of naturalization laws in the Middle East, see George Dib, *Population Bulletin* 15, 1978–1979.

4. Nomads of the area have been naturalized by thousands since the 1960s. This process picked up notably in the 1980s, with the annual number of naturalization cases well above 10,000 between 1982 and the Iraqi invasion of 1990 (Table 3.5). Combined with the very high natural increase among the Kuwaitis— 40.6 persons per 1,000 population (RSP No.1)—this policy accounts for the exceptionally high rate of annual population growth among the native inhabitants. Since 1957 this rate has never been lower than 3.8 percent. At its highest, it reached 9.6 percent in the inter-census period of 1961–1965 (RSP No.1).

TABLE 3.5   Number of Cases of Naturalization, 1979–1988

Year	Number of cases	Year	Number of cases
1979	8,976	1984	13,191
1980	10,141	1985	16,673
1981	9,921	1986	16,933
1982	14,356	1987	14,647
1983	12,908	1988	14,980

Source: Kuwait, *Annual Statistical Abstract*, 1989.

5. In 1995, a decree granted the Kuwaiti-born sons of naturalized citizens the right to vote and to run for elections. The same rights were not granted the fathers themselves.

6. Not to be confused with *Bedouins*.

7. The 1959 Aliens' Residence Law stipulates that among the categories exempted from the application of the law provisions are "Tribal members entering Kuwait by land from places where they used to do so for the purpose of performing their ordinary business" (Art. 25, official translation). It was only in 1987 that this article was amended (Ministerial Resolution, No. 649) and the tribes had to enter and exit Kuwait through border checkpoints like everyone else.

8. This applies only to the *bidoons* of Sunni bedouin background. Those who are Shia (originally from Iran or al Hasa) were not allowed to serve in the army

and the police. For these *bidoons*, the possibility for naturalization was practically nil.

9. *Arab Times*, April 8, 1989.

10. This figure was confirmed in 1991 by a Kuwaiti human rights organization, *The Committee for the Defence of Prisoners of War*. Before the Iraqi invasion, no figures about the *bidoons* were available. In fact, the authorities were reluctant to discuss the subject at all, and I met with deliberately vague answers from Kuwaiti officials of the Ministry of Interior. Privately, however, people discussed the matter with much concern. But no one seemed to have any clear idea of how many *bidoons* there were, nor where they worked. It was generally agreed that they were concentrated in the outskirts of Kuwait in the lower-middle class areas where settled nomads lived. The children, who always gathered around me when I was on a visit in such areas, used to explain spontaneously without my asking: "I am a real Kuwaiti, not an Iraqi," or "This is my best friend; he is not an Iraqi." Upon inquiry, it was explained to me that the children meant to say that they were not *bidoon*. Clearly, there was a widespread opinion by the late 1980s that many Iraqis tried to pass as "Kuwaiti stateless" and, in certain areas of Kuwait, *bidoon* and *Iraqi* were used interchangeably. This accounts for the predicament of the *bidoons* after liberation in 1991, since they were automatically suspected of sympathy, if not actual collaboration, with the occupying forces (see Lawyers' Committee for Human Rights 1992).

11. Each Kuwaiti male received KD 2,000 on his first marriage to help him pay his bride-price, provided he married a Kuwaiti girl. In the late 1980s, the exchange rate for the Kuwaiti dinar varied between US$3 and US$4.

12. In 1985, the total monthly rent for apartments—the type of dwellings most commonly rented by expatriates—amounted to KD 12,757,580. Equivalent rents for "villas" and "traditional houses," two categories associated with the Kuwaiti population, were respectively KD 670,822 and KD 2,314,405 (ASA 1989:119).

13. For example, Article 8 of the Rent Law stipulates that "[the lessor] shall, during the term of lease, carry out the necessary repairs, particularly the required works and maintenance of the roofs, stairs, lifts, water pipes and any leakage of drainage and septic tanks" (official translation, p. 6). This is a provision frequently violated by local landlords. The solution suggested by the law in that case ("In the event of his delay to do so after his notification accordingly, the lessee may secure a permit from the judicial authority to carry out the said works and then deduct the relevant costs from the rent" (ibid.)), it was indeed often resorted to by the expatriate tenants. However, if the landlords refused to deduct the costs from the rent, there was not much the expatriates could do. They could, of course, sue the owners, but a lawsuit was likely to be too expensive and time-consuming, in addition to other more subtle hurdles related to the sponsorship system. See Chapter 4.

14. After liberation, the government's decision to reduce the number of migrant workers by half entailed great losses for real estate-owning Kuwaitis. We have here a striking illustration of the Kuwaiti private sector's economic dependence on the presence of the migrants, not only as workers but also as consumers.

15. The other GCC countries do not have systematic data on population and labor migration. Unlike in Kuwait, censuses there are either sporadic (in the case of Bahrain, the UAE, and Qatar) or of difficult access (Saudi Arabia). The data that exist are mostly gathered by outside sources (e.g., Birks and Sinclair 1980, the World Bank, the United Nations). They indicate that in the UAE, Oman, Bahrain, and Qatar the number of non-Arab Asian (mostly Indian) migrants exceeded that of Arab migrants (Table 3.6). Saudi Arabia also had a large population of Arab migrants, but their influence was never as important there as it was in Kuwait.

TABLE 3.6   Percent Distribution of Arab and Asian Labor Force in GCC
             States, 1980

Country of residence	Arabs	Asians
Bahrain	13.3	76.2
Kuwait	64.4	34.1
Oman	12.4	83.2
Qatar	25.2	72.2
Saudi Arabia	80.2	16.1
UAE	21.8	75.0
Total	58.1	38.5

Source: Kuwait, *Research Studies on Population*, No.5, 1987.

16. Neither Pakistanis nor Bangladeshis worked in the other low-salaried group, that of domestic helpers, because it consisted mostly of women and there was, in both countries, an interdiction against labor emigration by unskilled women.

17. *Zakat* refers to the alm-tax, one of the principal obligations in Islam. Each Muslim must give *zakat* to the needy, especially during the holy month of Ramadan. In Kuwait, instead of being given by the private citizens, the money was provided by the state. *Beit al Zakat* or the House of Zakat had two main functions: to help the needy in the country, in particular the new Muslims (non-Muslims were not included), and to finance missionary work abroad.

18. Jobs as drivers were very popular, especially among the settled nomads. Those who were not employed in the government offices usually worked as taxi drivers.

19. *Arab Times*, November 2, 1989.
20. Approximately US$ 1,800.
21. Approximately US$ 2,400.
22. Approximately US$ 1,600.
23. The only exception was in the field of construction. Here the Arabs lost out to two giant Asian companies, the EPI (Engineering Project India) and Korea's Hyundai.
24. Interview with the Asst. Undersecretary for Statistical Affairs at the Ministry of Planning, April 2, 1989.
25. Interview with Fouad Mulla Hussein, Secretary-General of the Higher Planning Council, January 19, 1989. Mr. Hussein also suggested that the government should support through subsidies those companies "with high productivity, which employ highly skilled expatriates, which give jobs to a large number of Kuwaitis, and which produce for export" (*Arab Times*, January 9, 1989).
26. Described by Darwiche as "the most spectacular financial crash of recent years," the collapse of this unofficial stock market in 1982 left a trail of paper debt totalling KD 27 billion, five times the level of Kuwait's total bank credits. Practically all the Kuwaitis had speculated in the Manakh. Five years after the invasion and more than ten years after the crash took place, its impact still mars the social and political scene of the country.
27. The traffic in slaves in Kuwait came to an end officially in 1924 (Dickson 1951). But domestic slaves (*mu`alid*) were commonly found in all well-to-do Kuwaiti families until the late 1950s. The *mu`alids* were slaves, mostly of African origin, born of slave parents who had often been in a family for several generations. Their ownership was an important status symbol for the family and consequently they were usually well treated. Female slaves were often incorporated into the family through the mechanism of concubinage, which was permitted by Islam. This tradition may play a certain role in accounting for the widespread sexual abuse suffered by many female migrant domestic workers at the hands of their male Kuwaiti employers nowadays. But it is certainly not the only, or even the main, explanation as can be seen from the fact that abuse was also carried out by non-Kuwaiti male employers. It is obvious that the main explanation for this phenomenon lies in the legal organization of the domestic sector which ensured the total power of the sponsor/employer over the migrants and the latter's utter lack of legal protection (see Chapter 4).

4

The Structure of Dominance: The Sponsorship System

> *A Kuwaiti, a Palestinian, and an Egyptian are engaged in a boasting contest.*
>
> *The Egyptian says:*
> *"I painted the Red Sea."*
> *The Palestinian says:*
> *"I killed the Dead Sea."*
> *The Kuwaiti says:*
> *"I sponsor the Indian Ocean."*
> A popular joke in Kuwait

Undoubtedly the most important form of institutionalized relationship between Kuwaitis and expatriates was that of employer–employee. A unique significance was attached to this relationship so that it extended well beyond the economic sphere, where it commonly aggregates in other societies, and noticeably spilled over into the symbolic sphere. Since a non-Kuwaiti could enter and reside in Kuwait only if he or she was employed by a Kuwaiti institution or a Kuwaiti citizen, the employer–employee relationship had implications on many levels: for the general labor situation in Kuwait, for the migrants' employment and life opportunities, for the state of ethnic relations in this plural society, and, last but not least, for the employers' as well as the employees' perception of self and others.

To understand these multiple strands of organization, practice, and representation, we must start by looking at the way the employer–employee relationship was conceptualized and institutionalized and how it was acted out.

The *Kafala*

This relationship can be summed up by the term *kafala*, which is ordinarily translated as *sponsorship*. The *kafala* is an institution characteristic of the Gulf region; curiously enough it has been ignored by most research on labor migration to the area.[1]

It seems that we have here an instance of Kuwaitis applying to a concrete post-oil situation an organizational device with deep roots in their history. The noun *kafala* comes from the root *k-f-l*. Some of its derivative verbal forms mean (1) to feed, to provide for; (2) to vouch for, be responsible for; and (3) to be legal guardian of (Wehr, *Dictionary of Modern Written Arabic*). It has been suggested that this socio-cultural institution originated from the age-old Bedouin custom of granting strangers protection and temporary affiliation to the tribe for specific purposes (Beaugé 1986).

Opinions differ as to whether the *kafala* requirement had existed since the late 1940s, when labor importation started. According to some testimonies there may have been a practice whereby migrants were vouched for by a respected resident of Kuwait.[2] If this was the case, then the practice was not formalized in the first decades of labor importation, since the text of the Aliens' Residence Law issued in 1959 and amended in 1963, 1965, and 1968 made no mention of it. The 1960 Law of Commercial Companies did stipulate that foreigners might not establish businesses in Kuwait except with Kuwaiti partners who, in turn, were required to have 51 percent ownership. This requirement of partnership, however, was not strictly the same as the requirement of sponsorship, which, as we will see presently, entails that the foreign workers depend on their Kuwaiti employers for their entry visas as well as residence and work permits. Furthermore, the stipulations of the Law of Commercial Companies were restricted to the field of business partnership only. Throughout the 1950s and 1960s, immigration practices seem to have varied according to the origin of the immigrants: natives from other parts of the Gulf could enter and settle freely in Kuwait (Joukhadar 1980), whereas Indian migrant workers had to have a visa and a guarantee from their employer (in other words, sponsorship). As for the Palestinians, periods of visa requirement (mostly in the 1950s) alternated with a more liberal policy (late 1950s to early 1960s), only to be followed again by a more restrictive practice (Russell 1989b; Ghabra 1987). By 1969 the universal visa requirement was an established rule and, in general, all migrant workers had to be vouched for by their Kuwaiti employers (Joukhadar 1980;

Russell 1989a). It is obvious that the practice of the sponsorship or *kafala* had become common then. Yet the Aliens' Residence Law still did not make explicit mention of it. It was in the major 1975 amendment that the *kafala* was finally included in the legal text through the detailed reference to the kinds of document required for the various categories of workers (public, private, and domestic sectors) in order for them to obtain an entry visa. All these documents had to be duly signed by the prospective employer.[3] For the first time, the *kafala* was mentioned and the role of the *kafeel* (sponsor) was explicitly identified with that of the employer. In the years since 1975, the *kafala* institution had become the very key to in-migration. Yet nowhere and at no time had the notion of *kafala* and the relationship between the *kafeel* and the migrant worker been clearly explained, not even in the various detailed explanatory memoranda that accompanied the law and its amendments. As Beaugé (1986) suggests, failure to elaborate on the content of the *kafala* could be due to the fact that the practice was well-anchored in Kuwaiti tradition and was, therefore, widely understood and taken for granted by the native population.

By the 1980s, the *kafala* was a general and absolute requirement: each and every foreigner in Kuwait who originated from a country outside the GCC states had to be under the sponsorship either of a private citizen or a private or state institution. By private citizens the law, of course, meant *Kuwaiti* citizens. However, certain categories of expatriates were allowed to sponsor dependents and, in some cases, one domestic servant, provided they themselves met the minimum monthly salary require-ment.[4] Finally, some expatriates, in particular the Yemenis, enjoyed the privilege of being self-sponsored (Nancy 1985).

Strictly speaking, the sponsorship system consisted in the employer's signing a form issued by the Ministry of Social Affairs and Labor whereby he (or she)[5] declared that the foreigner worked for him (her); the employer undertook to inform the Immigration Department of any change in the labor contract (expiry, renewal, cancellation) or in the worker's domicile; the employer also undertook to repatriate the employee at his own expense upon termination of the contract. It was only on the basis of such a document that the migrant worker was issued a residence permit. If both parties agreed to renew the work contract after it expired, the sponsor/employer had to confirm in writing that the employee still worked for him.

Power: The View from Outside, Above, and Below

As will become increasingly obvious to the reader, the *kafala* was a relationship in which the sponsors/employers, through their ability to affect the fate of the migrants by determining their employment opportunities, unmistakably qualify for the role of dominant actors. By contrast, the workers' range of choices about their own lives was narrowly dependent on the sponsors' decisions, which placed them in a subordinate position. These are asymmetrical relations and, if "power" means the source of "the capabilities of agents to bring about intended outcomes of action" (Giddens 1984:173), the Kuwaiti sponsor undeniably exercised power over the expatriate worker.

We can approach the *kafala* from this external, onlooker's angle, in which case there is no dearth of empirical material to support the claim of power imbalance in favor of the *kafeel*. A power relationship, meanwhile, involves various actors, each positioned in specific sociohistorical circumstances, each faced with a different set of constraints and opportunities, and each engaged in his own construction and interpretation of the power relationship in question, shaped by what he perceives as being "in his interest."

The onlooker's view has its advantages: it can in principle claim an impartiality that is denied the participants and that, at best, allows the observer to make a more objective and complete description and assessment of the causes and consequences of dominance. The onlooker's view, meanwhile, is never as impartial as it claims to be: As a rule, it is not content with being the *onlooker's* view, since it is often assumed to be—or is presented as if it were—the point of view of the dominated actor as well. A full understanding of a power relationship, therefore, requires that the analysis be built on a threefold approach: a description of the situation "from the outside," as seen by the onlooker, an account of the point of view of the dominant actor, and an account of the point of view of the dominated. If we conceptualize all relationships, including power relationships, as consisting of various "events" defined as "outward appearance of behavior" (Barth 1992), this approach allows us to discover the actors' *intent* and *interpretation*, which turn such events into "acts."

"Dominance" and "compliance" may not always be perceived as such by those whom the anthropologist identifies with these behaviors. What is described as "power-wielding" by the researcher and/or the subordinate actor may well be perceived as something entirely different by the power-wielder himself. Likewise, "compliance" by the subordinates may not be meant as compliance, but as pragmatic strategy or covert resistance clothed in the public language of conformity (Scott 1985). In neither case do actors' self-understandings necessarily modify the actual power imbalance and its objective material consequences. In fact, more often than not, they contribute to stabilizing and reproducing the status quo by redefining as more manageable a reality that might otherwise be much more difficult to endure. To achieve an adequate understanding of the dynamics of the power relationship, not least its endurance and reproduction over time, it is therefore essential to grasp the opposing actors' definitions of their own action.

The assumption that elites, as a rule, tend to rationalize their action in order to legitimate it is one that most of us will find easy enough to accept. On the other hand, to substantiate a claim that non-elites view their own compliance as anything else than just compliance may require solid, empirically based demonstration. Such a claim, indeed, challenges the insights of those theorists who define power primarily as the ability "to engineer consent" among the powerless (Miliband 1969). According to this view, elites not only dictate the behavior of those whom they dominate, they also form their consciousness by imposing their (the elites') own image of a just social order (Lukes 1974). This ideological hegemony is achieved through the elites' control of what Gramsci (1971) calls the "ideological sectors" of society, namely, culture, religion, education, and the media. The subjugation of the non-elites by the elites thus rests solidly on the former's acceptance of the latter's rule as legitimate—in other words, on what Marxists refer to as "mystification" or "false consciousness."

This assumption of imposed consensus through the manipulation of the non-elite's consciousness has been questioned by, among others, Scott in his 1985 study of Malaysian peasants. Armed with an impressive array of empirical data, Scott demonstrates that what is usually taken to be the peasants' compliance vis-à-vis the landowners is in fact a strategy of covert resistance against the imposed social order. He shows that, far from subverting the peasants' minds, the landowners find themselves caught in a "silent struggle" against an enemy force all the more elusive as it is compelled by circumstances to use strategies of evasion rather than strategies of confrontation.

An entirely different critique of the thesis of the dominant ideology is raised by Abercrombie, Hill, and Turner (1984). These authors argue that in interpreting the work of sociology's founding fathers, modern sociologists have greatly exaggerated the role that Marx, Durkheim, and Weber actually assign to ideology in their writings. Thus, Marxists who speak of "dominant ideology" and "false consciousness" and non-Marxists who speak of "a common culture" share the same mistake: they both explain the continued class and socio-economic divisions by referring to the integrative power of ideology. What they have neglected to read in the great sociologists' work, Abercrombie et al. claim, is its emphasis on what Marx calls "the dull compulsion of economic relations."

Abercrombie et al.'s critique—rejected by some writers as "economism"—is diametrically opposed to Scott's position which advocates a phenomenological or ethnomethodological approach to the study of power and resistance and centers particularly on the experience and consciousness of human agents. Yet, I find that both insights are relevant to the study of power relations between Kuwaitis and migrants.

Along a line rather similar to the one followed by Abercrombie et al., I will argue, on the basis of empirical illustrations, that the combination of material constraints on the expatriates ("the dull compulsion of economic relations" that are, upon closer scrutiny, not merely economic but also cultural)[6] with the *kafala* creates such a firm structure of Kuwaiti dominance as to make recourse to ideology practically redundant. The stock-in-trade of ideology consists of core cultural items of a symbolic nature, such as beliefs, values, metonyms, metaphors, and rhetoric. The imposition and embracement of a dominant ideology presupposes a degree of sharing of these items, a feat that seems rather difficult in a plural society ruled by the politics of exclusion. If we subscribe to the dominant ideology thesis, the simultaneous occurrence of *ideological dominance* and ethnic and social *exclusion* is a contradiction, since exclusion, whatever its negative outcome, also implies that those excluded retain a measure of autonomy of mind. Exclusion thus undermines ideological dominance. Our working hypothesis, therefore, must be that, insofar as there is dominance in a plural society such as Kuwait, its weapon is unlikely to be ideological.

However, as Bottomore cautions the reader in his foreword to Abercrombie, Hill, and Turner's book, we must not throw the baby out with the bath water: to assign to the *dominant ideology* the prime merit of creating and maintaining order and cohesion in class societies is one thing; to entirely write off the role of ideology *tout court* in social relations, including those of dominance and subjugation, is another. It is here that Scott's uncovering of rampant resistance disguised as compliance is illuminating. In what follows, we will see that, although the migrant workers indeed submitted to the Kuwaitis' dominance, it was not as a result of blind fear and compulsion, or a fatalistic embracement of the social and ethnic worldviews of their masters. The expatriates' submission to the Kuwaitis' dominance and their politics of exclusion arose from decisions reached within a context of opportunities and constraints and in the light of carefully weighed priorities. It was a strategy the rationality of which can be grasped when we consider the circumstances that surrounded the migrants' lives, both in their home countries prior to outmigration and in Kuwait. To claim that there is a parallel between Scott's and the present case studies is not to say that there is a similarity in the ways actors in Malaysia and Kuwait respond to power. It only means that my analysis owes much to Scott's warning against taking the compliance of the weak at face value, and to his attempt to explain this compliance from the vantage point of the actors' experience and consciousness.

In this chapter, I will present the point of view of the onlooker through a description of the working of the sponsorship system. Woven into this account are descriptions of the position of non-Kuwaitis, their predicaments, and some of their strategies for coping which adumbrate their perception of the power relationship between the Kuwaitis and themselves. Expatriate views on this relationship and on life in Kuwait in general will be further explored in Chapter 6. In addition to the observer's understanding, the reader will find in this chapter the point of view of the majority of Kuwaitis as well.

As already mentioned, there was an important difference between sponsorship by state institutions, which was the case of public sector employees, and sponsorship by private individuals and companies. Under the system of state sponsorship, the relationship between employer and employee was based exclusively on the exchange of a specific type of work for remuneration, with both clearly defined in the contract. By contrast, private sponsorship, by which was meant all types of employment contract entered into between a migrant and a private employer resident in Kuwait,[7] was characterized by a web of expectations of prestations *not* stated in the work contract and regulated by a mixture of codified modern labor laws and unwritten customs and practices.

Each migrant worker carried an entry visa identified with the sector where he or she was to be employed: "Visa No.17" was that of employees in the public sector; "Visa No.18," that of employees in the private sector; "Visa No.19" was carried by professionals, tradesmen, and craftsmen who were either self-employed (i.e., self-sponsored) or in business partnership with a Kuwaiti; and "Visa No. 20" was for workers in the domestic sector.[8] For an employee in one sector, say, the private sector, to go over to a job in another sector, say, the public sector, he or she had first to leave the country and re-enter with the new type of visa.

In what follows, I will focus on the last three categories (visas No.18, 19, and 20). They share in common the fact that the *kafala* here bound the employee to a private individual employer rather than to an institution.

The *Kafala* in the Private Sector ("Visa No. 18")

In principle, the condition of the private sector employees was regulated by the 1964 Private Sector Labor Law; with the Aliens' Residence Law, this Law was undoubtedly the best-known piece of legislation in Kuwait. This is hardly surprising since the private sector, where the majority of the non-Kuwaiti labor force was employed, registered many more labor conflicts than the public sector; hence the private sector workers' constant preoccupation with the law's stipulations.

In addition to being inspired by similar laws existing in Bahrain, Iraq, Lebanon, and Syria at the time of its adoption, the Kuwaiti Labor Law was based on recommendations of the Arab League and the International Labor Office. In other words, the law had an excellent legal pedigree, which is confirmed by even a superficial reading of its articles. Like all labor laws, it aimed at protecting in a fair manner the interests of workers and employers, through a thorough and careful definition of work conditions, wages, employment of women and juveniles, labor accidents and occupational diseases, arbitration of labor disputes, and so on. Much attention was also devoted to the organization of trade unions.

The most striking feature in the original text of the 1964 law is its failure to take into account a single but critical fact, namely, that practically all the employees in the private sector were non-Kuwaitis, for whom many of the law's stipulations could not be implemented without taking into account the *kafala* relationship that bound them to their employers. This relationship was left to be handled in the Aliens' Residence Law, in the form of a crucial requirement, namely, the sponsor's agreement and confirmation in all cases of issuance, renewal, and/or cancellation of residence permits. The gap between the Labor Law and the Residence Law was considerable.

It was only in 1989 that the Labor Law unambiguously faced the consequences of the predominance of non-Kuwaiti workers in the private sector by addressing directly in a sweeping ministerial resolution (No. 87/1989) the matters of issuance, transfer, and cancellation of labor permits within the framework of the *kafala.*[9] Until then, the Labor Law seems mainly to have fulfilled the function of a liberal showcase that testified to Kuwait's subscription to modern law making, while leaving the actual task of policing the non-Kuwaitis' working conditions to the Residence Law. Hence, the paradoxical relationship between the Labor Law and the Residence Law: while the Labor Law, until 1989, spelled out in a universal discourse the ideal conditions under which labor relations were to take place (with a few resolutions here and there during the 1980s on specific aspects of the non-Kuwaiti laborer's condition),[10] the Residence Law, with its exclusive concern with non-Kuwaitis, drew up the actual framework within which these relations took place. The fact that in all cases the Residence Law took precedence over the Labor Law is undeniable. Here is one vivid illustration:

Stella, a Filipina, had been in Kuwait for ten years. In late 1987 she signed a two-year contract as a seamstress in a dressmaking atelier. After 18 months, following a conflict over long working hours, her employer terminated the contract verbally and announced that he would cancel her visa and repatriate her.

According to the provisions of the Labor Law (Arts. 53 and 54), Stella was entitled to end-of-service indemnities since the employer was the one who revoked the contract before its expiry. The employer, however, ignored her requests.

Stella could go to court and sue him (Art. 88 of the Labor Law). But a court case was a long-drawn process and, while it was pending, Stella had no lawful means of earning her living in Kuwait, since both the Residence Law and the Labor Law explicitly stated that an expatriate could only work for his or her sponsor. Through friends, she could have secured herself a new job and, according to the Labor Law, she was entitled to a job transfer, since she had resided continuously in the country for ten years (Art. 17 of Ministerial Resolution No. 87/1989, Labor Law). But a job transfer was permissible only if her present employer agreed to give her a letter of release. Everything, in other words, depended on the sponsor's goodwill.

Stella did not want to leave Kuwait. Her husband was also working there, and he had a good job, earning many times more than he would have in the Philippines. Together they were the breadwinners for both his parents and her younger brothers and sister. Instead of going to court, Stella decided to try to improve her relations with the sponsor, and perhaps also persuade him to grant her the release, by stressing, among other things, that he would save himself repatriation expenses if he allowed her to transfer to another job in Kuwait instead of sending her back to Manila.

She did not get her release, but the sponsor agreed to keep her in his service. In Stella's own words: "He knows I am his best seamstress; and now he also knows that I do not let myself be bullied. He is more polite to me." But when I asked whether the working hours had become shorter—after all this was the bone of the contention between them—she admitted that they had not.

The following letter was published in the "Legal Clinic" column of the *Arab Times*, May 22, 1989:

I am in my ninth year of service in a private company. However, after completing six and a half years, my services were terminated. At the same time, I was re-hired on a new contract—a post-dated one, making it appear that there was an interruption in my services, when in fact I worked continuously. Under the new contract terms, my salary and benefits were substantially reduced. What action can I take to compel my employers to rectify the mistake, if such an act can be called a mistake?

Your valuable advice is earnestly sought.

Signed: T.D'Souza

Here is the answer of the *Times'* lawyer:

Actually several employees face a similar problem. You have asked a good question. Let me assure you that the law does not look kindly on those who circumvent it. The law and courts in Kuwait do not accept a change in contract while [the employee is] on the job. In a court of law, you'll be able to get your back pay and the dues that are entitled to you from the date of [your] first contract. Your employment must be on the previous terms and conditions, as long as they are the most beneficial for you. Let me assure you that if you take legal action, an option open to you, you'll win the case. In this case, you can ask for the salary that you were getting at the start of service nine years ago.[11] The difference between the old and the new wages can also be obtained. *However, let me warn you of the consequences of legal action. If you file a case, your employer might not take it kindly and might object to your continuing in the job. He may, and can, fire you. Are you prepared to lose your job?* (italics added).

This exchange between the *Times'* reader and the lawyer provides us only with an empirical question and a rhetorical answer. What D'Souza eventually decided to do will remain unknown to us. The point of this example is that it unambiguously shows the precedence of the Residence Law over the Labor Law in the case of non-Kuwaiti employees. It also gives us a glimpse of the framework of opportunities and constraints within which many migrants made their choices and acted. And the framework seems indeed to vindicate Abercrombie et al.' s argument that what underlies social order is the dull compulsion of economic relations. This is a matter to which I will return.

One must not, of course, underestimate the advantage for private sector employees of having a legislation like the Labor Law, which provided them with an officially acknowledged legal protection. As the *Arab Times'* lawyer in the case above pointed out in his reply, the aggrieved worker could go to court, and the chances that he would win the case were good. Nor must one underestimate the official mechanisms for arbitration of labor conflicts that were offered by the Ministry of Social Affairs and Labor. By allowing them to fight for their rights in the public arena of the law courts, these mechanisms (which included free legal assistance when need be) gave workers the means to counter the power of the sponsors/employers and to opt not only for overt but also legitimate strategies of resistance. On the other hand, the benefit of the system was severely restricted by the sponsorship system and other factors that I shall now review.

According to sources from the labor courts, there was, each year, an increase in the number of cases of non-Kuwaiti workers suing their employers. In the opinion of my Arab informants who had gone through such an experience, the plaintiffs stood a fair chance of winning if their cases were well-grounded—unless their employers happened to be particularly influential citizens, in which case the workers usually knew better than to sue them. It appears that the majority of those who chose to go to court were educated, white-collar Arab workers who were familiar with the system and could afford to rely on their own financial resources while the case was pending. Low-skilled workers, especially non-Arabs, on the other hand, did not have the same access to written information contained in the laws, nor could they easily seek such information from alternative sources. Hence the importance of the "Legal Clinic" column in the *Arab Times*, although it must be added that, according to the *Times'* journalists themselves, only a small segment of the expatriate population used their services. Most represented were the educated migrants from India and Pakistan; there were far fewer Filipinos and Sri Lankans, most of whom could not afford to buy the newspaper on a daily basis.[12]

For many migrants, one of the greatest problems was their uncertain knowledge about their exact rights and duties relative to their employers. In principle, the relationship between employer and employee was built upon the terms of the contract signed between the two parties. The situation, however, was complicated by the fact that verbal contracts were accepted by the Kuwaiti Labor Law.[13] Besides, all contracts and other documents issued by the employer to his employees had to be written in Arabic; translations might be added, but in case of conflict between the Arabic and the foreign versions, the Arabic text prevailed (Art. 14). Upon recruitment in their native countries, the migrants signed a contract in English presented to them by the local recruiting agent. The signature of the employer might or might not be on such a document. When they arrived in Kuwait the migrants were asked to sign another contract in Arabic, which was the document acknowledged by the Ministry of Social Affairs and Labor. Although this was usually a mere formality, the Arabic contract supposedly being the exact equivalent of the English one, the employee could not be entirely sure unless he or she read Arabic. When conflicts arose, some found that the terms in the Arabic text did not correspond to those in the English one. Arab migrants were less vulnerable to this kind of treatment, although they were, just as often as the non-Arabs, forced to sign entirely new contracts at any moment of their career in Kuwait.

In the letter sent by the worker T. D'Souza to the *Arab Times* we have glimpsed one instance of contract manipulation by the employers. Throughout the 1980s, as the effects of the Souq al Manakh crash worsened under the impact of the Iran–Iraq war and the 1986 oil crisis, working conditions for the expatriates became harsher. The private sector witnessed a growing number of cases of employers/sponsors who openly followed the practice of having their workers sign new contracts agreeing to lower wages and longer working hours with minimal overtime pay. In many cases the new contracts also stated that the workers took upon themselves the burden of covering their own costs of accommodation and living, contrary to what had been agreed upon in the original contracts. Often, the sponsor/employer directly deducted an amount from the workers' wages to make sure that the expenses would be covered by the workers themselves. Moreover, as the case of D'Souza made clear, by signing a new contract long-time resident workers lost the benefits[14] accumulated throughout previous years. Whether the workers agreed to sign new contracts depended mainly on their individual circumstances and the alternative options available: for those burdened with debts contracted to finance their out-migration, for example, there was no real choice, since the alternative to signing was loss of employment and repatriation. The employers, on the other hand, were well aware of the workers' dilemmas and, given the conditions of the international labor market, knew that they could press their demands quite far without running any risks of losing manpower.

This brings us back to the problems that lay at the heart of the *kafala* relationship, namely the goodwill of the *kafeel* and the willingness of the employees to risk their employment chances by standing up to the sponsor in case of dispute. By making the expatriate workers entirely dependent on the *kafeel* for their residence and work permits, the Residence Law barred many of them from the possibility of using the Labor Law's provisions to defend their legitimate rights. As the *Times'* lawyer cautioned in his reply to D'Souza, the sponsor's displeasure as a result of a law suit might cost the Indian his job. Keeping in mind that he earned more in Kuwait than in his native Goa and that he most probably had dependents back home who lived on his remittances, D'Souza was likely eventually to adopt Stella's strategy of conflict avoidance vis-à-vis his sponsor.

The *Kafala* in Business Partnership ("Visa No. 19")

I have already touched upon this relationship when describing the private sector. The Kuwaiti business partner of an expatriate was also by law his sponsor. The following case illustrates some of the dilemmas involved in this form of sponsorship.

Najeeb was from Lebanon. In 1977, fleeing the civil war on the outskirts of Beirut, he moved to Kuwait under the sponsorship of Abdel Rasoul S., an acquaintance of Najeeb's cousin who had been living in the emirate since 1954. Abdel Rasoul was interested in entering into partnership with Najeeb to start a trading company specializing in the importation of quality bathroom furnishings from France and Italy. The sponsor provided most of the capital required, while the Lebanese, a graduate in business administration, provided the professional expertise. He was paid a monthly salary by Abdel Rasoul. Both Najeeb and the sponsor were Shia, and they got along well together and trusted each other. Abdel Rasoul helped Najeeb in many ways during the first years, and the grateful Lebanese looked upon him more as an older relative than as a sponsor. Their partnership was harmonious and mutually profitable.

Abdel Rasoul was a "sleeping partner," i.e., he lent his name to the company and signed its transactions but left the actual running of the business to Najeeb. It was agreed that during the initial years the profits would be reinvested in the company. In 1980, as the business prospered, Abdel Rasoul started getting one-third of the profits. In 1985, the sponsor suddenly died in a car accident, and his son took over as owner of the company and Najeeb's sponsor.

Thirty-year-old Hussein was not content with being a "sleeping partner." He wanted to run the company himself. His major decision was to cut down expenses by lowering the employees' wages: he reduced the salary of the Lebanese accountant (a man from Najeeb's village) from KD 260 a month to KD 200, and he replaced the Egyptian truck driver by a Pakistani one who earned KD 70 as compared with his predecessor's KD 110; the salary of the Indian messenger and coffee-maker dropped from KD 60 to KD 40. Hussein also fired the company's part-time public relations man, a Lebanese of Palestinian origin who had lived in Kuwait for twenty years and had all the right connections in the Ministry of Commerce and the Customs authorities. Finally, Hussein decided to increase his own share to half of the profits. In 1987, the profits were noticeably lower than in the previous years. Admittedly, no businesses were doing very well in Kuwait at that time. However, Najeeb was convinced that Hussein's decisions had made things worse than they needed to be. Until the Iraqi invasion in 1990, he watched helplessly as the businees deteriorated. But there was little he himself could do. Of course, he could withdraw from the partnership and take his share with him. But then he would lose Hussein's sponsorship. With the recession, it was difficult to find another reliable Kuwaiti ready to start a new business. If he left Kuwait, Najeeb was not sure to be able to return, even if he found another sponsor at a later stage. He was a Lebanese Shia, and after the series of Iranian-inspired terror actions on Kuwaiti territory,[15] the authorities had been less than eager to admit Shia expatriates within their own borders. Besides, with a wife and three children, where could he go? Lebanon held no future for him, and few countries in the world would give him an entry visa, let alone a residence and work permit. So Najeeb wisely decided that a decreased income under Hussein's sponsorship was better than no income at all. Like Stella the Filipina, and probably D'Souza the Goan, Najeeb the Lebanese opted to bow to the demands of his sponsor.

The *Kafala* in the Domestic Sector ("Visa No. 20")

Unlike other categories of workers, holders of Visa No. 20, known in law as "domestic servants and the like," had no claims to the protection of any labor laws. At the same time, they were subjected, like all other non-Kuwaitis, to the requirements of the Residence Law.

Employees of the private sector ("Visa No.18") were granted residence on the basis of their work contracts signed under the auspices of the Ministry of Social Affairs and Labor, which was also responsible for the general supervision of labor relations and arbitration of labor conflicts. Domestic servants, on the other hand, could not have recourse to the arbitration of the Ministry of Social Affairs and Labor, nor could they appeal for its assistance, because they were subjected to the sole authority of the Ministry of Interior. Since this Ministry was responsible for the maintenance of internal security and law and order and was unconcerned with labor matters, problems arising in connection with the work situation of holders of Visa No. 20 were automatically classified and dealt with as "law and order problems" and not as "labor conflicts."

No reasons were given for the exclusion of this category of workers from the Private Sector Labor Law.[16] However, there was an implicit, matter-of-fact assumption that since the domestic employees' place of work was the home of the employer, the particular conditions surrounding their work made it difficult, if not impossible, for the authorities to control the implementation of the stipulations contained in the Labor Law. Indeed, the trademark of the domestic sector was precisely the private nature of the locality where the workers performed their tasks. In addition, the requirement that the name and address of the employer be recorded in the servant's passport[17] was generally interpreted as an expectation that "domestic servants and the like" were to be attached to the person of the *kafeel* and be accommodated in his home. In other words, all household personnel had to be "live-in" employees. Thus, not only the labor but also the lives of this category of worker were concentrated within the private homes of the employers. The concept of "home" in Kuwaiti society implied a pronounced sense of privacy related to traditional sexual segregation. Until the advent of the oil industry, houses were built so as to shield the women of the household (the *hareem*) from the eyes of visitors. Tradition still survives in the form of the omnipresent *diwaniya*, or male only reception room. Although sexual segregation no longer officially existed in public places, the Kuwaiti home was still viewed as the sanctuary into which outsiders never entered unless explicitly invited. It was within this context of guarded privacy that the rule of the *kafala* in the domestic sector was operationalized. In this private context, the implementation of the law's requirements about adequate treatment of the workers, their right to one day's rest per week, to holidays, yearly home-leave, and so on, were left entirely to the discretion of the employer.

The following case was fairly typical:

Letter to the *Arab Times*, October 21, 1989:
I am a housemaid and have been working here for about one year and ten months. My employer has not paid my salary since July. I have asked him several times, but he never responds, and if he does, he asks me why I need the money, since they provide me with everything. I need the money to send to my family back home. I'll complete my contract in two months' time. I've asked him to send me back to the Philippines. But he is not ready to do that either. I don't know what to do.

The *Times'* reply:
Domestic helpers are not covered by the labour law. If your employer has not paid four months' salary, you can seek your embassy's help. Your embassy's officials may be able to persuade him. The best thing would be to explain your situation to your employer and *gain his sympathy so that he feels it is important that he pays your salary* (italics added).

Deprived of institutional protection and support, the holders of Visa No. 20 were left to their own devices to handle the intensely personal and direct interface with their employers. This relationship was nearly always complicated by problems of communication, since the workers here were uniformly non-Arabic-speaking Asians. Educated urban Kuwaiti employers communicated with their household personnel in a mixture of English and Arabic. Elderly Kuwaitis and those with less education spoke only Arabic, a situation that frequently engendered notorious instances of mutual misunderstanding[18] and forced the migrants to acquire as quickly as possible a rudimentary knowledge of Kuwaiti Arabic. This task was not facilitated by the fact, already pointed out, that the rate of illiteracy and semi-literacy was highest among this category of workers.

Linguistic communication, however, was not the only problem. The above case, which was extremely common, illustrates this claim. On the basis of the lawyer's reply, there seems to be a discrepancy in the way the sponsor/employer and the domestic worker defined their mutual relationship. To the non-Kuwaiti domestic worker, this was a contractual relationship, and she expected her services to be remunerated strictly according to the terms written down in the agreement between them. The lawyer, on the other hand, advised her to try to gain her employer's sympathy, a notion which has no pertinence or relevancy under contract law. That the advice was of a pragmatic nature is obvious: given the legal constraints on their status, the workers classified in the category of "domestic servants and the like," had indeed no other options than those outlined by the lawyer: to ask for their embassies' assistance or to appeal to their employer's sympathy. But the lawyer's advice also clearly indicates that many Kuwaiti sponsors/employers had not fully understood the modern notion of salaried work and its implications. As I will show later when discussing the Kuwaitis' views of the *kafala*, their conception of their rights and duties toward their employees were in terms of the relationship that prevailed between employer and laborer in the pre-oil economy.

The strategies resorted to by the workers carrying Visa No.20 to handle a *kafala* relationship that had turned problematic (and most *kafala* relationships in this sector were bound to do so at one time or another) were necessarily informal; they ranged from placating the employers and appealing to their goodwill and compassion (compliance), through work boycott, sloppily performed tasks, and sullen silence (passive resistance), to open confrontations resulting in the work contract being rescinded and the worker being repatriated or, as a last resort, absconding (overt resistance).

The Power of the *Kafeel*

Whether in the private sector, in business partnership, or in his home, the native sponsor had considerable power over the expatriates. In general, this power was founded not so much on what the laws said about the *kafeel*'s role as on what they did not say. The Residence Law posited the *kafala* as the basic requirement for the migrant's residence and work in Kuwait but, as already pointed out, it did so without explicitly clarifying the nature of the institution of the *kafala*. By failing to do so, the law also failed to draw up clear guidelines for both employer and employee, and, most importantly, it failed to restrict the power of the sponsor over the worker. In other words, the law indicated what the *kafeel* had to do vis-à-vis the authorities (answer for his employee, inform the authorities, and so on), but seldom what he could not do vis-à-vis the workers. Thus we find in the Residence Law many gray zones, areas of interaction between *kafeel* and employee left unregulated, where actors were expected to resort to common sense and customary practices to deal pragmatically with the situations.

The major gray zone included the mutually related questions of (1) the limits of the sponsor's power to control the life of his or her employees and to expect from them extra-contractual prestations, and (2) the personal autonomy of the migrants. In the absence of formally codified rules, the Kuwaitis had built, throughout the past fifteen to twenty years, a series of practices that were more or less openly supported by the authorities and were well on their way to becoming "customary law." Two such practices, which critically enhanced the *kafeel*'s power, were the keeping of the worker's passport and deportation.

Keeping the Worker's Passport

As a rule, and regardless of their occupations, expatriates were expected, shortly after their arrival, to hand over their passports to their sponsors, in whose possession they remained for the rest of the workers' stay in Kuwait, except when the workers traveled on job assignments or on leave. The document they carried on them while in the country was the identity card (*hawiyya*), which was delivered by the local authorities upon request by the sponsor.

The keeping of passports by the employer was a common practice, which, although not based on any written legal requirement, was explicitly recommended by the Ministry of Interior, whose spokesmen issued statements at regular intervals reminding both employers and employees of the importance of following the practice. To the authorities this measure was a way of restricting the expatriates' mobility and monitoring their movements. In this sense the measure was meant as a deterrence against expatriate criminality, since it was practically impossible for a foreigner who had committed an infraction to flee the country and escape from the law without his or her passport. To the individual employers, this practice provided the added security of knowing that their employees would not quit their jobs before the end of the contract period and leave the country, or resign against the employer's will and look for better work conditions elsewhere, since, in both cases, they would need to have their passports released by the sponsor. This practice had engendered its own logical consequence: an employee who was in conflict with the employer but who was not allowed to leave his service, had sometimes no other means of breaking up the relationship than by absconding. The newspapers in Kuwait regularly carried announcements similar to this one:

> A. H. Dexter Fernando, Sri Lankan waiter, holding passport No . . ., has left his work and is still under Aralyia Restaurant's sponsorship.
> We warn all those employing and hiding him of legal responsibility. Anyone knowing of his whereabouts should inform the nearest police station or call . . .

Absconding was more widespread among non-Arabs than among Arabs. It affected in particular the low-waged, low-skilled workers in the private sector and, most acutely, the domestic sector. This explains why among the non-Arabs, Indians, Sri Lankans, and Filipinos were overwhelmingly represented in cases of absconding, as compared with Iranians, Pakistanis, and Bangladeshis who practically never worked as servants. According to the law, absconding from work was a crime that the sponsor had to report immediately to the local police.

Absconders could not retrieve their passports unless they turned themselves in to the authorities and made an official complaint against their employers/sponsors. When doing so, the majority turned to their embassies for assistance; in fact, "to turn oneself in" commonly meant that the absconder, having nowhere else to go, found the way to his or her embassy. The embassy had to contact the police. Together they reviewed the case and had to return the worker to the employer if the worker's complaint was deemed insufficiently well-founded. Otherwise, the worker was advised to file an official complaint. In most cases, the sponsor eventually chose to forsake his worker and return the passport, usually after lengthy negotiations in the course of which a sum of money, to be paid to the employer by the embassy in exchange for the passport,[19] might be agreed upon. The absconders had to pay for their own tickets home, since, by absconding, they had freed the sponsor from his contractual responsibilities.

Not all absconders turned themselves in. Many decided to "go illegal" in Kuwait and to look for another job. The risk of being discovered by the police was not serious enough to discourage the absconders from opting for this way out, especially if they could count on a solid social network ready to give them shelter and help them find a new job. The longer an ethnic community had been in Kuwait and the more established it was, the easier it became for an individual who belonged to this community to find such network support, as is illustrated by the case of Rosie the housemaid.

> When Rosie, an Indian woman, fled from her employer in 1986, she knew where she would go: to the friends of her uncle, Joseph and Felicity Pereira, who had been living in Kuwait since 1961 (the uncle himself had gone back to India a few months earlier). They sheltered her the first few months. Through Felicity's sister-in-law, Rosie found a job as part-time cleaner. The sister-in-law worked as a maid for a European family. She had heard from her "Madam" that a Belgian family was looking for a maid but that they did not want a live-in one. This suited Rosie perfectly: a part-time arrangement did not raise the tricky question of sponsorship. No one needed to know that she was a runaway maid, and she could always tell the Belgian family that she had a nominal Kuwaiti sponsor to whom she paid a fee once a year in exchange for his sponsorship.
>
> Soon after, Rosie found another part-time cleaning job with some European friends of her employers, and then yet another one. She could now rent a room with a family related to the Pereiras and earned more than she ever did as a live-in maid.

Absconding had contributed to creating a shadowy population of illegal aliens in Kuwait. Among these were also people whose contracts had run out but who had stayed on in the country. According to sources from the embassies of the main labor-sending countries, the majority in the latter group were Arabs, especially Egyptians, while Asians made up the majority in the absconder group.[20] The authorities were fully aware of the existence of this population and, every four to five years, declared a general amnesty: within a period of three months the illegal aliens were given the chance to present themselves at their embassies, get a laissez-passer if they could not recover their passports, and leave the country legally. Without these cyclical amnesties, it would have been impossible for the illegal aliens ever to leave the country, since to do so they needed an exit visa issued by the Kuwaiti authorities.[21] The last time such an amnesty was declared before the 1990 Iraqi invasion was in October 1987. Of the approximately 20,000 to 30,000 illegal aliens believed to be in the country at the time, at least 10,000 took advantage of the amnesty to leave.[22]

In Kuwait, absconding can be described as the "weapon of the weak" (Scott 1986) *par excellence*. It was the most efficient form of illegitimate resistance available to those who were too vulnerable to seek the help of the labor courts, or to whom this help was unavailable. It was efficient because it was overt; at the same time, if successful, it shielded the worker from immediate and direct retaliation by the employer (unlike strikes and other open confrontations). Also, it was efficient because it deprived the employers of the workers' labor, while creating much trouble and irritation for them. But even successful absconding (as in the case of Rosie) was a costly solution, and the absconder sometimes had to live with its high price—the impossibility of leaving the country and the risk of being arrested—for a considerable number of years. Finally, the absconders represented a pool of labor even cheaper than the average migrants for those employers who were willing to override the legal prohibition against recruiting them. Over and beyond the control of the expatriates' movements and crime deterrence, the temporary confiscation of the worker's passport by the sponsor had an important symbolic significance as well. As an event occurring at the outset of the interaction between sponsor and employee, namely upon the employee's arrival in Kuwait, it set the premises for the dyadic relationship of power and dependency that was to characterize the interaction between the two parties. In the eyes of the expatriate employee it emphasized the superordinate position of the *kafeel*, who held the formidable power of extending or withdrawing the expatriate's residence and work permits. By the same token, it also stressed the constraints of the workers' subordinate position, their restricted ability to assume legal responsibility for themselves, and their dependence on the goodwill of their sponsor. I will return to this topic below.

Deportation

While the temporary withholding of the workers' passports was stipulated nowhere in the legislation, regulations about deportation were already explicitly spelled out in the original text of the 1959 Residence Law. Unlike other matters related to the expatriate presence in the country, however, the rules about deportation had been taken up for revision only once, in 1965.[23]

According to the law, deportation of an alien could be a judiciary or an administrative decision taken by the authorities in the three following cases: (1) if the alien had been convicted and the court had recommended deportation; (2) if he or she had no means of sustenance; and (3) if the Ministry of Interior objected to his or her presence on the national territory for security or moral reasons.

A person who had left Kuwait on a deportation order could never be granted another entry visa to the country. The legislation about deportation seemed clear enough on paper. Practical implementation, meanwhile, uncovered many questions and ambiguities. According to sources from the Ministry of Interior,[24] most deportation cases were judiciary, i.e., ordered by a court of law after the alien had been found guilty of an offence and had duly served his or her sentence. In principle, therefore, expatriates did not need to fear deportation unless they had committed a crime.

Yet, deportation cast a disproportionately large shadow over the daily life of non-Kuwaitis, even the most law-abiding ones. Fear of being deported was universal in the various expatriate communities, from the Arabs to the Asians and even the Westerners. The way everyone spoke about it might easily give the impression that deportation was a more frequent occurence than it actually was. One reason was that the law considered the violation of "moral" norms as valid grounds for deportation. Article 16 speaks of concern about "public interest, public security, or public morals." The explanatory memorandum clarifies that "crimes of a public moral nature" are those where "the behaviour of the alien contradicts the customary criteria of an ordinary man's behaviour" (Residence Law, official translation). The phrase "customary criteria of an ordinary man's behaviour" was generally taken to mean the customs and norms that were common among the Kuwaitis. Thus moral norms were cultural norms prevailing among the native population. This made non-Kuwaitis feel particularly vulnerable, especially when the above stipulations were coupled with the asymmetrical bond tying the expatriates to their private sponsors. The general feeling was that there were two main dangers: the danger that the expatriates might commit a cultural gaffe, that is, that they unknowingly acted in a way that might be interpreted as a deliberate norm violation; and the danger that the sponsor would use the rather vague notion of violation of cultural norms as a pretext to get rid of troublesome employees. The vagueness of the norms in question only increased the risk of the expatriate violating or being accused of violating them—or so the migrants firmly believed, as is illustrated in the following case:

> At a private school for non-Kuwaiti children, a dispute had arisen on the various matters of incompetent teachers, overcharging for school uniforms, deplorable hygiene, and rumors about the sponsor's appropriation of the school funds for his personal use. After several months of smouldering discontent, the conflict broke out in the middle of the school year, dividing parents and teachers into two camps, the majority siding with the headmaster, the minority siding with the Kuwaiti sponsor. After a week, however, the majority camp began to lose supporters.
>
> First to defect were the teachers, who had planned a strike in protest against the replacement of some colleagues by others whom they claimed were less qualified but more willing to accept lower wages. The teachers' change of mind was due to the sponsor informing them unambiguously that strikes were illegal and that they risked arrest and deportation if they persisted in their hostile attitude.
>
> Not only the teachers, whose jobs were directly threatened, but also the parents gradually changed their minds. Many were frightened by the mere idea of taking part in an open confrontation with a Kuwaiti citizen. Although, unlike the teaching staff, their jobs did not depend on the school's sponsor, there was much concern among the parents about how their own employers would react should it become known that the parents had been "making troubles" at the school. That the school's sponsor belonged to a well-known merchant family—as did all sponsors of private schools for non-Kuwaiti children—was another source of worry: "What if my sponsor and X are good friends?" asked a nervous father at a parents' meeting. To which another parent replied: "Even if they aren't, they will support each other against a group of expatriates. Making troubles will not solve the problems. It might even land some of us in administrative deportation."
>
> In this particular case, the parents' fears were largely groundless. Yet the mere mention of the word deportation sufficed to alarm those present to the extent that many chose to give up the fight. Some parents preferred to move their children to another school, even if this meant that the children had to follow instruction in another language.[25]

Deportation, meanwhile, might be more than merely an assumptive fear on the part of the expatriate workers. It was often brandished by some sponsors in the private sector as an explicit threat against their low-skilled, mostly non-Arab employees, usually in conjunction with the forced signing of new contracts. Taking advantage of these migrants' limited knowledge of the local laws, an unscrupulous sponsor could easily convince them that his ability to bring about an order of deportation was practically unlimited. The fears of the expatriates were fed by countless stories among the non-Kuwaiti population of people being dragged to the airport and put on the first flight out of Kuwait on the basis of false accusations and evidence planted by their sponsors. It was difficult to verify the accuracy of such stories, but whether they were true or not might be beside the point. What matters is that people believed them and this belief contributed critically to shaping the views, behaviors, and strategies of the expatriates in their daily lives.

As a mechanism of control, the importance of deportation resided less in its actual implementation as a legal sanction against crimes and violations than in its pervasive presence as a *threat* and in the unclear contours of its modalities: what may trigger deportation, who may take the decision, and under what circumstances. As a long-time resident in Kuwait commented, "deportation is to the expatriates what the sword was to Damocles."

The *Kafala*: A Control Mechanism by the Civil Society

Because of the small size of its native population, Kuwait did not have at its disposition a state apparatus large enough to administer and control the substantial expatriate presence on its territory. Through the *kafala*, the state solved the problem by delegating to citizens the functions that, in other countries, usually belong to state institutions (Beaugé 1986). In other words, the Kuwaiti State delegated to its citizens most of its power to decide about, and the daily administration of, matters related to the presence of aliens on its territory: the granting of entry visas and residence permits to the expatriates by the authorities depended, in many cases, upon the granting of a work contract by a Kuwaiti employer; the length of the worker's stay in the country and his or her departure from it could be arbitrarily decided upon by the employer; as long as the workers were present in Kuwait, the law expected the sponsors to be aware of their whereabouts and to report to the authorities any changes in the workers' work and residence status. The responsibilities of the sponsor could therefore be seen as a kind of civic duty. By shouldering these responsibilities, the native sponsors were actually carrying their share of the collective task of alien surveillance, which, given the demographic imbalance between natives and migrants, would otherwise have been an impossible burden on the state infrastructure.

We have seen that one of the paramount concerns of the *kafala* was security. The sponsor kept the worker's passport in order to circumscribe the latter's freedom of movement in and out of the country and as a way to deter the worker from breaking the law. The other major concern was to maintain the stability of the labor market.

The sheer volume of labor in-migration and the very tolerant attitude manifested by the authorities regarding employment practices by employers throughout the Gulf had given rise to the persistent popular myth that the labor market in the region was a free-flowing market. Although employers were indeed free to recruit their workers from wherever they pleased and at a price that they themselves could set nearly at will, the employees, once in Kuwait, were by no means free to move from one job to another or to offer their labor to the highest paying employer (Beaugé 1986). As we have seen, in order to switch jobs they needed the written permission of their first employer in the form of a release letter. By seeking to immobilize the workers in their occupational positions and attaching them to their sponsors (the old system of indenture practised, among other places, in the colonies), the law prevented the development of a competitive labor market where workers could also participate in regulating the wages and the working conditions. Such a participation would have disrupted the stability of the labor market and negatively affected the prevailing optimal conditions for the employers.

The effectiveness of the *kafala* as a control mechanism lay in the restriction imposed on the migrant worker's right to act as a judicial person and the delegation of this right to his or her sponsor.[26] Indeed, a prerequisite for the *kafala*'s smooth functioning was that the worker's freedom—of movement, labor, and judicial action—had not only to be restricted but also handed over to the sponsor. In the private and domestic sectors, the sponsor was thus the repository of several powers: (1) his own, *qua* employer; (2) the one delegated to him by the state to use on the migrant; and (3) the one the migrant workers had to surrender to him to allow him to act on their behalf. Before the law, therefore, the sponsor represented not only himself but also the state (vis-à-vis the migrant worker) and the migrant worker (vis-à-vis the state).

Power and Powerlessness: The *Kafala* Seen by Kuwaitis

Through their constant attempts at balancing long-term interests with immediate ones in their interaction with their employers/sponsors, the expatriates clearly showed that they were acutely aware of the dominant position of the Kuwaiti *kafeel* and his power to steer the course of their lives. Likewise, their obsession with deportation was an eloquent expression of the way they conceived of the asymmetrical relationship between themselves and their sponsors.

Students of power commonly present the point of view of the powerless and attempt to understand the circumstances leading to their revolt or their quiescence. They have less frequently addressed the question of how the power-holders perceive their own role in the power–powerlessness constellation. To do so does not mean condoning the asymmetry of power relations, or negating its existence. It is, as I suggested earlier, intended to enhance our understanding of the maintenance and reproduction of the power relationship.

During my own stay in Kuwait, especially before I initiated fieldwork in 1987, I had not for one moment doubted that we have here a clear-cut situation of power and powerlessness and that the expatriates were undoubtedly characterized by the latter. Seen from the onlooker's point of view, power—whether in terms of behavior, decision-making, conflicts or interests (Lukes 1974)—unmistakably belonged to the Kuwaitis. Whether the latter agreed with this view was a question I did not ask myself at the early stage of my research. During fieldwork, however, I became increasingly aware that whereas the expatriates (and I) perceived the *kafala* as a device that undeniably secured the Kuwaitis vast power over their migrants, most Kuwaitis themselves did not see it in the same light. In fact, many described their own situation vis-à-vis the aliens in terms of powerlessness. Although they would agree that the *kafala* allowed them a certain control over the large migrant population, the Kuwaitis considered this control to be vastly inadequate. This was principally because they did not perceive the *kafala* as primarily a power relationship between employer and worker.

A Burdensome Mechanism of Self-defense

What most Kuwaitis spontaneously said was that being a sponsor employing expatriates was a burden: to bring from abroad a totally unknown stranger entrusted with a job in one's company, one's shop, or even worse, one's own home, was always a problematic and worrisome decision. The fears of the prospective employer were not very different from those of the prospective employee. "It's a lottery," said one Kuwaiti informant. "There are all the questions that remain without answers: are they good people? are they honest? how safe can we feel we are with them? Can we entrust them with our homes? our children? We get the answers only after they have arrived, and if the answers are negative, then it is too late."

Furthermore, there were all the responsibilities entailed by sponsorship: the costs could be high, in terms of money, time, and, not least, unpleasantness if the employee was lazy, inefficient, or dishonest to the extent that the employer had no alternative but to repatriate him or her and get a new one. This view of the *kafala* was shaped, to a certain extent, by the practical entailments of the structural position of the *kafeel* as mediator between the state and the individual migrant.

The employers saw the custom of keeping the workers' passports as only a natural precaution, a step toward gaining a sense of security that was seldom, if ever, complete. A few Kuwaitis admitted that depriving workers of their passports and threatening them with deportation were harsh measures, but, as a Kuwaiti woman said, "Look at it as an expression of our fears and helplessness. We are few, they are many; we cannot afford to be trusting."

Lack of security was the constant *leitmotiv*. The presence in their midst of a vast population of migrants whose backgrounds were unknown to them generated among the Kuwaitis pervasive suspicion and a constant feeling of being under siege. Perceiving migrant workers first and foremost as a threat against their own stability, security, and cultural identity, the nationals' dominant concern was with the ways and means of protecting themselves. The *kafala* seemed the most natural, though somewhat burdensome, solution, not least because indentured labor had been an old and proven practice in Kuwait from the pre-oil days.

The Historical Factor: Indentured Labor Before Oil

The organization of labor relations in Kuwait's pearl-diving past provides ample support to this claim. It is commonly agreed that pearl diving (*al ghaus*) was among the most harrowing occupations ever practised. The men dived without protection and with the most primitive gear (a nose-clip to help them hold their breath, a stone tied to the foot to speed the descent to the bottom of the sea and a basket). As an observer recounts:

> When the season was over, the diver has weathered the impossible; he has probably completed over 3,000 dives in from 30 to 50 feet of water, and has spent over 50 hours under the surface of the Persian Gulf—that is over a full forty-hour week without air, valiantly striving to gather all the oysters he can see through his blood-shot and irritated eyes, which become less sensitive with each dive . . . After they have been at it for many weeks, the divers are apt to get convulsive shivers when they come out of the water for their rest, even though the temperature may be 110° F and their tenders are covered with a lather of sweat. (LeBaron Bowen 1951:173)

The economy of pearl diving rested on a system of debts that bound the divers to their captains, and the captains to the boat-owning merchants (Ismail 1982; Rumaihi 1986; Villiers 1940). Since captains and merchants often came from the same families, it was particularly at the level of the divers that one can speak of debt bondage and indentured labor. Succinctly, at the start of each pearling season, the merchant or the captain gave a loan (*salif*) to the divers so that their families had something to live on while the men were at sea. At the end of the season, the profits were distributed among the captain and the crew, who then paid their debts to the merchants. Unless the season had been exceptionally good— which was a rare occurrence from the 1930s onwards with the depletion of the pearl banks—there were never enough profits to allow the divers to come home with money in their pockets. As a rule, the debts were larger than the shares, and once started, the spiral of debts never ended; so that at the end of each pearling season, the diver had to pledge to work for his captain again the following season. If he died in the meantime, his brother or his son inherited his debt and had to dive in his place. Since a diver worked during the rest of the year as a sailor on a merchant ship, his diving captain could not use his services without written permission from his merchant captain.

The Kuwaitis saw pearl diving as one of the most fundamental institutions of their cultural past. Although they acknowledged the existence in those days of debt bondage and indentured labor, the Kuwaitis with whom I discussed the subject did not think the system itself was unfair. On the contrary, they saw the *ghaus* as the symbol of the solidarity that once characterized the Kuwaiti community. In those days, even the poorest families knew they could rely on someone better off to help them make ends meet. Among the older generation, who had experienced the hard pre-oil living conditions, this view was not simply due to a glorification of the past that tends to place pre-oil poverty and hard work on a pedestal. Rather, it arose from the vivid recollection of the constraints poverty imposed upon the lives of men and women who had to make do with whatever means of livelihood were available to them.

Abu Khaled, a man in his late sixties who remembered clearly his last pearling expedition as a diver in 1948 and who otherwise refuted all the nostalgic rhetoric about "the good old pre-oil days" as "strange talk" (*kalaam ghareeb*), repeatedly cautioned me against looking at pearl diving outside its historical context. The following excerpt from our conversation in October 1988 illustrates Abu Khaled's view of indentured labor and the relationship between employers and laborers in the old days:

ANL: What was deducted from the diver's share at the end of the *ghaus*?
AK: First of all, his *salif* (loan), and this could be quite large if he was a good diver and his captain a generous man. Second, the amount spent on the food and water consumed by the diver during the season.
ANL, surprised: Are you really saying that in addition to working under such hard conditions the divers also had to pay for the little they ate? [27]
AK, shaking his head: Listen, you make it sound much worse than it really was. Remember that people had no choice. They had to make a living either from the desert or from the sea. The *salif* was not a bad thing because the diver did not have to pay it back. No one expected him to, and the captain had no right to demand to be paid. What he was entitled to was the diver's work. As long as the diver worked for him, it was all right. If the diver wanted to go to another captain, he had to ask this new captain to pay for his release. If he simply left, the diver would be arrested for absconding.
ANL: So, either way, the man was owned, he was not free?
AK, slightly puzzled: What did he want to be free for? There was no other work! Pearl diving kept him alive. He benefited from the system.
ANL: Didn't the merchant benefit more than the diver?
AK: On the contrary, the merchant bore the cost of the whole expedition. He had to pay for the boat, the food, the water, a thousand things! And he had to give *salif* to everyone, from the captain to the divers, the tenders, down to the helpers. If the catch of the season was bad, the merchant got nothing out of it. If the season was good, if they found *danas* (large pearls), everyone made a profit.

And Abu Khaled added gravely: "When you write about this, you must not do like other foreign writers, and see only the bad side of the *ghaus*.

You must also tell about its good side. Without it, people would have died. The rich did not only make the poor work for them, they also took care of them, gave them enough to eat. And remember: when you are poor, you see things differently."

One must be cautious not to draw an exact parallel between the pre-oil indentured labor in pearl diving and the modern-day *kafala* system. There are, nonetheless, striking similarities in the ways both systems were organized. Among other things, the labor market was regulated, then as now, through freezing the laborer in his relationship to one employer. This system allowed the employer to appropriate the labor of his employee through an understanding that was, in theory, mutual. In exchange for this appropriation, the employer was expected to provide for his worker's needs.

The conceptual framework within which Kuwaitis thought of the modern organization of employer–employee relationship today was still strongly colored by the old tradition of indentured labor that lasted until the 1950s. It was a conceptual framework that emphasized the laborer's lack of choice and the employer's paternalist role, and de-emphasized the exploitative aspect of the relationship. This approach to labor relations makes the question of power rather irrelevant in the Kuwaitis' eyes. One problem with this conceptual framework is that it rested on the assumption of a degree of cultural commonality between employers and workers that allowed for some mutual identification and accountability. According to Abu Khaled's and other elderly people's accounts, this commonality had existed between the merchants and captains and their divers in the pre-oil days. It did not, meanwhile, seem to exist between most present-day Kuwaiti employers and their non-Kuwaiti employees. Moreover, cultural commonality ran counter to the politics of exclusion that consisted in defining non-Kuwaitis as irremediably different. This contradiction and the post-oil social context had not led the Kuwaitis to reformulate their conceptual framework around labor relations and the *kafala*. On the contrary, the old conceptualization was still operative, whereby the Kuwaitis still defined their role as that of paternalist employers. What had changed nowadays, in their view, was the nature of their employees, people in whom they could no longer place the same trust as before when this kind of relationship was established among members of the same community. In other words, for the majority of Kuwaitis, the relationship itself had not changed, what had changed was one element in the equation, the employees.

Ultimately, the organization of employer–employee relationships that prevailed in Kuwait today was simply viewed by most Kuwaitis as the *normal* way labor relations are. The fact that, historically, this organization can be traced back to the pre-oil tradition of indentured labor is worth noting, since it facilitates the espousal by Kuwaitis of an organizational pattern articulated in a familiar cultural idiom. It should not, however, be taken as a license for the anthropologist to reach out for historically or culturally deterministic explanations: the ease with which the pre-oil organization of labor relations had persisted among Kuwaitis under post-oil circumstances cannot be accounted for simply by reference to past practices. The parallel with the past may dress labor relations in a reassuring discourse of cultural continuity; the stuff that made up the relations themselves spoke of social discontinuity. The explanation must be sought in the present-day social context, more specifically in the interplay between the politics of exclusion and the way ethnicity was conceptualized and practised in ordinary day-to-day life in Kuwait. This will be the topic of the next chapter.

The Economic Factor: The Kafala as a Source of Income

Finally, the *kafala* was also construed by many citizens as an easy way of making money. This could be done legally in the various ways described above (through business partnerships, private sector activities, and so on) where the sponsored expatriate worked for a Kuwaiti; or it could be done illegally, through the so-called "sales of visas," whereby a Kuwaiti citizen declared himself the sponsor/employer of an expatriate but, in fact, did not employ him or her. In exchange for this nominal sponsorship, the expatriate paid him a fixed amount per month or per year. The amount could vary widely. In 1987–1989, it ranged between KD 200–300 and several thousand dinars per year, according to who the expatriate was and how imperative it was for him or her to be in Kuwait. Although this practice was strictly prohibited by law and could entail imprisonment and fines for both sponsor and migrant, it was common and widespread. "Sales of visas" were a lucrative and easy way of making money, most actively used by lower-middle-class, unskilled Kuwaitis. Here was one area where the mechanism of control, shared between the state and its citizens over the aliens, broke down and where native sponsors and migrant workers cooperated closely together against the authorities. Both parties had a common interest in keeping the relationship alive; both derived clear advantages from the arrangement, and the sponsor, constrained by the illegality of his action, had little lati- tude to exercise control or power over the expatriate. It was here that the *kafala* came closest to being a mutually balanced transaction, not only freely entered but also freely maintained. In contrast to the cases reviewed above, in this particular instance the parties involved focused on the practical and financial advantages of the deal rather than on the social content of the relationship. Although dominance loomed large in the case of legal sponsorship and tended to overshadow the material pro- fits the system engendered, the same cannot be claimed about illegal sponsorship. For the illegal *kafeel*, the sponsorship was a purely econo- mic activity from which he could not expect to derive direct personal gratification in the form of private exercise of power or public social recognition. What it did provide him were financial means to achieve other goals unrelated to the relationship itself.

If legal sponsorship was the "main gate" through which contacts between natives and migrants flowed, the visa trade was the most impor- tant backdoor where these two groups met and dealt with each other.

I have dwelt extensively on the empirical aspect of the *kafala*, tracing in some detail the modalities of the institution, because of its rather unique character: although asymmetry in labor relations is found else- where in the contemporary world, we seldom see it erected into a cogent system, sustained by state regulations and implemented by state institu- tions. At least in the eyes of the employers, but not infrequently also in those of the employees, this system was justified, even legitimated, by the impervious logic of short-term labor migration and national identity. Combined together, these two principles strengthened arguments in favor of the exclusion of the migrants who, as transient aliens, were expected to accommodate themselves to the role of marginals, which, not surpris- ingly, was also the role of the powerless.

The *kafala* was undeniably a power relationship where the *kafeel* could, if he wanted, take advantage of the constraints created partly by circumstances in the migrant's life situation and partly by the Kuwaiti legislation itself to press the expatriates into a pattern of submission and docility that, more often than not, resulted in material profits for the sponsor. I have suggested, meanwhile, that a complete understanding of this relationship requires that we investigate not only the objective work- ing of the system and the viewpoint of the expatriate workers, but also the viewpoint of the Kuwaiti employers. Whereas the migrants viewed the *kafala* relationship in terms of constraining power exercised by the sponsor over the worker, practically all the Kuwaitis perceived the system differently—as a way of protecting a vulnerable minority native population against the onslaught of alien in-migration, as a natural state of affairs, and/or as a source of income for the private citizens.

The structure of dominance in Kuwait rested on the convergence of several factors that were primarily anchored in material circumstances: the conditions in the international labor market, the migratory pressures in the labor-sending countries, and the organization of labor relations in Kuwait ("the dull compulsion of economic relations"). By comparison, ideology played a rather modest role in maintaining the Kuwaitis' superordinate position, all the more so as the plural context of Kuwait was likely to defeat attempts by the elite to impose their views on the alien non-elite.

We have also seen that the *kafala* had an important non-economic function, that of shifting the state's power of control over the migrants on to the Kuwaiti civil society. Through this delegation, dominance was no longer merely a property of macro relations between the state and its migrant population but a central component in the relationship between individual natives and individual migrants.

If we keep in mind the image of the politics of exclusion as a wall-building process whose ultimate purpose was not to shut off interaction but to shape and control it, the structure of dominance reviewed here sets the stage for this interaction: it was not the laws themselves but the daily social exchange between actors within the framework of these laws and the cumulative effect of this exchange that actualized the power relationship between Kuwaitis and non-Kuwaitis and thereby shaped their perceptions of self and other. I will now turn to the day-to-day ethnic relations informed by the rules of exclusion and dominance.

Notes

1. For a significant exception, see Beaugé 1986.

2. Peter Lienhardt (1993) writes that the British Foreign Office, in charge of Kuwait's external affairs until its independence in 1961, "scrutinized (visa) applications very carefully in order to exclude as many as possible of the opportunists and tricksters any oil state attracted, for whose misbehaviour the British might have been blamed . . ." (1993:30). According to Lienhardt's account, it was the Foreign Office, and not the Kuwaitis, that instituted the sponsorship custom, mainly for practical reasons: "The Foreign Office . . . made it a condition of granting a visa that any visitor to Kuwait should first find a host there,

because the hotels were at that time very simple indeed, and the Political Agency did not want to be used as a general emergency rest-house" (ibid.).

3. For the employees in the public sector, the document needed was a certificate issued by the government authorities or public institution in question (Art. 3 of Ministerial Order No. 22 of 1975); for the employees in the private sector, a permit issued by the Ministry of Social Affairs and Labor duly signed by the employer (Art. 4); and for "domestic servants and the like," a no-objection certificate (NOC) issued by the Administration of Nationality, Passport, and Residence, duly signed by the employer (Art. 5).

4. KD 450 if they were employed in the public sector and KD 600 if employed in the private sector.

5. Most sponsors were male Kuwaitis, but occasionally female citizens also sponsored migrant workers. If this was not a frequent occurrence, it was because most Kuwaiti women were either married or lived with their families. In these cases, their husbands or their fathers took over the charge of the sponsorship. For a more detailed study of the legal position of Kuwaiti women, see Chapter 7.

6. This point will be elaborated in Chapter 6.

7. In both the private and the "domestic" sectors.

8. The numbers attached to the various types of visas referred to the number of the specific article in the Aliens' Residence Law that stipulated the conditions of entry for each category of employees.

9. Here again, the term used in the official translation was "employer" and not "sponsor." While the amendment showed that the lawmakers were operating with the *kafala* in mind, they kept to the habit of not making explicit references to this institutional relationship in the text of the Labor Law.

10. For example, the whole series of ministerial resolutions adopted between 1982 and 1984 on the issuance and validity of labor identity cards for non-Kuwaiti workers.

11. Employment conditions were more advantageous for migrant workers in the 1970s and early 1980s, and the level of salaries used to be higher then.

12. All newspapers cost 100 *fils* (ca 40 cents) before 1991.

13. "Employment of a labourer shall be made under a contract in writing or verbal, showing in particular the date of appointment, the value of relevant wage, the term of contract, if fixed, and the nature of the job. In the event of a verbal contract, the labourer or employer may prove his right by all evidential methods" (Art.12, official translation).

14. These consisted of: end-of-service indemnities ("a ten day wage for every one year of service during the first five years, and fifteen day wage for every one year for the following years," Art. 54 of the Labor Law); and leave ("every labourer who has completed one year of continuous service with the employer shall be entitled to a leave of 14 days with full pay, which shall be increased to 21 days after the fifth year of continuous service," Art. 38).

15. These included the bombing of the French embassy, an attempt on the emir's life, and the highjacking of a Kuwait Airways passenger plane.

16. It is interesting to note that when it comes to control over immigration in general, responsibility has shifted several times between the Ministry of Social Affairs and Labor and the Ministry of Interior. Prior to 1965, it was under the Ministry of Social Affairs and Labor; from 1965 to 1974, it was under the Ministry of Interior; in 1974, it was transferred back to the Ministry of Social Affairs and Labor (Russell and Al-Ramadhan 1994). As a rule, whenever responsibility lay with the Ministry of Interior, control over entry, exit, and conditions of employment was tightened. Throughout those years, however, domestic servants have always been under the jurisdiction of the Ministry of Interior; their exclusion from the Labor Law dates from 1964.

17. "The data of a residence permit granted to a servant duly indicated in his/her passport shall include the name and address of his/her employer" (Art. 2 of Ministerial Resolution No. 84/1977, Residence Law, official translation).

18. This situation was unanimously confirmed by everyone I have interviewed: employers, employees, the police authorities, the embassies from the non-Arab labor-sending countries, and the recruiting agencies.

19. Interview with the minister counsellor of the Philippine Embassy, October 25, 1987.

20. Interviews with the labor attachés of the Egyptian, Indian, Philippine, and Sri Lankan embassies in December 1987.

21. There was a widespread conviction amongst Kuwaitis that an unknown number of illegal Arabs had become permanent residents in the country by mixing with the *bidoon* population.

22. *Kuwait Times*, February 1, 1988.

23. The amendment concerned Article 18 and was related to the length of time the authorities could detain an alien while the order of his or her detention was being executed.

24. Interview with Col. Ahmed Rujaib, Ministry of Interior, May 15, 1989.

25. Each ethnic community usually had only one school. See Chapter 6.

26. If an expatriate was arrested and detained, for instance, the police immediately got in touch with his or her sponsor. As a rule, no actions were taken to deal with the charge against the migrant before the sponsor had personally shown up. Even if the arrest turned out to be a mistake, the expatriate was not set free before this formality had taken place.

27. Divers ate very little in order to be able to dive. Their meals consisted only of dates, boiled rice, and tea.

5

Conceptualizing "Us" and "Them" Through Everyday Practice

In their daily lives, people in Kuwait were acutely aware of their own and others' national origin. Even under the most occasional and fleeting interaction, actors began by automatically registering the national identity of the other party. When this identity was ambiguous, they would often ask explicitly, "Where are you from?" In most cases, however, people could easily pinpoint each others' ethnic origin.

In this chapter, I will look into the way ethnic and national differences were expressed in Kuwait and how recognition of ethnic signalization impinged on the flow of social interaction and contributed to the definition of the situation. The purpose is to attempt to disentangle the intricacies of ethnic identity and identification in this plural society, a task which will be carried out against the background of the overarching categorization described in Chapter 3. Central in this chapter are two concepts that are notoriously elusive, namely, ethnicity and identity. As I hope that an implicit definition of ethnicity will gradually emerge through the presentation and discussion of the empirical material, I will attempt, at this initial stage, to explain succinctly my use of the concept of identity.

The identity under focus in this study is primarily *ethnic* identity, that is to say, one actualized in the course of relations between individuals and groups that perceive themselves as different in terms of their imperative characteristics. Identity, in its most general sense, is closely related to *role* and *status*. A person's identity is defined, embraced, and expressed through the set of roles and statuses he or she holds in society. Thus, role and status are constituent parts, while identity, "essentially a concept of synthesis" (Epstein 1978), is related to "the process by which the person seeks to integrate his various statuses and roles, as well as his diverse experiences, into a coherent image of self" (1978:101). It must be added, however, that insofar as identity arises from the sum of roles and statuses it cannot be conceptualized only in terms of actor's consciousness of self, but also in terms of perceptions of the actor's self by others in relation to whom he or she holds these roles and statuses. In other words, identity, especially ethnic identity, is not only self-defined and assumed; it is also ascribed and imputed. Because this type of identity is imperative and inclusive, it tends to take precedence over other identities. As a result, both assumption and ascription of ethnic identity are peculiarly constraining upon the choice of roles and statuses a person can make beyond those assigned at birth; in Barth's formulation, ethnic identity "defines the permissible constellations of statuses, or social personalities, which an individual with that identity may assume" (1969:17).

In the light of this approach to identity, the reader will find that my use of the concept is not clearly delimited in relation to the concepts of roles and statuses. As this chapter deals almost exclusively with the sphere of articulation between Kuwaitis and non-Kuwaitis, actors' identities must be understood not so much in terms of consciousnesss of self as in terms of ascription and imputation by others.

Group Differentiation and Group Identification

There are no clear phenotypical differences between the native population of Kuwait and the majority of the expatriate population. Although the northern Arabians, especially Bedouin nomads, have sometimes been described in the literature as distinct from most other Arabs ("taller" and "more resilient"), those descriptions hardly apply to the native population of Kuwait today. Strictly speaking, there are no particular physical traits that distinguish a Kuwaiti from any other Arab. Moreover, centuries of migration and contact with Ottoman Iraqis and Persians, on the one hand, and with the people around the Indian Ocean, on the other, have left their imprint on the physical traits of those known today as Kuwaitis: Iranian, Turkish, African, Indian, and even Southeast Asian (particularly Indonesian and Malaysian)[1] features are visible among the native Arab population. In other words, ethnic boundaries separating Kuwaitis and non-Kuwaitis are not built primarily upon differences of a phenotypical nature, and ethnic relations in Kuwait cannot be expressed in terms of race relations in the way that they may be between, for example, blacks and whites in the USA, South Africa, or the Caribbean. The racial distinction between the three main categories of the population (Kuwaitis, Arabs, and non-Arabs) is so negligible that it was imperative for Kuwaitis to resort to diacritical signs other than the biological ones in order to carry out their politics of exclusion. In other words, one can claim that the diacritica used in Kuwait to categorize and stratify groups were of a wholly and unambiguously socio-cultural character.

I am aware of the view according to which race is also a socially constructed principle of stratification, insofar as "racialization attributes meanings to certain patterns of phenotypical variation" (Miles and Phizacklea 1980, quoted in Rex and Mason 1986:98–99). I do not claim that phenotypical variations and the diacritica used in Kuwait are qualitatively different. What I suggest is that they differ in their degree of *malleability* and *negotiability*: boundary-crossing is, in principle, a lot easier to achieve where the criteria of group differences can be transformed, concealed, or disguised. Gross phenotypical differences, on the other hand, are much less easy to manipulate. What is of concern to us here is the relationship between the malleability/negotiability of the diacritica used in Kuwait and the overall structure of dominance embedded in the power asymmetry between natives and migrants.

An important point to keep in mind is that group identification did not have the same meaning for Kuwaitis and non-Kuwaitis. In the case of the former, the logic of exclusion prevailed; its ultimate purpose, as I will argue in more detail in Chapter 7, was the building of a national identity consonant with the Kuwait of the post-oil era. In other words, for Kuwaitis, especially since the 1970s, group identification has been essentially a political project, to which the state contributed actively. In the case of non-Kuwaitis, except for the Palestinians, who were more a community of refugees than a community of migrant workers, group identification was characteristically spontaneous and unorganized. The migrant population was atomistic, with a high rate of personnel turnover and subject to strict legal constraints. Group identification, in this case, was the combined result of administrative categorization and informal relations between individuals (mostly close friends and families). As will be shown in the next chapter, ethnic associations existed, but only for specific and limited purposes. The formality of Kuwaiti group identification thus stood in contrast to the informality of group identification among the various migrant nationalities; at the same time, the two processes presupposed each other's existence.

Signaling Identity Through the Dress Code

Much has been written in the popular literature (Bulloch 1984; Izzard 1979) about the way male citizens of the Gulf countries, and particularly the Kuwaitis, use their traditional robe, the *dishdasha*, to signal their identities. The social scientific literature, meanwhile, has mostly ignored the study of the dress code in the Gulf countries, rather disdainfully relegating it to the crude folk repertoire of lay actors and amateur observers. Only the women's veil has so far been an object of sociological analysis (e.g., Wikan 1982). My contention, however, is that the dress code is a crucial key to our understanding of the kinds of meaning that inform daily action in Kuwait. In the absence of clear racial distinctions, the dress code played a major role in ethnic signalization. This was all the more so as Kuwait's Asian population could not use more subtle signals such as variations in the Arabic accents and dialects and Arabic names as clues for ethnic identification.[2]

The Dishdasha

With very few exceptions, when in Kuwait, all Kuwaiti men wore the *dishdasha* and the headdress.[3] Since time immemorial the *dishdasha*, under varying forms and different local names, has been identified with the inhabitants of North Africa and the Middle East, from the Sahara in the west to the Arabian Peninsula in the east. With modernization and the introduction of Western fashion in the twentieth century, its use receded in many Arab countries and is, today, commonly associated with old and traditional people, peasants, and the urban poor, rather than the educated middle class and the elite. In the Arabian Peninsula, meanwhile, the use of the *dishdasha* has been remarkably persistent. To Kuwaitis, it was an integral part of their material culture, and wearing it was a natural thing to do, a custom untainted by any particular negative connotations. On the contrary, since the oil boom, whatever connotations are attached to it have become overwhelmingly positive in the Kuwaitis' eyes.

Non-Gulf Arab expatriates seldom, if ever, wore the *dishdasha* in public. Neither did the non-Arabs. Most expatriate men wore European-style clothes, although unskilled laborers from the subcontinent and Egypt sometimes wore their own native clothes.[4] There was a curiously strong sense among foreigners that the use of the *dishdasha* was a uniquely Kuwaiti preserve; this view was so clear that it deserves some attention. There were no explicit rules that prohibited the wearing of the *dishdasha* by people originating from outside the Gulf. Nor were there rules that imposed its use on the Kuwaitis. Yet, as a matter of course, young Kuwaiti men systematically went over to wearing the *dishdasha* around the age of eighteen to twenty. The two following examples can give us some clues as to why they did so.

> Tariq was on his way home from the cinema one evening when he was stopped by a police officer and asked to show his identity papers. In his jeans and T-shirt, Tariq looked like any Arab expatriate. His clothes and the fact that he was walking (and not driving) in Salmiya, a neighborhood mostly inhabited by expatriates, gave away few indications that he was Kuwaiti. When the policeman saw his Kuwaiti ID, he apologized and said: "Next time, save yourself unnecessary trouble. Wear the *dishdasha*."
>
> In a grocery store, expatriate customers stood around waiting to be helped by the two salesmen, an Arab and an Indian. A man in a *dishdasha* walked in and said *"Salam aleikum."*[5] He then turned to the Arab salesman and enquired about the prices of several types of nuts. The salesman gestured to the expatriate customer he was serving to wait, and turned his full attention to the man in the *dishdasha*. None of the other customers protested, and when the Kuwaiti wanted to pay, they all moved aside to make room for him at the cash desk.

A Palestinian, an Egyptian, a Syrian, or a Lebanese would not wear the *dishdasha*. Considering the privileged treatment the use of this distinctive dress could confer to its wearer, it is surprising that Arab expatriates did not adopt it. Many non-Kuwaiti Arab men scoffed at the thought of wearing the *dishdasha*. Hassan, an Egyptian real-estate agent, had very strong opinions about it: this long, white[6] robe was hopelessly impractical, he said. "To keep it immaculate in this heat, you have to change clothes several times a day. Or else, you must secure yourself a job in a nice, air-conditioned office, from which·you can send people here and there running errands for you." He admitted that the *dishdasha* could be much more comfortable than the Western suit in the heat, but said, "In Egypt, only *fellaheen* (peasants) go around dressed in long robes and headscarves. They are old-fashioned. No one in his right mind would do so if he is educated and has a serious job to do." Among male expatriates, the use of non European-style clothes (mostly by Egyptians and Pakistanis) was associated with low-paid, unskilled laborers particularly within the construction sector.

Nabil, a Palestinian oil engineer born and brought up in Kuwait, shrugged when I asked him on this subject. "I work most of the day out in the oil fields. Can you see me wearing a *dishdasha* to do that? Even my Kuwaiti colleagues come to work in ordinary clothes." The difference between them was that after working hours, the Kuwaiti oil engineers went home and changed into the *dishdasha*; not Nabil, who assured me that his idea of comfortable clothes was closer to that of a Westerner. It was only much later that Nabil told me about the football match incident. A few years back, as he was about to graduate from high school, Nabil went to a football match with his Kuwaiti friend Fahad. Both teenagers attended the exclusive American School at the time, and had a cosmopolitan circle of friends who considered Nabil to be as Kuwaiti as Fahad. Nabil was very attached to Kuwait and felt that this was where he belonged. His father and mother were among the first Palestinian teachers who came to Kuwait in the late 1940s and had contributed to setting up the Kuwaiti school system. For years, influential Kuwaitis had suggested that they be granted nationality as a token of gratitude (ironically, the family became Kuwaiti the very year Nabil turned twenty, which meant that unlike his younger brothers and sisters, he was left out of the naturalization process). Nabil said that, in his younger days, he spoke Levantine Arabic, mixed with many Kuwaiti colloquial expressions. The match Nabil and Fahad were to attend that day was between the Kuwaiti national team and an Egyptian team. Football was enormously popular in Kuwait, and the atmosphere was one of national celebration. The stadium was filled with Kuwaiti men in *dishdashas*. Nabil also wore a *dishdasha* and he vociferously supported the Kuwaiti team. After the match, as he and Fahad were making their way to the parking lot, some of Fahad's cousins drove past the two boys and called out from their car: "Hey Nabil, nice *dishdasha* you've got there. Are you getting ready for naturalization?" They all laughed as the car drove away. Nabil's comment on the episode: "That was just a silly thing boys would say and I did not pay much attention to it then. But for some reason or another, that sentence remained stuck in my mind. As I grew older, I realized that all the while I thought of myself as a Kuwaiti, others saw me as a foreigner. So I decided that instead of being a half-baked Kuwaiti, it was better to be a full-blood Palestinian. Except that this is also difficult since Kuwait is the only place I really am familiar with. This is where I have all my friends, where I got married, and where my children were born. Like it or not, this place means more to me than anywhere else."[7]

Nabil's younger brother Maher, also born and raised in Kuwait, became Kuwaiti when their father was naturalized. Unlike Nabil, however, Maher did not feel particularly attached to Kuwait. He could not, for instance, bring himself to wear the *dishdasha*, although he realized that it would have made his life much easier: for example, when he married a Palestinian girl and went to the Ministry of Interior to register her name on the list of candidates for naturalization through marriage, the Ministry's officer thought Maher was his wife's brother and refused to consider her case. "You must come back with your husband," he told her, "not with your brother." "But I am her husband," protested Maher. The man behind the desk eyed him with suspicion: "Is that so? Then why are you dressed like a Palestinian?" Something similar occurred when Maher went to an office in the Ministry of Defence to enroll for national service. He was told to join the line of non-Kuwaiti recruits and it was quite a while before anyone took the trouble of checking his identity card. Again, it was his failure to wear the *dishdasha* that led the Kuwaitis to classify him as an expatriate.

Arab expatriates did not adopt the use of the *dishdasha* partly because they associated it with a lack of modernity. For some, this association was anchored in prejudices from their native countries; for others, it was a vague reaction against the unwritten norm that kept the use of the *dishdasha* exclusively for Kuwaitis. That such a norm existed was beyond any doubt, as was clear from the cases presented above. The public use of the *dishdasha* by any person from outside the Gulf region was viewed as an attempt at pretending to be Kuwaiti, or what Goffman (1959) calls "passing," an activity that was normatively reprehensible. The example of the police officer who advised Tariq to wear the *dishdasha* next time in order to save himself the unpleasantness of being stopped and checked and the case of Maher show that not only passing from non-Kuwaiti to Kuwaiti, but also failing to "identify" oneself as Kuwaiti, could be negatively sanctioned. It also confirms my contention that group identification among the Kuwaitis was a highly official affair in which the state intervened actively with a battery of legal sanctions and unwritten norms. The sanction against Kuwaitis who would let themselves be identified as non-Kuwaitis consisted in their risking the loss of their national privileges. Exactly what the sanctions against non-Kuwaitis who systematically tried to pass as Kuwaitis might be I cannot say, since I have never come across such instances. On the basis of Nabil's case, however, public ridicule seemed to be the most likely strategy, all the more so as the "passer" would have to master the Kuwaiti accent and manners—a feat that, according to the Kuwaitis themselves, was never successful: "We always spot the phony accent," a Kuwaiti told me. "Even people from the Gulf do not speak Kuwaiti like Kuwaitis. How can an Egyptian or a Palestinian fool us?"

As both Hassan's and Nabil's statements indicate, there was another symbolism attached to the *dishdasha*. In their eyes, this immaculately white robe stood for a life-style associated with idleness and luxury. To the extent that it was worn by workers, it was well suited only to certain types of occupations—the term "white collar" comes inevitably to mind and seems particularly appropriate. The occupational association of the *dishdasha* connects it back to the whole sphere of employer–employee relationships and, of course, to the *kafala*. One may be tempted to explain the reaction of deference that the sight of the *dishdasha* instantaneously triggered in non-Kuwaitis in terms of situational roles. Under normal circumstances, natives and migrants interacted within very precise contexts in which both parties played a limited set of roles: the former as (1) representatives of the authorities, (2) sponsors/employers, or (3) customers; and the latter as (1) aliens answerable to the authorities, (2) sponsored employees, or (3) providers of services. In all three roles, non-Kuwaitis were in a dependent situation where they had no choice but to be polite and deferential and to take their cue from the Kuwaitis. Yet roles (2) and (3) were relations which, at least in principle, implied reciprocal and not necessarily asymmetrical transactions. In themselves, therefore, they could not account for the quasi-instinctive deference on the part of non-Kuwaitis. Only by connecting these relations with the structure of dominance embedded in the sponsorship system can we grasp the string of actions and reactions in the migrant–native interface, where ethnic and occupational identities were fused together.

The *dishdasha* was the most eye-catching emblem of male Kuwaitiness. In a crowd it immediately singled out Kuwaitis from non-Kuwaitis. It did not matter what the individual wearing it actually looked like; the *typical* Kuwaiti was defined first and foremost by his dress code and his demeanor (the way he wore his headdress, the way he carefully readjusted it now and then, the way he nonchalantly played with his prayer beads, and so on); under "demeanor" we may also include the use of the Kuwaiti dialect, a diacritical sign of particular significance for the Arabic-speaking expatriates. Dressed in European-style clothes, the Kuwaiti could be mistaken for a Western Arab, a Turk, an Iranian, a native of the subcontinent, or a Westerner.[8] Dressed in a *dishdasha*, his identity was unmistakable. And this identification immediately set in motion a chain of reactions—always the same—among the people he interacted with, especially if they were expatriates. This in turn informed him of, and confirmed, his identity, one that was firmly anchored in social privilege and power.

The Abaya

The *abaya* is a black cloak that envelops women from head to ankle. It is worn over a white headscarf and a long, loose dress. While practically all Kuwaiti men wear the *dishdasha*, not all Kuwaiti women wear the *abaya*.

As a rule, urban women from the merchant class dress in the Western fashion. The *abaya* is something they put on only on special occasions, as when paying condolence visits or when shopping in the old *souq*. This is true for most upper-class women younger than fifty, the vast majority of whom are educated. Among non-urban women, by whom I mean the less-educated Bedouin women who live mostly in the "rural" neighborhoods and the outlying governorates of Jahra and Ahmadi, the use of the *abaya* and the *burqa* or the *niqab* (two types of face veil) was common in the late 1980s. Among urban women, the use of the face veil was extremely rare,[9] if only because it was forbidden in conjunction with car driving, an activity that was particularly widespread among urban Kuwaiti women.

Yet it would be misleading to look upon the use of the *abaya* as a criterion to draw the line between urban and non-urban and educated and less-educated Kuwaiti women. Although I have heard a few Kuwaiti women speak of the *abaya* in the same derogatory terms used by Hassan the Egyptian when he spoke of the *dishdasha*, describing it as a symptom of traditionalism and even backwardness, this was an exceptional view. Even when they personally dressed in European style, most urban women did not dismiss the black cloak in negative terms. Nor have I heard anyone complain that she was forced to use the *abaya*. In Kuwait, women who were *muhajjibat* ("covered") wore the *abaya* willingly and proudly. If, for a while in the 1960s, European-style clothes seem to have gained popularity among younger women, the traditional dress code with the use of the *abaya* reemerged throughout the 1980s, most noticeably among the young urbanites, many of whom were educated and working women.

Like the *dishdasha*, the *abaya* was identified with the Gulf area (including Iraq and Iran) and, as a rule, was not worn by expatriate women. Non-Arab women wore European-style clothes and some women from the subcontinent wore saris. Arab women wore European-style clothes or what is customarily referred to as the Islamic costume and which consists, as elsewhere in the Middle East, of a long dress and a headscarf. In many ways, the *abaya* elicited the same reactions of deference and service in the non-Kuwaitis as did the *dishdasha*. Deference in this case meant, in addition to general politeness, a special kind of consideration, namely sexual consideration.

To understand this situation, we must consider it within the context of labor migration in Kuwait. As indicated in Chapter 2, the only expatriate community that registered a balanced sex ratio was the Palestinian community (100.0 in 1983, according to Shah and Al Qudsi 1989). Among the other expatriate communities, there was a clear imbalance, most acute in the age groups between twenty-five and fifty-nine, which affected particularly the non-Arabs; in 1985, the sex ratio for non-Kuwaitis was 160.8, compared to 98.9 for Kuwaitis (RSP No.1). The imbalance would have been even greater if we remove the Palestinian community from the non-Kuwaiti group. Although 70 percent of the migrants were registered as married in 1985 (RSP No.1), many did not live as a family unit in Kuwait. The condition for the migrants to bring in family dependents was that they earned a minimum monthly salary of KD 450 in the public sector or KD 600 in the private sector. It was to get around these regulations that many expatriates resorted to illegal sponsorship to bring in their wives.

The presence of a large population of single male migrants in the country was a constant source of worry to the Kuwaiti authorities. An expression of this worry can be found in the municipal regulation forbidding *azaab* or "bachelors" (in this particular context only unaccompanied expatriates, whether married or not, fell within this category) from being housed in residential areas predominantly occupied by Kuwaitis. This explains why, in this officially unsegregated society, one would find public places that could not be visited by "families" and "bachelors" on the same days of the week (for instance, the popular Entertainment City, north of Kuwait, was forbidden to "bachelors" on Fridays). The idea was to protect the female population, especially native women, from the predatory sexual behavior of the "bachelors." Fears were fueled by nearly daily reports in the press of so-called "sexual crimes" committed by non-Kuwaitis.

The reemergence of the *abaya* in the urban areas reflected the concern of Kuwaiti women with making a clear statement about their national identity and status that they intended all foreigners, in particular the men, to understand wholly and unambiguously. Parallel to the adoption of laws constraining the activities of migrants, the emphasis on an exclusive dress code signaling a privileged identity contributed to the creation of a zone of security within which the native population could move without fear and that allowed them to hold on to the myth of continuity in the face of sweeping change. When wearing the *abaya*, native women had nothing to fear from foreign men, who were fully aware of the consequences of harrassing a Kuwaiti citizen.

The use of the headscarf among expatriate Arab women had a somewhat similar effect. It signaled their identity as *Arab* women, that is, women who lived in Kuwait surrounded by a protective network of kin and relatives. As pointed out in Chapter 2, a considerable number of Arab female expatriates were in Kuwait as dependents, whereas the majority of Asian women were in the emirate in their capacity as unaccompanied workers, in other words, without the protection of a husband, a brother, or a father. In most cases, Arab women had a male relative to whom they could turn when in need. Both Kuwaitis and Arab expatriates operated within a common cultural ideology that assigned to the male head of the family not only the right but also the duty to protect and defend his female dependents. Even though their social status may not have been as privileged as that of the Kuwaitis, the ethnic status of Arab women, signaled through the headscarf, did provide them with an effective measure of protection.

Although the presence of a large population of male migrants inspired real concern among the natives, one should not exaggerate the implications of this concern. In reality, everyone in the country was aware that the specter of the predatory "bachelors" was a half-empty threat: before the 1990 Iraqi invasion, life in Kuwait was so secure that people seldom locked their doors. The migrant population in Kuwait was a surprisingly disciplined one, and foreign men seldom allowed themselves overtly improper behavior, knowing fully well the sanctions that might result from it. Thus, to say that the Islamic dress code aimed at protecting its wearers from unwanted sexual attention was to uncover only one of its purposes, the functionalist purpose that was not necessarily the one with the deepest resonance for the female actors themselves.

The uneasiness created by the presence of the male migrants was only one of several events that led to a collective mobilization among the Kuwaitis. This mobilization has had consequences on the political scene, and it is on this outcome that analysts have focused most attention. In the early 1980s the religious forces registered a remarkable advance in Kuwaiti national politics.[10] This is commonly seen as part of the wave of Islamic revival that swept across the Middle East from the late 1960s onwards, and more particularly in conjunction with the revolution in Iran. The complex phenomenon known variously as "Islamic revival," "political Islam," or "Islamic fundamentalism" springs from a range of sources in the many societies that make up the Muslim world. Common for most of these societies are the problems of demographic surge since the 1960s, urbanization, and the inability of the state to cater to the population's socioeconomic needs, in particular employment for the generation between fifteen and thirty. In most countries in the Gulf, the situation is different. Although population increase and urbanization are real enough here as well, we are dealing with phenomena that are radically dissimilar in degree and sometimes also in substance. Population increase in Kuwait entailed not only demographic change but also a change in ethnic composition and a cultural pluralization of a dimension unknown elsewhere outside the Gulf region. Urbanization of this city-state under the prosperous oil conditions, on the other hand, cannot be compared to urbanization in Egypt, Iran, or Algeria, where it invariably goes hand in hand with the appearance of slums and the breakdown of basic infrastructures and public services. Finally, the state in Kuwait had, so far, been able to cater more than adequately to the needs of its population in the areas of health, education, and employment. Therefore, to use the cluster of usual factors (population increase, urbanization, and unemployment) to account for the revival of Islam in politics in Kuwait would be misleading. Another explanation that has been offered (e.g., Burgat 1995) regarding Islamism is that return to Islam is return to what the actors involved perceive as a way of life and a mode of thought that are their own rather than being imported, borrowed, or imposed from the outside. This perspective is particularly appropriate to the understanding of the situation in Kuwait.

In 1981, after nearly a decade of frenzied and erratic development accompanied by the staggering influx of migrant workers from outside the Arab world, the Kuwaitis' capacity for cultural absorption seemed to have reached a point of saturation. Drowning in the midst of aliens from East and West, the small native population was desperately looking for ways to shield itself and to preserve a sense of cultural identity. As an elderly Kuwaiti put it, "Imagine seeing strangers everywhere around you, including in your own homes (i.e., the servants). We used to know all the

Kuwaitis, and to trust each other. In the old days, when someone made a promise, you knew he would keep it. We were like a big family. Now, everyone is a stranger. You don't know whom to trust anymore." Also the younger generation experienced a sense of being under a cultural siege, as the following statement by a woman in her early thirties shows: "You have been to Abu Dhabi and Dubai, haven't you? How many local people did you meet in the streets there? One? Two? They are so few compared to the expatriates that they have surrendered the streets to them. Sometimes, I think we should do that too, withdraw to a ghetto where we would be only amongst ourselves. It would have been easier, less tiring. But we are more numerous than the the Emiratis. And we are not shy like them. We want to retain our streets, to keep them Kuwaiti. We want to hear Kuwaiti spoken out there, see Kuwaiti people and Kuwaiti manners around us. This is our home. We don't want to lose it. We want to be able to live here in our own way."

Reading the Signals

Signaling identities through the dress code was a highly efficient means of inter-ethnic communication in Kuwait. But signals are seldom attached to just one meaning; there are at least two: the one assigned to the signal by its sender and the one assigned to it by its receiver (Tambs-Lyche 1991). The two need not coincide. On the other hand, when a sign or a symbol is conventionalized, the variety of meanings are reduced to just a few or even a single meaning, which then becomes the one shared by a large majority of the population. National flags are a typical example. The *dishdasha* in Kuwait was also a conventionalized sign with a relatively simplified meaning. It achieved this status partly by accident (after all, it was the dress that Kuwaiti men favored and that many foreigners did not find practical, hence its natural association with the privileged native minority) and partly as a result of an ideological mobilization under the aegis of the state: the formation of a national identity epitomized by the Kuwaiti male was an official part of the Kuwaiti nation-building project. Through the exclusive use of the *dishdasha*, Kuwaiti men symbolically appropriated the monopoly of social power vis-à-vis non-Kuwaitis, a fact that was legally embedded in the sponsorship system. This appropriation was consistent with the actual social asymmetry experienced by natives and migrants in everyday life and was, therefore, the object of a practically general consensus. Through the use of the *abaya* Kuwaiti women symbolically appropriated a monopoly of sexual morality, but the consensus here was more uncertain.

To most non-Muslim expatriates in Kuwait, the message of the *abaya* and the headscarf was exclusively about the wearers' ethnic origin and social status, not about their sexual morality. If foreign men respectfully kept their distance from the "covered" women more than they usually did from the "uncovered" ones, it was not primarily because they believed the former to be morally respectable and the latter morally lax. It was, rather, because they knew that in the case of the "covered" women the sanctions against harassment meted out by the authorities or the women's own kin would be much more severe. The *abaya* and the Islamic dress had the same function as the distinctive paraphernalia that surrounded members of the wealthy upper class, regardless of their ethnic and national origins. This function consisted in heralding their protected social status relative to an underprivileged population. In other words, to non-Kuwaitis the message of the *abaya* and the headscarf was a secular, not a religious one.

Most Kuwaitis, in particular the "covered" women themselves, had a different view. To them, the *abaya* and the headscarf were not only elements in a particular cultural dress code. They were also an integral part of the traditional Islamic discourse on female modesty that linked the covering of hair and bodily shapes with morality, and lack of covering with sexual laxity. Thus, although the *hijaab* (literally the "veil," by extension, all that covers[11]) may originally have been a pragmatic device to solve a topical problem, it was not a device without consequences for the moral evaluation and moral ranking of groups in the Kuwaiti social discourse.

Through the process of covering themselves with the *abaya* to signal their national identity, Kuwaiti women had progressively come to create in their own eyes and possibly those of some other Muslims a sharp contrast between themselves and the "uncovered" alien women around them, a contrast that was easily conceived of in terms of divergent sexual morality: a European-style dress, skirt, or jeans, or a sari easily looked "immodest" next to the black, all-enveloping *abaya*, as did the sight of female hair left uncovered. The very fact that non-Kuwaiti clothes were colorful made the wearers look frivolous. When this "frivolity" combined with patterns of gender interaction that differed from those prescribed by Islam, as in the case of Christian women from Kerala, Goa, and the Philippines, it reinforced the negative ethnic stereotypes about these women's sexual morality.

In this society, strictly stratified in terms of class and ethnic origin, women used variations in the public projection of sexual image as a key index of moral definition by self and others. Here, as in the case of male power, the Kuwaitis, who set the norms and defined the criteria, had the widest margin of action. Since these norms and criteria were cultural and were drawn overwhelmingly from the structure of the labor market, they could also be used advantageously by the Arab expatriates, although in a more restricted way. They were of the least use to the Asians, many of whom did not share in the Middle Eastern/Islamic culture and also ranked lowest on the occupational hierarchy. Yet, unlike the symbolic appropriation of social power by Kuwaiti men, the symbolic appropriation of sexual morality by Kuwaiti women was neither absolute nor unchallenged.

For one thing, the Quranic connection of the *hijaab* made it impossible to exclude female Arab expatriates from such a sphere of sexual morality. Moreover, since membership of Islam is an open category, even non-Arab women married to Kuwaiti men had a claim to the dress-code-based sexual morality if they converted. They could, therefore, wear the *abaya* without being ridiculed or accused of attempting ethnic passing.[12] As already pointed out, it was much more usual for Kuwaiti women to dress according to Western fashion than for Kuwaiti men. The fact that those who did were overwhelmingly educated women of the upper and middle classes introduces a dimension of class into the analysis, not between natives and migrants this time but among the Kuwaitis themselves. Insofar as the "covered" Kuwaiti women sought to define sexual morality as their own ethnic prerogative, they found themselves in conflict with the educated elite, who tried to define female Kuwaiti identity in terms of criteria of modernity (for example, education and participation in public social life) rather than in terms of sexual morality. These women did not find protection behind cloaks and veils but behind their class status, frequently expressed through material riches. From this perspective, one may conclude that the *abaya* and Islamic dress were claims to social regard made overwhelmingly by Kuwaiti women from more modest social origins, who did not have the means to signal their ethnic status through material riches.

Ethnic Identities and Gender Identities

Social power can be conceived of as a property arising from the rights a person can exercise directly or indirectly over others who depend on, or are subordinate to, him or her: actors have social power when they can positively or negatively affect the objective life situation of others, while others cannot seriously affect theirs. Autonomy—the ability to decide for oneself—and a degree of unreachability through action on the part of subordinates characterize social power. From this perspective, we may work out an analytical model whereby gender identities in Kuwait varied according to ethnic identities and the positioning of these on a vertical scale of social power. Thus, we may claim that, in Kuwait, social power was the characteristic feature of the status of the Kuwaiti male. The rights of which we are speaking here are both legal rights explicitly enunciated in the legislation and moral rights arising from customs and norms.

The social power of the Kuwaiti male derived from his being entitled to the maximum number of rights that an individual could have in this society: personal rights according to the family law, the right to sponsorship, the right to all the welfare benefits, and, in the case of "first category" citizens, political rights. He was empowered to decide for his wife and other female dependents, his children, and his employees. The only formal authority to which he was answerable was that of older male kin and the state.

The Kuwaiti female had no political rights. As to her personal rights, they were subordinated to her husband's or, if she was unmarried, to her father's. Her access to the welfare benefits (in particular housing) as well as her right of sponsorship were conditional upon her being a widow in charge of young children (a childless widow or divorcee returned to her parental home). Otherwise she acceded to them only via the male on whom she depended. Lack of autonomy was thus associated with the female status and was opposed to autonomy associated with the male status. However, Kuwaiti women were not entirely without social power: while they held a subordinate position vis-à-vis Kuwaiti men, they held an absolutely superordinate position vis-à-vis the expatriates in their capacity as employers and citizens—the same kind of "male" power associated with Kuwaiti men. Thus, most native women had both a "female" and a "male" status, according to whether they acted in the Kuwaiti-only sphere or in the sphere of Kuwaiti–non-Kuwaiti interaction. In this latter sphere, and particularly when they emphasized their ethnic identity through the use of the *abaya* or other mechanisms, Kuwaiti women projected the image of, and were commonly perceived by non-Kuwaitis as, repository of "male" social power. The abstract "male" status had been substituted for the woman's biological female status.

Non-Kuwaitis, finally, had no absolute legal autonomy. They were all subordinate to their Kuwaiti employers/sponsors in what was to them one of the most important aspects of their lives, namely, work. Additionally, strictly speaking, they did not have the right of sponsorship.[13] Whatever social power they had could therefore never be so extensive as the Kuwaitis'. This power was exercised over other non-Kuwaitis who either depended on them, for example wives and children, or worked under them. Arab expatriates, who were often accompanied by dependents and were employed in managerial and skilled positions, had frequent access to this type of power. Like most Kuwaiti women, therefore, many Arab men and women moved between contexts where their status alternated between "male" and "female"—"female" vis-à-vis the sponsors to whom they had to defer legally and, in the case of women, to their male kin; and "male" vis-à-vis their dependents and/or their non-Kuwaiti subordinates. This also applied to the skilled non-Arab workers in similar life and occupational situations.

At the bottom of the social and occupational scale, the semi-skilled and unskilled non-Arab workers had little power and were subjected to others' power. Their legal autonomy was strictly circumscribed and there was usually no one in Kuwait over whom they could exercise their authority: in principle they had no dependents with them, nor had they any subordinates at work. Whether men or women, their status was a thoroughly "female" one in most contexts of inter-ethnic articulation. As a result, it was usual for Kuwaitis and Arab expatriates to perceive Asian men in low occupations merely as an embodiment of "female" status whose biological sex was irrelevant—a view that could be compared to that of the expatriates, who looked upon Kuwaiti women as the repository of "male" social power. A process of "desexualization" of social actors took place at the same time as a gender constructed along ethnic lines was being ascribed to them by those surrounding them.

This was most clearly illustrated by the way Indian men were employed in certain occupations where an observer would have expected to see only women. The typical example is that of domestic servants.[14] Most servants in Kuwait were women. Men, practically always from

India, were employed as drivers, cooks, or so-called "houseboys," who did odd jobs *outside* the house itself. Some Kuwaiti families, meanwhile, employed male Indian domestic servants to perform the same type of housework as the female servants: clean, tidy up, wash and iron the laundry, and similar tasks. These men were introduced directly into the heart of the domestic sphere, where they were in close daily contact with the *hareem*, or the women of the household. Had they been Arabs or Muslims, such a job in such a setting would have been unthinkable. But as male Asian expatriates embodying a "female" status, they did not represent any danger; they were, in Hansen's (1990) fitting description, merely "part of the household inventory."

Another job where Indian men were unexpectedly employed was that of salesmen of women's lingerie. David was such a salesman.

A friendly, smiling man from Kerala, he could be seen during all the years I lived in Kuwait at the Union Trading Company department store in Salmiya. The UTC sold everything from electrical appliances, bathroom towels, and suitcases to school uniforms, fake jewelry, cosmetics, and clothes. David had been through various departments before he ended up on the upper floor, in the lingerie department. Here he excelled in selling silk pyjamas, flowered nightgowns, delicate stockings, and laced female underwear. His customers were from various ethnic groups and walks of life but mostly lower middle-class Kuwaitis and Arab expatriates, who were the main targets of the store's low-pricing policy. I have often observed the Indian engaged in lively discussions with his Kuwaiti customers, swathed in black, over some fragile looking pieces of female lingerie. David, with great persuasive authority, counseled the women on the best choice, and together they discussed detailed questions of quality, size, and color, without either party showing the slightest sign of being self-conscious about the sex barrier between them.

Not only the UTC but many other lingerie boutiques in Kuwait employed Indian, and only Indian, sales*men*. When they were not Indian, the salespersons were of various nationalities, but they were always women. Arab men—mostly Palestinians, Lebanese, and Syrians—often worked in shops and boutiques selling women's clothes. But I have never seen an Arab salesman in a lingerie store.

In Kuwait, persons and groups were assigned roles and statuses according to the principle of sponsorship relationship and to where they belonged in the ethnically divided labor market. Inevitably, social power and social subordination were distributed along ethnic lines. In such a system even the most basic of identities, gender identity, was subordinated to ethnic identity insofar as the latter was an index of (male) autonomy and (female) lack of autonomy. It may be useful to conceptualize gender in Kuwait not as a permanent, inalienable, either/or identity, but as a variable ascription, more or less independent of the personality of the actors themselves, which shifted according to the situational context in which ethnic relations took place.[15] Thus gender identity could be perceived as a scale along which the various ethnic groups—Kuwaitis, Arabs, Asians, and Westerners—defined themselves and were defined by others according to the degree of power they wielded in society or, alternatively, according to the degree of subordination to which they were assigned.

Seen in this light, only two groups, the top and the bottom, had a "stable" gender identity. Kuwaiti men, who under practically no circumstances had to defer formally to the power of decision of either women or expatriates, were therefore always "male." At the other end of the continuum, almost as stable in their gender identity, were Asian women: with few exceptions, they seldom found themselves in a position where they exercised formal power over others; at the same time, they were subordinate both vis-à-vis their employers and vis-à-vis their male kin, if they had any. For this reason, they were almost always "female" (figure 5.1). This latter statement, meanwhile, needs to be qualified, because one did find Asian women in skilled occupations, especially in the health sector (head nurses in government hospitals were often Indian women) and the hotel and restaurant sector.

In between, we have Kuwaiti women, Arab men, Arab women, and Asian men, whose gender identity could vary from more or less "male" to more or less "female."

FIGURE 5.1 Scale of Gender Identity in Kuwait

"Male"	*"Female"*
Kuwaiti men	
Kuwaiti women	Kuwaiti women
Arab men	Arab men
Arab women	Arab women
Asian men	Asian men
	Asian women

Ethnic Stereotypes

It is important to stress that the ascription and self-ascription of "male" and "female" statuses according to ethnic identity was characteristically a *group* phenomenon, arising from, and strengthened by, social distance between the various nationalities and the fact that interaction between them took place mostly within the restricted context of market services, where actors participated in only one role, practically always the same. Ascription of gender status could be viewed as part of a wider process of ethnic stereotyping. Ethnic stereotypes have been defined as "cultural constructions in which certain signs and symbols, perceived as 'ethnic,' acquire their context-related meaning" (Tambs-Lyche 1991: 141).[16] Stereotyping is the way in which

> social psychological processes contribute to the texture of an "objective" intergroup social situation. They do not create such situations; on the contrary . . . not only the origins of stereotypes but even their contents cannot be dissociated from the prior existence and the special characteristics of a conflict of interests. However, once they are in existence, they become in their own right one of the causal factors which needs to be taken into account in the analysis of intergroup relations. (Tajfel 1978:6)

Stereotyping also achieves a purpose similar to that of habitualization, a process studied by Berger and Luckmann, whereby

> any action that is repeated frequently becomes cast into a pattern, which can then be reproduced with an economy of effort and which, *ipso facto*, is apprehended by its performer *as* that pattern . . . In terms of the meanings bestowed by man upon his activity, habitualization makes it unnecessary for each situation to be defined anew, step by step. A large variety of situations may be subsumed under its predefinitions. The activity to be undertaken in these situations can then be anticipated. (1981:71)

What is being habitualized in this concrete instance is not an "action," properly speaking, but an idea about a certain group of people and their moral and social assessment by others. Instead of being varied, nuanced, and contextualized, the idea Kuwaitis had of, say, Indians was reduced to just a few monolithic characteristics borrowed mostly from the situation on the labor market and widely generalized.

Stereotyping is particularly salient in situations of social flux, where people from various cultural backgrounds cross each other's paths at a heightened tempo. The ascription of identities and the ethnic stereotypes that steered expectations and judgments and defined interactional situations in Kuwait did not simply reflect the objective relations on the labor market. They were also effort-economizing and stabilizing devices in a society where the level of personnel turnover was high and people frequently found themselves having to deal with new faces. Both for natives and migrants, ethnic stereotyping became necessary in order to chart their way through the maze created by the fact that so many of those they had to deal with, directly or indirectly, were total strangers to them. Similar situations were observed by anthropologists in the Copper Belt in the 1950s and 1960s (Mitchell 1974).

When confronted with a stereotyped image of self by others, groups and individuals react differently according to whether the stereotype is positive or stigmatizing. In the first case, one usually observes embracement of the stereotype by actors, who mobilize resources to live up to, and reproduce, it. In the latter case, actors commonly try to impose an alternative image of themselves, inasmuch as they dispose of the social and material resources to do so. Let us consider the case of Tariq, whom we met at the beginning of the chapter:

At the time he was stopped for police control in Salmiya, Tariq had just returned from a five years' stay in the USA where he had earned a Ph.D. in sociology. He was a self-declared social democrat who firmly believed in the value of hard work and personal merit. He dreamed of a more just society in his country and saw the development of Kuwaiti human resources as the only way to achieve this goal. Upon his return, Tariq took a job at the Ministry of Social Affairs and Labor, one of the least glamorous institutions in the whole government sector. He lived with his young wife in a modest government house in Bayan, a middle-class residential area, and drove a Japanese car.[17] His brother, who was in his late twenties, and his parents lived in villas in Abdullah al Salem, Kuwait's most exclusive neighborhood. His brother drove a Jaguar and worked in the Ministry of Information, a hothouse for ambitious young Kuwaitis. Tariq's family and friends did not understand that, with an American Ph.D., Tariq was content with such an anonymous and austere existence. "He could have had any well-paid job at the university or with KISR[18] and lived in a palace," his brother sighed. "Instead he earns a pittance in an obscure ministry and lives among Bedouins!"

For three years, Tariq held on to his beliefs. But gradually he began to give in to the pressure around him. When he started wearing the *dishdasha* also after office hours, it was, in his own words, because he was "fed up with being pushed around." Then a private bank offered him a job at a critical moment, when he was feeling increasingly frustrated at the lack of efficiency in the ministry. "Nothing ever gets done there," he complained, "the bureaucratic system stifles all motivations." He accepted the bank's offer and left the civil service. When I met Tariq again after the war and we reminisced about the old days, I reminded him of his social democratic ideals. Tariq smiled rather wistfully. "Basically they were good, and I still believe in them," he said. "But this is not how things work here. If you want to get things done, you have to play according to the rules. In a suit, no one took me seriously. In a *dishdasha*, I get things done twice as rapidly. You see, people expect the Kuwaitis to behave in a certain way. If you don't, the rules get all mixed up."

Most people had, for example, difficulties accepting the idea of a Kuwaiti actually doing manual work to earn his living, and when this happened they had to find some plausible explanations for it. The case of Jassim bears this out:

Jassim graduated as a landscape architect in Holland in the mid-1980s and returned to Kuwait to practise his trade: he did not only administer foreign gardeners from an air-conditioned office, but actually went out to the various gardens; dressed in his working outfit, he measured the terrain, assessed the quality of the soil, and personally supervised his employees even in the summer heat. His behavior was considered so exceptional that he became something of a celebrity. Newspapers interviewed him and there were many speculations as to who and what he really was. People—especially expatriates—who knew he was Kuwaiti were puzzled by his behavior until they learned that he was engaged to be married to a Dutch girl. "That explains everything", was the relieved commentary. "He has become half foreigner!" In his work, Jassim was often mistaken for a non-Kuwaiti. Being of Turkish/Iraqi ancestry, he was relatively fair and had blue eyes. "My Caucasian looks save me," he used to say jokingly. "If I had been dark with curly hair, I would have been treated as an Egyptian" (many gardeners were Egyptian). "In which case," muttered an Egyptian who happened to hear Jassim's good-humored statement, "he probably would have given up 'playing gardener!'"

Similarly, an Indian banker or a Filipino civil engineer could be the cause of much cognitive dissonance. Unlike the Kuwaitis who had the choice between drifting into the comfortable role everyone associated with their ethnic identity or withstanding the pressure and sticking to the "degraded" role associated with expatriates, the non-Kuwaitis were not free to step into an "upgraded" role. They were systematically pushed into a "degraded" role. Here are some strategies used by actors who were caught in this and other types of identity-related predicaments.

Opting Out: The Never-Never Land of Western Identity

Mr. and Mrs. Jha moved to Kuwait in 1986. Mr. Jha was an economist who had graduated from a Western university. He was offered an excellent job in a private Kuwaiti bank, whose owner had studied with him. Unlike the majority of the Indians in Kuwait, who were from the southern states, the Jhas came originally from New Delhi. They had also spent most of their married life in the United States.

"We are shocked at the way we are treated here," said Mrs. Jha. "The Kuwaitis and other colleagues at my husband's work are nice enough. They know who we are so they are usually considerate. But it is the others, especially the Arabs, who are incredibly rude to us."

She recounted one of many unpleasant episodes that occurred when she and her husband went to register at the Immigration Office. The bank had sent an Arabic-speaking clerk with the couple to help them through the process.

"We stood in the line, like everyone else. It was fifteen past twelve, and we knew that the office closes at half past. Our turn came, but then the Arab man behind us waved to the woman behind the counter and spoke to her in Arabic. I don't know what he said, but the woman nodded and gestured to him to come forward. Do you believe it, he just walked ahead past us! We protested, the clerk from the bank protested, but no one cared. Of course, when the Arab had finished, it was closing time. We protested again, but the woman just shrugged and said: 'Come back in the afternoon.'"According to Mrs. Jha, they would not have been treated in this way had they not been Indian: "They believe that all Indians are laborers," she complained. "So you must all the time show that you are from the middle class." This she did by surrounding herself with obvious signs of wealth: "I dress up even to go to the supermarket. And I always ask my husband to send the car over with the driver, even though the shop is just five minutes' walk from the house."

As far as the composition of their social networks was concerned, she said that they shunned both the Arabs and the Indians. They preferred to mingle with what Mrs. Jha called "the cosmopolitan crowd," that is to say, people who had the same class background as themselves, regardless of their ethnic origins, were widely traveled, and who subscribed to a vaguely Western life-style. But on the whole, the couple was not happy in Kuwait, and when Mr. Jha was offered the chance to renew his contract two years later he declined and they left for India.

The predicament of the Jhas was not unusual, although their final strategy, exit, might be more so. The middle-class expatriates who remained in Kuwait for lack of what they perceived to be better alternatives in their own countries invested great efforts in defining themselves out of the stigmatized non-Kuwaiti identity that was associated with working-class migrants. Like Mrs. Jha, the majority tried to correct the perception others had of them not so much by underplaying their ethnic identity as by over-emphasizing their class identity. In the case of Mrs. Jha, because she and her husband felt alienated from most of the other Indians (from the southern and western states) and because they had lived abroad for many years, she felt that she belonged with the educated cosmopolitans rather than with any particular ethnic or national groups.

The "cosmopolitans" were a population of skilled migrants of diverse nationalities who had entered the life of expatriates by choice or accident, usually a little bit of both. Among them was a core of European businessmen and professionals and their families, who had been drawn to the Gulf during the golden 1970s. With the boom a thing of the past, they kept speaking about packing up and going home, yet they could not make up their minds to leave for a variety of reasons that often seemed unclear even to themselves. The most common explicit reason was the growing costs of the children's education: most of the "cosmopolitans" came out as young professionals with little children who, by the late 1980s, were all attending expensive universities in Europe or the USA. Others, like the Palestinians and Lebanese, had nowhere else to go and had ambivalent views of Kuwait as both a haven and an exile, or a haven in exile. The middle-class expatriates from the subcontinent (Pakistanis and especially Indians), some of whom had been in Kuwait for almost as long as the Palestinians, seemed to be those who found it hardest to return home—"what with all the social and economic problems there," as they used to say.

This ethnically composite population shared one common feature, a "creolized" expatriate culture with elements from multiple origins expressed in a major Western idiom—mostly English, occasionally French—and coalesced around values that were perceived as Western. In the context of ethnic articulation between the various components of the total population, Western identity was a third option for middle-class migrants who could not claim the privileged Kuwaiti status but who, at the same time, refused to be caught in the ordinary category of migrant workers and its derogatory connotations. On the one hand, "Western" did refer to a cultural world that could be identified with Europe and the USA: people thought it "Western," for example, to drink alcohol, to have mixed parties, to dance (to the tune of Western music), and to practise sports in a mixed environment (for example, in the exclusive sporting clubs of the Western international hotels). Upon closer scrutiny, however, these activities were not necessarily nor exclusively Western. But they *were* un-Kuwaiti. Alcohol was indeed prohibited in Kuwait, as were discotheques, but the authorities often ignored the violations if drinking and dancing took place in private homes. In the Kuwaiti sporting clubs, men and women did not mix when practising the various sports activities, and private parties in Kuwaiti homes were also often sexually segregated, with men attending the typical male-only *diwaniya* meetings while women had their own gatherings.

At the same time, activities designated as "Western" were "Western" and not simply "non-Kuwaiti" precisely because they could not be identified with the general population of ordinary migrants. To many, especially expatriates from the Philippines and Goa, drinking, dancing, and mixing between men and women were no more Western than any other social activities. Yet the working-class migrants could not indulge in them because, in Kuwait, such activities took place in private or exclusive settings that were the preserve of the middle class. Thus "Western" in this context was the particular feature of a social class rather than any national or regional culture. It was a category unattached to any particular geographical area, and whose meaning must be investigated against the backdrop of class stratification and ethnic relations between natives and migrants in Kuwait. In this sense, the "Western world" was a "Never-Never land," the invention of an expatriate population in its effort to solve the problem of stigmatized identity rooted in the structure of dominance and the Kuwaiti politics of exclusion.

"Western" identity may have given the middle-class non-Kuwaitis a feeling of membership in a group that was unstigmatized in the non-Kuwaiti context, but it hardly reduced the barrier that separated them from the Kuwaitis. Although classwise, that is, in terms of wealth and occupational ranking, the privileged marginals were closest to the urban Kuwaitis, "off-duty" contacts between the two groups were not particularly extensive. An important reason here was the predominance of

Levantine Arabs among the expatriate middle class and the perceived cultural distance between them and the inhabitants of the Arabian Peninsula.

The Definition and Perceptions of "Us" and "Them"

Throughout this study so far I have used the term "non-Kuwaiti" as if this were an actual ethnic category. In reality, of course, "non-Kuwaiti" was only an abstract administrative designation that lumped together a disparate population whose shared characteristics were all defined in contradistinction to the Kuwaitis. Yet, this abstract distinction had such a force that it was always present in people's minds, as was obvious from the way expatriates adjusted their behavior according to whether they were dealing with a Kuwaiti or another foreigner.

At the same time, the non-Kuwaitis were a population that was itself divided in terms of ethnic origin and class. While the middle-class expatriates tended to close ranks across nationalities, united in their eager embracement of "Western" identity, the working-class migrants usually held themselves firmly within their own ethnic boundaries. In the lower-paid occupations, recruitment of workers took place on a group basis rather than individually. Cleaning companies, for example, tended to recruit all their workers from one country, frequently from the same area within a country. Here coworkers were also countrymen or even neighbors from back home. Added to this were lack of language skills and lack of social opportunities to widen their social networks. For these reasons, working-class migrants tended to remain among themselves.

Considering the vast differences in backgrounds among the non-Kuwaitis, one can hardly expect the perceptions and definitions of "us" and "them" to be uniform: a person's definition of in-group and out-group depended on much more than his or her own nationality or ethnic allegiance, as can be seen from the following example:

> The Indian manager of a Punjabi restaurant was telling me about his customers. "At lunch," he explained, "we have mostly Indians, Pakistanis, and sometimes Afghans and Iranians. The Kuwaitis usually come in the evening. On Fridays, we have many foreigners." I was surprised at the term "foreigners" and wondered to whom it might refer. Since the manager was very busy that day, I could not ask him to elucidate his cryptic words, so I came back the following Friday to find out myself. In addition to Asian and Kuwaiti customers, the restaurant was filled with non-Kuwaiti Arabs,

as far as I could see from the dress styles and hear from the accents. The Indian manager apologized that he did not have a single table that was available, and said: "I told you: Friday's the day of the foreigners!" He smiled broadly, obviously satisfied with the state of his business.

As an Asian in Kuwait, he had his own definition of who the outsiders were: the "foreigners" were neither the Asians, for obvious reasons, nor the Kuwaitis, who were the native population, but the Arab expatriates.

We have seen in Chapter 3 that the Kuwaitis conceived of various degrees of foreign-ness. Most alien to them were the non-Arabs (*ajaanib*), then the Arabs (*ghair kuwaitiyin* or non-Kuwaitis), then the Gulf people (Iranians, Iraqis, and the GCC citizens). Arab expatriates, for their part, were keenly aware of the various Arab nationalities but, like the Kuwaitis, tended to see non-Arabs as an undistinguishable group; the only clear ethnic difference here was the one between Asians (of whom there were two major categories, the "Indians"—a euphemism for all from the subcontinent—and the "Filipinos," that is to say, all East Asians) and Westerners. To the Arabs, the foreigners *par excellence* were these non-Arabic speaking expatriates, especially the Asians, whose presence in most Arab countries, unlike in the Gulf, was of relatively recent date. Non-Arabs usually did not differentiate between the various Arab nationalities, only between the "*dishdasha*-wearing people" (whom they took to be all Kuwaiti men) and the others, the "foreigners."

Nor were the definitions of "us" always unequivocal. In relation to non-Kuwaitis, Kuwaitis had a clear perception of their group belonging, manifested through the use of the dress code, emphasized by the daily practice of exclusion and dominance, and glorified by the ideological apparatus of nation-building (education, information, activities of the "invention-of-tradition" type). Most important was the mobilizing effect of being a minority in their own country and in need of cultural survival. Among themselves, however, there were multiple sub-divisions of "us" and "them" (urban versus tribal, Sunni versus Shia, first category versus second category, and so on). The most obvious line of division was between urban merchants and settled nomads or tribals. A cause of discontent among the former was the government's policy of granting nationality to the latter, and I have heard prominent merchants argue that it would have been preferable to integrate Palestinians and other well-deserving and educated Arab expatriates instead. Although these same merchants seldom counted non-Kuwaiti Arabs among their close friends, their education, life-style, and worldviews were, in the 1980s, closer to the latter's than to their ex-nomad co-citizens'. The Palestinians also had a clear awareness of their group identity owing to the very special circumstances under which they lived: exile, the cause of Palestine liberation, and the presence of a thinly disguised political organization exceptionally tolerated and supported by the Kuwaiti authorities.[19]

Among the rest of the non-Kuwaitis, however, the perception of "us" as a corporate group with common interests varied from reasonably strong to practically non-existent. Very weak corporate ethnic identification was most typical for the small ethnic groups who were trapped in the lowest-paid occupations (e.g., the Bangladeshis and the Thais), and had practically no possibilities to meet regularly and enact their ethnic identities.

Ethnicity and Class

A traditional debate in anthropology and sociology, generally portrayed as a dispute between Marxists and non-Marxists, is the question of the relationship between class and ethnicity. At stake is the contention that either of the two principles of social stratification is to have an independent causal role. Non-Marxists, usually of Weberian inclination, are commonly accused of taking ethnic processes at their face value, stressing their quality as a social resource and overlooking the question of power imbalance (Jenkins 1986). Marxists, on the other hand, are said to be guilty of economic reductionism, intent on finding class interests behind each and every proclaimed yearning for the enactment of collective primordial sentiments.

Life in Kuwait was placed under the sign of ethnicity. If we define ethnicity as a property inherent in social relations, in the course of which groups systematically enact and reproduce their perceived cultural differences—an enactment and reproduction with consequences for their objective social situation—we may even claim that social life in Kuwait was an explicit effort, especially as regards the Kuwaiti minority, at maximizing ethnicity. This situation arose as the combined result of objective cultural pluralism and the embracement of the politics of exclusion by the native population.

Overshadowed by ethnicity, but equally present as a principle of social organization, was class. As is well known, the concept of class varies according to whether one looks at it from a Marxian or from a Weberian angle. In Marx's definition, classes are categories of persons occupying similar positions vis-à-vis the means and the process of production. The occupants share the same relation to the means of production and hence the same objective interests. The transformation of this class-in-itself to the class-for-itself, in other words from an economic category into a politically organized group with consciousness of solidarity, takes place through class struggle. Against Marx, Weber argues that position within the relations of production is not sufficient to determine class situation; rather, it is positions in the relations of distribution (market, life-style, and attendant status) and the relations of authority that are crucial for the formation of classes. Weber prefers to speak of "socioeconomic standings" based on the distribution of income, education, and prestige. In other words, Weber defines classes on the basis of *market* or *exchange* relations whereas Marx adopts a *production* relations definition.

In both perspectives, one can claim that the relations between Kuwaitis and non-Kuwaitis were relations of class that, at the same time, were also ethnic relations. Here, class and ethnicity were united through the institution of sponsorship: not only did Kuwaiti citizens own the means of production and appropriate the surplus value produced through the migrants' labor, but as sponsors, they also had absolute authority over the migrants and the legal ability to decide on their life situations while the migrants could not decide on theirs. Also, ethnic stereotyping, which can be taken as a major index of the rule of ethnicity, faithfully reflected the organization of the labor market and the sponsorship system.

The conflation between class and ethnicity was less clear if we consider the two dimensions in light of other determinants, such as education (a considerable number of non-Kuwaitis clearly ranked higher than many Kuwaitis), or economic resources (some Palestinians/Jordanians, for instance, were much wealthier than the average non-urban Kuwaitis). Nor was the conflation entirely well-grounded if, by ethnicity, we refer not to the Kuwaiti–non-Kuwaiti dichotomy but to the various national groups within the heterogeneous expatriate population. Although Arabs made up the majority of the middle social echelon in the three-tiered social pyramid, there were also many laborers among them, just as there were upper-middle class and middle class among the Asians. Yet, on the whole these were exceptions, and the class structure in Kuwait was an ethnically organized structure.

If we approach class not in economic terms but in terms of group identification, we see that the processes taking place among Kuwaitis

and non-Kuwaitis differed perceptibly. Whatever their internal cleavages, Kuwaitis had a clear awareness of being both an ethnic group and
a superordinate class with common interests to defend against non-
Kuwaitis. In relation to the latter, they belonged together.

The migrants were aware of the natives as a "them-group" whose status differed from theirs, but they did not have any active perception of
the category "non-Kuwaitis" as an "us-group" with clear common interests. "We, the expatriates" was a rhetorical identification that was seldom heard in Kuwait. To the extent that a sense of identification existed
among migrants beyond the narrow communal boundaries,[20] it existed in
reference to the workplace. "We, the employees of the Sheraton," for
example, was a more commonly heard phrase. However, this should not
be taken to indicate that the workers experienced a sense of solidarity
around perceived common interests that united them against the employers. If used at all, "we, the employees of the Sheraton" was more likely
to be a description of the sponsorship relationship of the workers to a
common employer than a reference to the relationship among the workers themselves.

Absence of active identification among the migrant workers was not
due primarily to competition between the ethnically distinct workers in a
"split labor market" (Bonacich 1972). This competition was indeed very
limited in Kuwait because it took place at the stage of recruitment which
happened abroad, prior to the workers' arrival in the emirate. All the
workers who were in Kuwait were already in possession of a job when
they arrived, and, the law of sponsorship being as it was, migrants were
not allowed to offer their labor on a free local labor market. Inter-ethnic
animosity, when it existed, arose from the generalized practice of diffe-
rentiating salaries according to the worker's ethnic origin. I have already
mentioned that Arabs were better paid than Asians (Table 3.3). This
difference also existed among the various Arab nationalities and Asian
nationalities. Thus, for similar jobs and equal qualifications, a Palestinian
would automatically earn more than an Egyptian, and a Filipino more
than a Sri Lankan. This differentiation was explained by the alleged
higher level of education and degree of general sophistication of both
Palestinians and Filipinos in relation to, respectively, Egyptians and Sri
Lankans.[21] In some cases, salary differentiation existed even though this
general assumption turned out to be unfounded. Animosities resulting
from this type of discrimination reinforced the tendency within each
ethnic group to abstain from establishing close contacts with the others;

beyond this, however, and as far as I could judge, they did not lead to particular conflicts. It appeared that the migrants were aware that the system of differential salaries was fixed by the Kuwaitis and was due to factors that were beyond the individual worker's control, such as the labor-sending country's economic situation and its willingness to export its human resources at low and competitive prices. In itself, therefore, the fact that the labor force originated from different countries does not entitle us to conclude that class solidarity among the workers was by definition impossible to achieve. To assume this, we need concrete evidence that ethnicity, and nothing but ethnicity, was the main hindrance to concerted action. I did not find any such evidence. At least one incident that occurred during my fieldwork seemed to point in the other direction: in 1989, a multinational team of construction workers consisting of Indians, Thais, and Chinese working on the Qorain construction project south of the capital went on strike after several months of non-payment. As far as I know, this was the second time in the late 1980s that such a concerted action had been carried out. A previous strike took place in 1987, also by construction workers of various nationalities, but went unnoticed by most people because, until 1989, the press had not been allowed to report on such occurrences. Strikes in Kuwait were acts of despair and frustration, since they were forbidden and strikers risked deportation. They were, therefore, viewed by the workers as a last-resort solution. Their infrequent occurrence cannot be taken as a conclusive sign that class solidarity was entirely absent, although it certainly makes it difficult to assess the degree to which such a solidarity existed or could be developed.

What is certain, meanwhile, is that the severe constraints imposed by the Kuwaiti labor laws, such as the absence of workers' unions, the prohibition against strikes, the lack of comprehensive legal protection and, of course, the sponsorship system itself, effectively impeded the development of an active identification among the expatriates, not as members of non-Kuwaiti ethnic groups but as members of a class of workers versus a class of employers.

At the same time, non-Kuwaitis were clearly aware of the existence of constraints preventing them from advancing occupationally and status-wise in this society; they were also aware of the barrier between themselves and the Kuwaiti employers/sponsors, of their differential access to power and privilege, and of their distinctive non-Kuwaiti way of life. Except among the privileged marginals, these various forms of awareness were widely expressed in an ethnic idiom, and reinforced by the way the migrants conducted their private lives (i.e., outside the area of work) within the boundaries of their ethnic groups, in near total separation from the Kuwaitis. But immediately underneath this ethnic discourse lay another, more covert one, in which migrants occasionally expressed their situation vis-à-vis the Kuwaitis in terms of class. Thus, when an expatriate had difficulties with his or her employer/sponsor, he or she was often the object of much sympathy from people of various nationalities and origins who obviously empathized because they could see themselves in the same situation. During the 1989 strike by the Qorain construction workers, there was an outpouring of sympathy toward the strikers and much indignation against the employers from practically all the non-Kuwaitis. Some even wrote to the newspapers to express their feelings, while others in the Indian community collected money to help the strikers.[22]

Nonetheless, in spite of this objective and subjective identification as a group against the Kuwaitis, expatriates, through their actions, showed that this perception affected neither the way the majority among them defined their priorities nor how they devised their plans. Here their status as transient migrants loomed large as an explanation, at least as large as the lack of an organizational frame to promote relations beyond the occasional social contact, and other constraints imposed by the Kuwaiti system. Being transient, non-Kuwaitis were not looking for an improvement of the labor relations in the long term, nor were they ready to endanger their present contracts in the pursuit of such an improvement. Gains were construed in purely personal, not collective, terms, and so were strategies to achieve them. Here it seems that concerns with both class and ethnic identifications were absent from the migrants' considerations: while the failure of this class-in-itself to become a class-for-itself can be blamed on the ethnically plural situation and the structural constraints embedded in the Kuwaiti legal and normative system, one cannot come to a full understanding of the phenomenon unless one also takes into account the deliberate decision by the majority of non-Kuwaitis to opt for individual strategies.[23] To do so, we need to ask what it was that the migrants defined as their goals in life and what they aspired to achieve by coming to work in Kuwait.

Throughout this chapter, the focus has been on the area of inter-ethnic articulation, mostly between Kuwaiti natives and non-Kuwaiti migrants. Both parties ascribed to each other identities that, although embedded in the reality of legal and economic dominance, also engendered their own non-legal and non-economic consequences. There is little doubt, meanwhile, as to who had the most constraining role in this ascription: in the sphere of native-migrant articulation, non-Kuwaitis had to enact whatever roles were assigned to them by Kuwaitis and espouse the status and identity that went with such roles. Whether these statuses and identities were consonant with their self-definition and habitual dispositions or not was a problem that the migrants had to solve on their own and that was of little relevance for the Kuwaitis. Ethnic relations in Kuwait were a process whereby the content of the local structure of dominance was given concrete form in the consciousness of both Kuwaitis and non-Kuwaitis through their everyday practice in the sphere of articulation. How migrants perceived their own situations and what moved them to choose strategies of non-confrontation and individual action are the topics I will turn to in the next chapter.

Notes

1. The Southeast Asian connection is mediated through contact and migration from the Hadhramout in Yemen.

2. An Arabic-speaking person, on the other hand, can easily distinguish a Kuwaiti from an expatriate Arab, and amongst the various Arabs themselves, using names and dialects as indicators.

3. There has been a slight change in this respect after the invasion. In 1995 the use of the *dishdasha* is less uniform, especially among young urban Kuwaiti men.

4. People from the Gulf and Iraq are not included among the foreigners here. Among Iraqis, both European-style dress and the *dishdasha* were common, while Gulf citizens usually stuck to the *dishdasha*. However, the fashion of the *dishdasha* varies slightly from one Gulf country to another, thus allowing an expert eye to recognize the origin of its wearer.

5. "Peace be with you." This is the traditional greeting by Gulf people. The other Arabs usually say *marhaba*.

6. The winter *dishdasha*, worn during the cold months of December and January, is cut in grey or dark blue woollen fabrics. For the rest of the year, the *dishdasha* is in dazzling white cotton.

7. During the Iraqi occupation, Nabil worked actively with a group of Kuwaiti resistants and saved the life of at least one of them. After liberation, when other Palestinians were mercilessly sent out of the country, he and his family were allowed to stay. The fact that his father was a Kuwaiti citizen

helped, of course. As a Palestinian, he lost his job in the oil sector but was offered employment in Fahad's private company.

8. The extreme malleability of ethnic identity in Kuwait was borne out by the fact that during the Iraqi occupation, many Kuwaitis fled the country disguised as migrant workers.

9. After the war, the face veil of the *niqab* type suddenly reappeared, notably among young female students. In November 1991, the dean of the faculty of medicine threatened to exclude *niqab*-wearing students, arguing that this was an impediment to laboratory tests and other medical activities.

10. The 1981 elections led to the formation of the most conservative National Assembly in Kuwait's recent history, with five Sunni deputies (from the Social Reform Society and the Islamic Heritage Society) and four Shia deputies. Among the motions the Islamists proposed were the following: to recognize the *shari'a* (Islamic law) as the main source of law, to restrict naturalization to Muslims, to ban public Christmas celebrations, to make the veil compulsory for Kuwaiti women, and to ban the use of alcohol by diplomatic missions (use of alcohol elsewhere was already forbidden). Only the motions on the *shari'a* and compulsory veiling failed. The religious conservatives also succeeded in voting down women's suffrage (Crystal 1992).

11. In the Gulf there is no consensus as to what the proper Islamic dress code is, beyond the fact that body and hair should be modestly covered. The use of the black *abaya* and the veiling of the face with the *burqa* or the *niqab* are more open to discussion. Strictly speaking, these are features of the local Bedouin tradition rather than of Islam. In the urban context, when a Kuwaiti woman is said to be *muhajjiba* ("covered"), it is usually understood that she wears the Islamic dress and the *abaya*. As already indicated, the *burqa* and the *niqab* were practically never worn by the urban women.

12. Among the East Asian women married to Kuwaiti men whom I knew, several wore the *abaya* when pregnant as they felt that they were granted "more respect" in shops and other public places. Note that, through marriage, a foreign wife could acquire Kuwaiti nationality (see Chapter 7). Note also that a *muhajjiba* woman is expected to be Muslim. From the Kuwaiti actor's point of view, the use of the *abaya* and headscarf clearly has a religious content. In this particular area, it is difficult to separate Kuwaiti identity from Islamic identity.

13. They had the right to sponsor family dependents but the right to sponsor employees (domestic servants exclusively) was granted only to very few categories of expatriates (see Chapter 3, under "Domestic sector"). In practice, many non-Kuwaitis violated the rule and employed servants without proper sponsorship.

14. This phenomenon has been observed elsewhere in the world, for instance in Zambia in the relations between African male servants and their white female employers (Hansen 1989).

15. This situation is by no means unique. In many cultures, including the Middle Eastern, post-menstrual women, for instance, are granted a status that could be said to be half-way between that of men and younger women (see Mernissi 1983). In a different context, alien women are sometimes defined as "men." This has often been the case with female anthropologists doing fieldwork in traditional societies with sexual segregation.

16. ". . . kulturelle konstrukt innen hvilket de enkelte tegn og symboler som tolkes som 'etniske,' får sin kontekstuelle mening."

17. In Kuwait, cars were a common indicator of class membership. Upper-class urban Kuwaitis drove European (German, Swedish, and the most exclusive British) cars, while middle-class and non-urban Kuwaitis usually drove Japanese makes. American cars were used almost exclusively as official cars in the public sector.

18. The Kuwait Institute of Scientific Research.

19. The PLO office in Kuwait had a clear overview of the Palestinian population in the emirate. It organized social assistance to the poorer among them (among other things, shouldering all or part of the school fees for the lower-middle-class and working-class children), and levied a 3 percent income tax paid by all Palestinian workers through the Kuwaiti authorities. Alone among the non-Kuwaitis, the Palestinians were allowed to have a pseudo-political organization.

20. Except for the privileged cosmopolitans.

21. Regarding the question of "sophistication," it was commonly said that Filipino women who worked as domestic helpers were "more modern" and more familiar with the use of electrical household appliances than their Sri Lankan counterparts. This was undoubtedly due to the fact that most Filipino migrants came from Manila itself or areas in its immediate vicinity, while Sri Lankans had both urban and peasant backgrounds.

22. The Indian community was most active because the majority of the strikers were from India. If only Indians among the strikers were helped by their community, it was because the other strikers were from the People's Republic of China and from Thailand, i.e., migrants without an established community in Kuwait. The fact that practical assistance was forwarded along ethnic channels of course weakens the point I am trying to make. Be that as it may, the mere existence of the case prevents us from concluding that in an ethnically split labor market class awareness is necessarily impossible.

23. Meanwhile, the possibility that, given time and stability, this class-in-itself might turn into a class-for-itself was present in the minds of the Kuwaitis, who took the necessary precautions to ensure the transience of the migrants. One obvious indication was the way in which the Labor Law had shortened the length of contracts throughout the years (five years until the 1970s, then three in the early 1980s, then two from 1989).

6

Expatriate Life:
Liminality and an "Ad Hoc" Way of Life

*Une des caractéristiques fonda-
mentales du phénomène de l'immigration est que, hormis quelques
situations exceptionelles, il contri-
bue à se dissimuler à lui-même sa
propre vérité. Parce qu'elle ne peut
pas mettre toujours en conformité
le droit et le fait, l'immigration se
condamne à engendrer une situation qui semble la vouer à une
double contradiction: on ne sait
plus s'il s'agit d'un état provisoire
mais qu'on se plaît à prolonger
indéfiniment ou, au contraire, s'il
s'agit d'un état plus durable mais
qu'on se plaît à vivre avec un
intense sentiment du provisoire.*[1]

Abdelmalek Sayad, *L'immigration ou les paradoxes de l'altérité*

A Migrant Career

Antonio left his native Philippines for the first time in 1979, five years
after he graduated as an electrician from a technical college in Manila,
with his mind bursting with plans for the future. He was to work for three
years in the Ministry of Electricity and Water (MEW) in Kuwait. The
salary—KD 200, with food, accommodation and transportation covered by
the MEW—was so good that Antonio simply *knew* that upon his return he
would be able to start his own company and make a good life for his wife,
Isabel, and their three children. In the beginning, things went the way
Antonio had planned. Early in 1982 his contract expired. There was a

moment of hesitation when he was offered the possibility of extending it. But homesickness prevailed, and the Filipino declined; he went home to his wife and children. From then on, however, events seemed to take their own course. In retrospect, he believed the mistake was in his decision to buy a plot of land in the vicinity of Manila and build a house instead of using his savings from Kuwait to start a company, as he had planned earlier. But then, he said, Isabel and the children had been living with his parents and his sisters while he was in Kuwait, and the situation had been most difficult for everyone. He felt his wife deserved a better life. As for his parents, Antonio not only repaired their house but also added a floor to it. After this, not much was left from his savings. And as hard as he tried, Antonio could not find a lucrative permanent job. By the end of 1983, with Isabel pregnant for the fourth time and expecting twins, he decided to return to Kuwait.

This time there were no jobs available in the public sector, so he signed a contract to work as an electrician in a hotel that offered reasonably good working conditions. The pay was lower, KD 120, but he was told that he could earn extra money by working overtime. With his usual optimism, Antonio assumed that if he worked during all his free days he could easily double his monthly salary. He promised his wife that neither she nor the children would be in want of money. True to his words, Antonio worked almost day and night in Kuwait. In addition to his job as electrician, he volunteered for extra duty in the hotel's laundry and room service after regular working hours. He took his day off only when the hotel had no extra jobs for him. The overtime hours were badly paid, though, and Antonio did not earn as much as he had hoped.

In 1986, things grew worse. Kuwait was going through a bad recession due to the combined effect of the oil crisis and the war between Iran and Iraq. The private sector was severely hit. As business almost came to a standstill, so did the hotel industry. The management of the hotel where Antonio worked decided that instead of paying employees who did overtime with money, it would, with a few exceptions, pay them with days off. This dealt a blow to the staff's morale; what they needed was money, not free time. Who was interested in days off, anyway, when there was "nowhere to go and nothing to do?", as one employee put it.

The worst, however, was yet to come. In 1988, the management announced that employees whose contracts had run out and who wished to remain in their jobs had to sign new open contracts. This meant that they could resign or be fired at any time and that their salaries might be adjusted independently of the number of years and benefits accumulated until then. The staff was stunned; they asked to be paid their indemnities before signing, but the management refused: indemnities, they were told, were paid only upon final departure. Rather than signing new open contracts, a number of workers preferred to leave the country.

As the expiration of his contract drew closer, Antonio went through an excruciating soul-searching. Outwardly still a cheerful man, he admitted to me that the last few years had taken their toll on his fighting spirit in a way that he previously had not thought was possible. His health had grown poorer. As a son, he had become responsible for his old and ailing parents. As a father, he was carrying an increasingly heavy financial burden. The school fees for his three oldest children were growing larger every year; soon the twins would join the others. Antonio and his wife wanted to give their children a good education, so they sent them to a private school in Manila, a great strain on their budget. To make ends meet, Isabel had started a tailoring atelier at home; in addition she had rented one room to a tenant. Aware that his family counted on him but knowing full well that there was not much he could do to improve his earnings, Antonio started to look for better opportunities elsewhere outside Kuwait. He was hesitant, meanwhile, to let go of his present job, as he did not know whether he would find anything really better. He toyed with the idea of trying to go to the United States. Isabel had a cousin working in California; he had recently got the Green Card[2] and was planning to bring his parents over. He had also promised to help Antonio, but so far nothing had materialized.

In addition to these worries, Antonio was wrestling with another type of problem. In 1987 he had taken his four weeks' leave of absence and gone home to see his wife and children. The family had kept in touch through letters, pictures, and, occasionally, messages that Antonio and Isabel recorded on cassettes and sent to each other via friends and acquaintances who traveled between Kuwait and Manila. But nothing had prepared Antonio for the change he found that summer. He hardly recognized his three oldest children, who were by now nine, ten, and eleven; as for the twins, this was the first time he saw them in the flesh. He realized that he was a stranger to his children, did not know how to speak to them, and became quickly irritated by their constant running in and out of the house. Most disturbing of all was the state of his relationship with his wife. Isabel had been through a hard time having to work and raise the five boys in his absence. She had changed considerably, Antonio thought, had become distant, and never seemed to have time for him any longer. Perhaps because of this, he said, he could not bring himself to tell her much about his life in Kuwait. When he left after four weeks to return to Kuwait, he did not know whether he was sad or relieved to go. Once back in Kuwait, he realized how much Isabel and the children meant to him, so he hurried to record a message in a cassette that he immediately sent home to them. But he was worried that the damage was already done and that the gap between them would grow as time went on. In 1988, the last thing Antonio wished was to extend his stay in Kuwait and venture into the uncertain coming years with an open contract. But he eventually decided to sign up for one more year, as news from Manila showed that employment prospects there were worse than ever.

This decision had a curious and unexpected effect on Antonio's state of mind. Whereas from 1984 until then "only half of me," as he said, had lived in Kuwait, the other half being in Manila with his wife and children, Antonio suddenly developed an interest for his social world in Kuwait. Previously, he practically never socialized with the other Filipinos, or anyone else for that matter. Life for Antonio could then be summed up in one word: work. Even after 1986, he had gone on doing overtime work because his was one of the exceptional cases that were still paid with money and not days off.[3] On his rare free days he was so exhausted that all he could do was to sleep. From 1988 on, however, he regularly took the one free day per week to which he was entitled. His health improved, and he felt like "being with people" again. He had now the opportunity to attend Mass at the Catholic church downtown, something he could practically never do before. At the church he met Filipinos other than his colleagues at work, and he began developing friendships with some of them. Whenever they could, the men met at a bowling center. Antonio rediscovered a sport in which he had excelled in his younger days in Manila. He threw himself into bowling with passion, as if to make up for all the years gone in between. He became so good at it that his friends suggested he enter his name for the next bowling tournament organized by the Filipino Association—which Antonio did. He trained intensely before the event and came second. Since then, Antonio had become an integral part of the Filipino bowling and sports community. In February 1990, he told me about his plan to arrange, later in the year, a friendly competition between Filipino and Indian bowlers. Since 1988, he had renewed his contract with the hotel on a one-year basis, forfeiting in this way his right to paid home leave every two years.

The bowling competition never took place because in August 1990 Kuwait was invaded and occupied by Iraq. After three months, Antonio decided to make his way to Baghdad and Amman, together with a group of Filipinos and Egyptians. From Amman, after a while, he was evacuated to the Philippines. I unexpectedly ran into him in Riyadh in April 1991, seven weeks after Kuwait was liberated. Thanks to his previous manager from Kuwait, who had moved to Saudi Arabia in the meantime and was now working in a newly opened hotel in the Saudi capital, Antonio had obtained a job as waiter in the hotel's coffee shop. Apparently, in January 1991 the manager had let his contacts in Manila know that he was interested in recruiting hotel employees with experience from Kuwait. Antonio applied as soon as he heard the news. By then he had been home for exactly three- and-a-half weeks.

Human Agency and International Labor Migration

The study of labor migration to the Gulf tends to treat the phenomenon from a structural point of view in which the central "actors" are the pull and push factors of economy and demography. Human beings, the people who migrate, are described in terms of "stocks," "flows," "deployment," or simply "labor force," an army of anonymous, faceless, and voiceless workers ready to be sacrificed on the battlefield of the international labor market. Undeniably, to map the larger structural causes and consequences is to lay the grounds for an understanding of international migration for what it essentially is, namely, a historical process within the context of world capitalism (Frank 1967). For our understanding of why and how it reproduces, however, knowledge about the structural framework alone quickly proves to be insufficient. We need to know something about the men and women behind the facts and figures, their plans, their priorities, their aspirations, how they intend to go about improving their lives, and how they assess the results as compared to their expectations.

By arguing for the need to bring the human actor into focus, I do not argue for a psychologistic and individualistic approach to migration that negates the importance of historical macroeconomic relationships and processes. On the contrary, I consider that to understand how structural factors and material constraints impinge upon the decision by individual workers to migrate is the most crucial step in the study of international labor migration. It is obvious that, when people go abroad because they cannot find jobs in their own countries, their decision cannot be explained without reference to a whole set of variables that are external to, and independent of, the individual actor. These variables include the general level and the policy of development in labor-sending and labor-receiving countries, the former's need for foreign exchange and the latter's lack of human resources, the disparity in wage levels, and the world economic situation.

At the same time, we must not forget the truism that not every potential candidate for migration does in fact migrate, nor do all migrants make the decision to "remain on the road" once they have started. There are more than structural incentives and impediments to account for these events: the definition of the limit beyond which "deprivation" becomes intolerable and thus necessitates drastic measures such as migration, as well as the definition of what is "good," "better," or "worse," "necessary," or "impossible" to put up with in the host country, are decided by human beings who appraise their own circumstances, and are not the work of abstract structural forces. The experiential basis of the decisions to migrate, to remain abroad, or to return home, is a subject that must be investigated and understood in its own right as urgently as must the structural factors that contribute to shaping the decisions themselves.

This chapter describes major aspects of the lives that migrants lived in Kuwait. It also asks how this "Kuwaiti experience," which, at the outset, was seen by practically everyone as temporary, a short transition, a liminal and bracketed moment in their lives, became in many cases their lives *tout court*. This chapter is a modest attempt to fill a void in the scientific literature on migration to the Gulf and thus throw some light on a, so far, rather obscure link in the migratory process to the region. The greatest methodological problem is how to deal with the heterogeneity of the expatriate population—heterogeneity not only in terms of national and ethnic origins, including the baggage of culturally transmitted knowledge, but also in terms of class and personal life experience. It would be naive to believe that the presentation of a few life stories, observed here and there and filtered through my own understanding, could ever cover and reflect the immensely varied experiences of the large population of migrants in Kuwait.

Yet, I believe this task to be worth undertaking, no matter how imperfect its results, because, through what I have described in Chapter 1 as my "double-positioned" observation, I have been able to identify recurrent patterns in the concerns expressed, and the strategies tried and chosen, by expatriates from the most different cultural and class backgrounds. It was the same types of concern that initially pushed the migrants to undertake their migration and set their course toward Kuwait. And the same structural circumstances encountered in the emirate—the sponsorship system, the politics of exclusion, the uncertain future—played an important role in determining the kinds of strategy available to both the skilled professional and the unskilled laborer. I will thus contend that, over and beyond the wide variety in nationality, culture, and class membership, the expatriates shared a loose commonality of dispositions, purposes, and, given the structural constraints, strategies.

I must hurry to add, however, that this was a commonality that the actors themselves, with few exceptions, did not acknowledge easily or willingly, separated as they were by perceptions of more or less radical ethnic and class-based distinctions. They might admit that they shared common aspirations and life-projects with their social peers, or perhaps with their countrymen if the national group was small and socially homogeneous. But the majority would not agree that they had anything in common with people who belonged to a different nationality and especially to a different class from their own. While it may be easy for an observer to see that a British bank manager who hoped to pay the mortgage on his house in Kent or Oxfordshire through his three years spent in Kuwait and a Sri Lankan maid who aimed at saving enough to buy an electrical pump for the well of the family's farm shared a commonality of purpose and strategy, the actors themselves might not be aware of this. And if they were, they might be reluctant to acknowledge it. The Kuwaitis, on the other hand, had no doubt that all the expatriates were pursuing the same aim: they all wanted money and that was why they were in Kuwait. Like the anthropologist, in a way, the Kuwaitis saw what the expatriates often could not see, namely, that they constituted a population of like-minded individuals, something that the ethnography presented here will, I hope, appropriately illustrate.

The selection of the cases discussed in this chapter needs to be clarified. I have deliberately chosen to direct the focus primarily, though not exclusively, on the "average" expatriate men and women, that is, people who belonged neither to the privileged upper-middle class nor to the class of unskilled laborers on the bottom rung of the social hierarchy (especially the domestic workers), whose plight has occasionally been described in the international press and discussed by the human rights organizations (e.g., Middle East Watch 1992). Both categories were minorities within the expatriate population. Concentration on the upper-middle class might divert our attention from the very real problems that the majority had to confront daily. On the other hand, a too focused concentration on the unskilled laborers can make us lose sight of the fact that migration to Kuwait was a real opportunity for economic improvement. Even when the positive outcome of migration might not be obvious to the observer, it was obvious from the expatriate actor's perspective. Unless we take this actor's view seriously and give it a central place in the analysis, we may easily end up with the kind of structural analysis in which agency is denied a role in labor migration and the human actor is, to borrow from Giddens (1979:52), a "structural dope," a plaything in the hands of economic forces. The fact that migration in many cases exacts a price that, to the anthropologist and other observers, may seem unreasonably high is analytically irrelevant. What is relevant in this regard is the assessment of their own situation by the migrants themselves.

I have also chosen to study the case of the less transient migrants, people who had remained in Kuwait for more than three years (the maximum length for one contract). Long-term residence not only lies at the heart of the problem of migration, as I will presently show; it also illuminates the subject that this chapter attempts to pursue, namely, the ambivalence of temporality and spatiality in expatriate life.

The "average" expatriates discussed in this chapter are mostly non-Arabs. This again is a deliberate choice: the living and working conditions of Arabs in the Gulf in general, and in Kuwait in particular, have been highlighted by the Arab media throughout the years and occasionally written about in the popular literature, often by authors who have themselves been migrants in the Gulf.[4] On the other hand, much less is known about the life circumstances of the Asians. As a result of the absolute numerical predominance of the Palestinians among the Arab expatriate population and of their considerable stability before the war, the circumstances around Arab expatriate life in Kuwait were rather similar to those found in migration cases elsewhere in the world. Insofar as we need to bring the actors in *Gulf* migration to life to see more than the facts and figures, it seems more urgent to start with the non-Arabs. My particular focus will be mainly on the Filipinos and the Indians.

A Population of Like-Minded Individuals

What kinds of people migrated to Kuwait? Research carried out throughout the 1980s has drawn a clear socio-economic profile of the migrants to the Gulf, one that was strikingly similar for most labor-sending countries. Migrants were recruited from among the most economically active age groups (20–45), were mostly male (with the important exceptions of Sri Lanka and the Philippines) with more often than not an urban background, and, in the context of their native countries, were relatively well-educated (Al Moosa and McLachlan 1985; Arnold and Shah 1986; Birks and Sinclair 1980; RSP No.3). Beyond these objective, quantifiable background data, there were also other characteristics that point to the existence of a commonality of purposes.

Migrants invariably came to Kuwait with a clear goal in mind, sometimes as specific as a target sum to be earned in order, for instance, to buy a farm, open a shop, pay a bride-price, or cover the education of one or several dependents. Even when the goal was not so specific, there was nevertheless always a sense of more or less urgent purpose. What the migrants had in common, therefore, is the fact that they had a life-project that they hoped to realize, partly if not wholly, through their stay in Kuwait. One might say that, whatever their national cultural backgrounds and personal convictions, the migrants arrived in Kuwait with one common credo: they believed in personal initiative and individual hard work and its rewards; otherwise they would not have migrated. The case presented above bears this point out. Antonio was from the Philippines, but there were many like him from the subcontinent and the Middle East who showed the same firm belief in the ability of individuals to make a difference in their own lives and the lives of their dependents.

Expatriates conceived of work in primarily pragmatic terms. It was an instrument through which to obtain a valued goal, frequently articulated in material terms, rather than a way of self-development. This has been brought out repeatedly by studies that show that, during their migration period, migrants seldom learn new skills that might lead to upward occupational mobility upon return, although there is often a lateral move from technical work to commercial activities (Al Moosa and McLachlan 1985; Birks and Sinclair 1980).[5]

While the valued goal itself differed from one migrant to another, the overriding concern behind it was very much the same and could be summed up by the term "life improvement." Especially at the start of their migrant careers, expatriates had a particularly optimistic view of social mobility, a quasi-obstinate will to change it for the better, if not for themselves, at least for their dependents. Because they believed in personal initiative, resourcefulness and opportunities were centrally valued concepts. The master key to the world of opportunities was education, by which was meant the acquisition and possession of concrete skills rather than abstract knowledge. Whether we deal with Palestinian academics or Asian female domestic workers, we find the same determination to give their children the best education they could afford, either in Kuwait itself or in their homelands. Again and again I have heard migrants who used half, and sometimes more, of their earnings to pay their children's school fees say that they did it because "the children are going to have a better life than ourselves." Palestinians, Lebanese, and other expatriates without a clear territorial anchor used to say that "education is the only thing no one can take away from us." In an uncertain world where material possessions, residence permits, jobs, and salaries could be lost overnight, what you know may well turn out to be all that you really ever possess. Rather like kinship relationships, education thus represented a (hopefully) secure fund of resources on which one could draw in situations of emergency and crisis, and it was this "fund" the expatriates wanted to make sure that their children acquired, almost at any cost.

In Kuwait itself, education was relatively accessible to the Arab expatriates: before the Iraqi invasion, all the private Arab community schools[6] were heavily subsidized by the Kuwaiti state,[7] a privilege removed after the war. In addition, the children of Arab civil servants had the possibility of attending the Kuwaiti public schools, which were free of charge.[8] Education was more costly for the non-Arabs, whose community schools did not benefit from subsidies from the Kuwaiti state and had, therefore, to rely entirely on the tuition fees paid by the students.

For those migrants whose families were not present in Kuwait, it was not education *per se* but remittances that took the lion's share of their earnings. Much has been written in the literature on labor migration about the role of remittances. Research on this topic leaves no doubt whatsoever as to the significance of the money transfers by migrant workers for their dependents and for the economy of the labor-sending countries—a fact amply borne out by the catastrophic consequences of the Iraqi invasion of Kuwait on these countries, in particular in the case of the Palestinians in Jordan and the occupied territories (van Hear 1992). The role of remittances was at least as important for the Asian labor-sending countries. In Sri Lanka, for instance, the value of remittances by migrant workers has, for some years, been second only to export earnings from tea (Eelens et al. 1992; Korale 1986). Although it is not possible to distinguish the part played by the Kuwait migrants in the data presented, Korale indicates that up to 80 percent of the value of private transfers consists of remittances and savings by Sri Lankans working in the Middle East. Similar observations have been made about the state of Kerala, whose remittances from the Middle East alone in 1981–1982 equaled the remittances by Keralese working in all other countries taken together. As far as the Philippines are concerned, the data presented by

Go and Postrado (1986) confirm my own findings: Filipino contract workers remit on average more than half of their earnings.

What does the preeminence of remittances tell us about the expatriates in Kuwait? At the very least, it shows that we are dealing with a population that, despite its ethnic diversity, shared a common pattern of consumption constrained by a concern with saving and, thus, with vicarious or delayed gratification: practically all the benefits of their earnings went to their families back home, and the economic and non-economic rewards of migration were reaped by the migrants themselves only upon their return. The expatriate population in Kuwait was, thus, a population with a developed sense of individual responsibility, economic and otherwise, toward significant others who lived elsewhere. As a result, it was a population with an intense degree of purposiveness and self-discipline in most aspects of life.

Life is a Place Elsewhere

This was most strikingly expressed in the deliberately austere lifestyle to which the majority of the expatriates subjected themselves. They were in Kuwait to work, not to enjoy themselves or to settle down. Since their stay was assumed to be short, no efforts and sacrifices seemed too great. Whatever their earnings,[9] the expatriates always reserved a (sometimes substantial) part of these either as remittances to send home or as savings that they would often invest elsewhere to prepare for the day they would have to leave Kuwait. For expatriates like the Palestinians and Lebanese, who sought not only economic opportunities but also residential refuge in Kuwait, security took the shape of a house or an apartment in Europe (usually England for the Palestinians and France for the Lebanese) or Canada: the possession of immovable properties in these countries gave them automatic access to entry visa and residence permits as well, the greatest need of these diaspora people in a post-Kuwait life. Concern with the future played a towering role in the expatriates' lives, as is illustrated by the case of an Indian family, the Sharmas.

> The Sharmas came to Kuwait in 1975, at the height of the boom period. Dev Sharma held a degree in statistics and had work experience in the public sector in Bombay. In Kuwait he was attached to the Central Statistical Office (CSO) at the Ministry of Planning. The family consisted then of Dev, his wife, Nirmala, and their two children, a daughter of five and a son of two. Life was comfortable for the Sharmas in Kuwait in the 1970s, and

they made many friends in the Indian community, where Dev was highly regarded. With a shrewd sense of business, Dev made some strategic investments in real estate in Bombay that turned out to be profitable. This additional income was something they could fall back upon, they said, in case Dev lost his job in Kuwait. Although the CSO valued his services, growing talk during the 1980s of "Kuwaitizing" the public sector was a constant source of worry for the Sharmas and hundreds of other expatriates. The most important thing to the Sharmas then was that Dev be allowed to remain in his job until the children completed their education. By education, they originally meant high-school education.

The Sharma children had had all their schooling at the New English School, considered to be one of the best English-language schools in Kuwait. They could have gone to the Indian School, like the majority of expatriate Indian children, but Dev and Nirmala had an almost religious faith in the importance of education, and they were determined that Devika and Bhagat would receive the best schooling their parents' money could provide. With a yearly fee of nearly KD 1,000 per child at the secondary level, their education was, in the late 1980s, the single most important item on the Sharmas' budget. When Devika graduated in 1987 with top grades and was admitted at Cornell University in the United States, the Sharmas did not have a single moment of hesitation: of course, Devika would go to Cornell, no matter what it cost. And since she had come that far, so would her brother Bhagat. In their plans, the Sharmas' connection with Kuwait was stretched one step further in the future: Dev simply had to remain in his present job long enough to see that the children completed their college education in the United States. The family's life-style, which had never been extravagant, became even more spartan. Dev and Nirmala scraped and saved every penny they could to allow Devika to have a proper standard at Cornell and to pay her ticket home to Kuwait once a year. Meanwhile, they saw with great concern that Bhagat was increasingly influenced by the spending habits of his wealthy friends at the English school, and they tried to restrain him. Bhagat, who lacked his sister's serious disposition, had a difficult time following his parents' advice. Then one January day in 1989 Dev suddenly collapsed at his office desk, the victim of a stroke and, according to his friends, of his multiple worries. With the excellent hospital facilities in Kuwait, he was quickly taken care of. The question was whether he would recover well and soon enough to be able to get back to his work before the Central Statistical Office found it necessary to replace him permanently. The strain under which the family lived during that January had a sobering effect on young Bhagat. The Sharmas' hope of remaining in Kuwait until their son had his college degree in hand was defeated by the Iraqi invasion. The family returned to Bombay after a grueling journey through Basra, whence they embarked on a ship sent by India to rescue her stranded citizens. Dev's health never recovered from the ordeal. According to the latest news I have from common friends, it seems that Bhagat did not make it to the United States. Instead, he has started engineering studies at the University of Bombay.

Migrants in Kuwait did not save for the sake of saving, in a Protestant-capitalist spirit, as it were. They saved for a very specific purpose, and they could spend generously for this purpose. The contrast between the long periods of austerity and the short periods of spending was sometimes striking. How much money Dev and Nirmala Sharma really had was a matter one could only speculate about, because they did not flaunt it. They lived in a modest apartment, drove an old car, and Nirmala never shopped in expensive stores. The only time they spent large amounts of money was before going home to Bombay on vacation, when Nirmala went gift shopping for their numerous relatives and friends.

Home visits were often ruinous affairs for the expatriates. All my informants concurred on this point. Najla, a Lebanese, said that "everyone expects a present from you when they know that you come from Kuwait. And you must be careful not to give more to the one than to the other, or else someone will be hurt." An Egyptian woman told me that her neighbors and kin expected to be entertained with a feast every night during the four weeks she was home in Cairo. "They came to my parents' house (where she was staying) to say hello and wish me welcome home, and they expected to be served a meal. What could we do? We could not disappoint them!" Jossie, a Filipina, had to cut her home leave short in 1988 and return to Kuwait because she had run out of money and could not lose face by refusing to receive friends in her home or to lend them money.

There was a certain *noblesse oblige* logic attached to the status of "Gulf migrant." People expect migration to entail upward social mobility, not only for the individual migrant but, in many cases, also for his or her family and kin (Go and Postrado 1986). The returnee was expected to be successful and wealthy, and the only way for others to assess this success was through the degree and pattern of his or her spending. In most Middle Eastern and Asian societies, wealth consumed through gifts and feasts enhanced the migrant's and his or her kin's status. Spending money during home leaves was not always the result of outward pressure, however. Lavishing gifts on loved ones, especially the children, was one important way to make up for the migrants' long absence from home. Home visits were, therefore, always costly. Yet, typically enough, they were perceived as a problem more by the long-time resident expatriates than by the new migrants.

At the beginning of their careers, the few weeks spent at home meant more than the months and years spent in Kuwait. Life in India, Egypt, or the Philippines was often more real to the migrant worker than life in the alien environment of Kuwait. At this stage only one thing mattered, namely, the necessity to earn and save. This sense of urgent purposefulness was so overwhelming that the migrants showed a characteristic indifference to social life in Kuwait. Their accommodation often reflected this state of mind. Expatriates usually lived in rented flats that most of them, when unaccompanied, preferred to share with one or two colleagues or friends from their native countries in order to cut down on the rent and avoid being lonely. The suitcases were sometimes only half unpacked, ready, as it were, for the journey home. The furniture was only basic, usually taken over for a cheap price from the previous tenants: who would want to invest in tables, chairs, cupboards, and china that were to be left behind in a few months or a couple of years from now? In addition to the refrigerator and the television, the only pieces of furniture, if one may call them such, that most expatriates were willing to invest in were a cassette player and a video cassette recorder. As with Antonio and Isabel, the migrants in the Gulf made frequent use of modern technology to communicate with their families. Although letters were still a common medium of communication, they were often complemented by cassettes and, among the better-off expatriates, telephone calls and video tapes. On the whole, everyone seemed to prefer sending and receiving cassettes to letters; the orality of the medium definitely made the message more alive, spontaneous, and immediate.[10]

The Social Content of Liminal Time

For most migrant workers, involvement in social life in Kuwait was not only a function of length of stay but also of how much free time and what opportunities they had at their disposal for meeting and entertaining friends and acquaintances. The mechanisms through which expatriates from various nationalities built their social networks varied mainly according to whether they were Arab or non-Arab.

Arab expatriates met among themselves in very much the same way as they did in their home countries, informally through their familial and collegial networks. Except for the various Palestinian socio-political associations gathered under the umbrella of the Palestine Liberation Organization, there were no formal Arab community associations. The purpose of such associations, which are invariably set up under the initiative of resourceful middle-class individuals, was seldom to meet the socializing needs of the community at large, only those of the middle class. Associations usually aim at providing a venue for isolated middle-class individuals and families, where they could meet with one another and carry out traditional collective rituals (secular and religious). Among the Arabs in Kuwait there was no need for such formal associations because the middle-class expatriates were well provided for when it came to private social networks. In regard to religious celebrations, Islamic rituals were common to the Arab Muslim expatriates and the native Kuwaitis: *ramadan, 'id al fitr, 'id al adha, mawlid al nabi,*[11] and other occasions were celebrated at the same time, if not exactly in the same manner. Because they were, in the main, well-settled in the emirate, Arab expatriates could use their own private homes as venues for social gatherings. As for the unskilled, low-paid "bachelors" without local family relations, they met in the popular coffeehouses scattered across expatriate and "bachelor" neighborhoods to smoke the water pipe, drink tea and coffee, watch television, and play dominos and backgammon while discussing salaries, job opportunities, and, sometimes, non-Kuwaiti politics. These coffeehouses, which charged very modest prices, are part of a tradition found all across the Middle East (Hattox 1985; Lienhardt 1993) and they seemed to be frequented by Arab expatriates only.

There were relatively few similar gathering places for non-Arabs. Those that existed were restaurants rather than coffeehouses and, as such, were more costly, therefore less popular. As a rule, unskilled Asian laborers could not afford to make these the regular places where they went in the evening to while away the time in the company of other expatriates; besides, they were often living in work camps outside the city. Not unsurprisingly, therefore, the customers of the Asian "ethnic" restaurants were mostly middle-range salaried employees. It was also for this category of Asian expatriates that all other social activities, formally or informally organized, were meant.

Among the unskilled Asian laborers, only the Catholics were fortunate enough to have a formal venue that represented a meeting point, though of an entirely different nature. This was the Church of the Holy Family in downtown Kuwait. On Fridays, from early in the morning until the evening, the church was filled with migrants, who came to attend Mass in different languages. It was the one day in the week when the city center was deserted by most of its Arab—both Kuwaiti and expatriate—inhabitants, and Kuwait seemed to revert to its pre-oil Indian Ocean past. This was particularly true around the area popularly known as "the Sheraton roundabout," located in front of the hotel of that name, at the junction of two main commercial avenues, and a few meters from the Catholic church. Here, every Friday, unskilled laborers, domestic workers and maids strolled in the streets or settled on the grass of the roundabout after Mass in the winter, when the sky was clear and the temperature mild. In the summer, the heat and sand storms made them flee indoors, looking for refuge in the air-conditioned coolness of the modern *souqs*.[12] It was during such informal gatherings that the migrants exchanged news, information, and experiences, that acquaintances were made, and remittances, letters, and cassettes were given to departing workers and received from newly arrived ones.

A study of expatriate life in Kuwait cannot ignore the role played by the Catholic church. This role, widely acknowledged, was much more important in the case of the Asian Christians than the Arab Christians (SanMiguel 1978). Whereas for the latter the meaning of the church remained pretty much the same here as in their home countries, for the former, it took on a disproportionate significance. In addition to its religious role, the church was a haven away from the daily drudgery and the alien environment, and a meeting place. It was run by priests of different rites (Roman Catholic, Greek Catholic, Maronite, Syro-Chaldean) and different nationalities (Lebanese, Indian, Filipino, Spanish) under the leadership of a bishop who, in the 1980s, was a Carmelite from Malta. The priests were aware that the zeal of the Asian Christians was related more to the Church's secular role than to its religious role. "They come to us with their social, practical, and emotional problems," the bishop told me on one occasion, "and I wish we had the means to help them. What we should have here is a team of social curators, not only priests. As things are, there is very little we can do, except keep the church always open for them." Not all the priests were happy that the expatriates used the church premises for purposes sometimes unrelated to religion. For instance, one Indian priest complained that "many go quickly through the ritual of Mass before settling down to what they really came here for, namely, socializing. Others don't even come near the church;

they just enter its grounds and spend their time in the garden, chatting." He saw it as his task to go around to check that people did not just loiter.

The priests' presence in the emirate was only half acknowledged. Officially, they entered the country under a visa that put them in the same category as the *mullahs* (Muslim preachers) contracted from Egypt to preach in the local mosques.[13] Their religious activities, however, were strictly limited to performing Mass, in principle only within the church compound in Kuwait City and in Ahmadi.[14] Their status as men of religion gave them no privileged authority in the society at large and, if they were Asian, they did not escape from the ethnic categorization into which all working-class Asians were placed. Father Jesus, a Filipino, who depended on being able to drive a car to visit the sick, could not make his case heard at the Traffic Department when he went there to apply for a Kuwaiti driving licence: to the Egyptian office employees he was a Filipino worker and nothing else (even though he tried to explain his special status as "Christian *mullah*"), and they refused to consider his case, citing the law that barred ordinary Asian expatriates from obtaining a driving licence.[15] Having exhausted all the licit repertoire of arguments, Father Jesus turned to the only possible solution in such situations: he appealed to his *wasta* ("connection") in the Ministry of Interior, a resourceful Christian Palestinian, who got him the driving licence within less than a week.

In all the non-Arab ethnic groups, middle-class expatriates used the associations as their most common social venue. In principle membership of these associations was open to all who were of that nationality. In reality, unskilled laborers seldom joined, because they could not afford to pay the membership fees. For example, the two Filipino associations, the *Kapisanang Pilipino Sa Kuwait* (the Association of Filipinos in Kuwait) and *Flassik* (the Filipino Ladies' Society in Kuwait) had the tacit policy of not accepting maids and other low-paid workers among their members. The same applied to the Indian associations. For expatriates who qualified for membership, the associations provided a good opportunity for meeting their countrymen. In addition to the celebration of the traditional festive rituals, the associations also organized cultural and sporting events, sometimes charity bazaars for their needy laborers[16] or good causes in the home country, and served as arenas for intra-communal discussions.

The Indians had the largest number of associations, organized along ethnic, linguistic, and religious lines. Not surprisingly, the largest one

was the Keralans' Union of Malayalee Organization. The UMO celebrated the traditional Indian and Keralan festivities (especially Divali
and the Bharath Mela), organized football matches, and played an important role in making sure that the Keralan politicians back home took care
of the interests of their migrant voters in Kuwait. Since the Indian community was a relatively well-settled community, the Indian associations
tended to be dominated by the older generation of "respected men"
(mostly long-time resident businessmen), and the members usually participated as families. The Filipino association, in contrast, was clearly an
association of "bachelors," both male and female. It provided an arena
where men and women could meet and socialize. Its relatively younger
and more "unsettled" character was manifested in its activities: the Filipino association delighted its members with *Fiestas Filipinas*, barbecues,
Valentine parties, and sports and baby contests. Dating between men and
women, sometimes leading to marriage, had happened as a result of its
members attending such occasions. Marriage in the Indian community,
on the other hand, often resulted from initiatives by the families back
home or in Kuwait itself. An Indian peculiarity regarding marriage was
the "matrimonials" advertisement column in the *Kuwait Times*. These
advertisements were usually placed by the family of the seeker, and were
intended to be read by the family of the prospective candidate. Among
the most highly appreciated assets were a clear complexion, high education, and employment in Kuwait or, even better, possession of an American Green Card.[17]

Time: The Making and Unmaking of Relationships

As long as they had their purpose clearly in mind and its fulfillment
seemed within reasonable reach, the migrants' perception of Kuwait as a
genuine social world was usually minimal. Feelings of transience made
them define themselves as marginal. But, as Antonio said, "Things do
not always happen the way we plan them." Indeed, while they worked
and saved in Kuwait, back home the migrants' children were growing up,
their parents were getting old, their houses deteriorated and were in need
of repair, the family farm required a new well, and so on. New needs
continuously appeared as the old ones were about to be met; plans never
seemed to be finalized, they only seemed to grow and expand into other
plans. Somehow time always ran faster than the working and saving.
After the second or third contract, many expatriates began to lose sight of

the time when they could leave Kuwait and return home permanently. What appeared at first as a neat and simple plan—three years' hard work, a sum to earn, a joyous homecoming, a new life from then on— became blurred and melted into a vague and widening project, the end of which was increasingly difficult to foresee. Assailed by uncertainties about the future, the migrants often had to fight off shapeless and muted fears about the present as well, especially about the state of their relationships with their loved ones back home (as in Antonio's case), which seemed sometimes to be directly threatened by the unexpected development of new relationships in Kuwait. It was usually at this juncture, when life no longer let itself be ordered into a neat plan and became, in the words of an Arab expatriate who had not been home for twenty years, "a big mess that gets out of control," that the migrants suddenly realized their *de facto* involvement with Kuwait.

Cora, a 38-year old Filipina, worked as a cashier at one of Kuwait's biggest privately owned supermarkets. She had been in Kuwait since 1985. Cora came to Kuwait very much against her will. She had had a good job in Manila, where she worked in the Gourmet Shop of the Manila Sheraton. Most importantly, she had three children, two boys and a girl, between twelve and nineteen, whom she did not want to leave. But Cora had serious marriage problems: her husband, a heavy drinker, drifted in and out of occasional jobs, and used to beat her and take her money. It was mainly to get away from him that she took the job in Kuwait. The agency that recruited her was a reputable one and charged only P. 5,500 in placement fees, while others charged up to P. 21,000. At the agent's, she enquired about the pay in Kuwait. They offered her KD 90, which was more than she had been earning at the Sheraton. Still, she tried to bargain up to KD 120, but they refused. She did not think KD 90 were really worth the hardship, but because she was having serious difficulties with her husband at that time and because she thought she might supplement her income with extra jobs and overtime work, she signed the contract and arranged for her mother to take care of her children while she was away.

Once in Kuwait, Cora discovered that, according to the law, it was strictly forbidden to take up extra jobs outside the supermarket. Moreover, overtime was not paid with money. Cora sent KD 80 every month home to her family and kept only KD 10 for her personal use (food, accommodation, transportation, and uniforms were all covered by the employer). Her monthly remittances sufficed to cover her family's current expenses and the children's school fees. Her children were Cora's pride, especially her nineteen-year old son who was doing computer studies in Manila. The boy had been a mother and a father to his brother and sister ever since Cora left. In addition, he had won a scholarship and hoped to be able to emigrate to Australia after graduation to take over his mother's role of breadwinner and allow her to come home. Australia had always been Cora's dream. In 1985, the family had applied for immigration there, but, because her husband was unskilled, their application had been turned down. Now she was also considering Canada and was trying to gather information about the possibility for her and her children to immigrate.

Cora met and fell in love with her coworker Dennis in 1987. Dennis was a thirty-year-old Indian from Kerala. Cora was, as a rule, wary of men in Kuwait, especially the Filipinos. They always tried to make contact with newly arrived girls, she said. Most of these men were unreliable. Many young Filipinas fell into the trap and became involved with men who did not really care for them and often were already married in the Philippines. Cora, who considered herself an "old woman," knew better. Anyhow, she did not have spare money to spend on nice clothes and restaurants, and she would not let any man pay for her. But Dennis was different. He was honest, kind, considerate; and he really cared for her, she said. Cora knew that her relationship with Dennis could not last. After six years in the Gulf, he was a rich man by Keralan standards and a most eligible bachelor. His parents had found the ideal wife for him in Mangalore and insisted that he come home to get married. So far, he had evaded their plea, finding always some excuse or another. To Cora he had said that if he ever married, he would marry her and no one else. But she knew that this was impossible, considering her nationality ("I don't think his family would accept a Filipina"), her age ("I am too old for him"), and her family situation ("I have three children, and besides, I cannot get a divorce"). She would have given anything to be able to straighten out the situation. As a Catholic, she said, she knew she was doing "something terribly wrong." She had stopped going to church, out of shame. Once in a while, at Christmas and Easter, for example, she went to the Protestant church instead.

Yet, all in all, life was not too bad in Kuwait, said Cora. She would have gladly stayed here if there had been any possibility for immigration. That, and labor unions, she added, through which workers could secure their jobs.

I last saw Cora and Dennis in February 1990. What happened to them after the occupation, no one seems to know. In December 1991 the owner of the supermarket told me that he would have liked to get Dennis and some of his best employees back in their old jobs—if only he knew where to find them.

Cora said that she longed for her children; at the same time she said that "all in all, life was not too bad in Kuwait" and that she would have "gladly stayed" here if she could. These obviously contradictory statements were an eloquent expression of Cora's dilemma; they also epitomized the ambivalent effect of migration on the state of social relationships. Cora's relationship with Dennis, which was possible only as long as both were in Kuwait, bore all the characteristics of their migratory situation: temporary, liminal, seemingly against the moral norm. Yet this relationship had also led Cora to redefine her experience in Kuwait from something utterly alien and negative to an almost ideal situation. Involvement with Kuwait through this type of relationship across ethnic boundaries and in violation of the actors' own cultural and/or moral principles created acute ambiguities in identification with lifeworlds. In such cases, the making of social relationships in Kuwait often seemed inevitably to entail the unmaking of social relationships in the home country. Nowhere was this dilemma more evident than in the migrant's marriage relationships.

In Cora's case, problems had already arisen prior to her migration. Generally, however, it was prolonged migration itself that had a destructive impact on marriage relationships, unless active efforts were made by the migrant, often the husband, to bring his spouse over. In this respect, the difference between the South Asians and the Filipinos was striking: a married Indian male migrant who remained in Kuwait longer than the span of one contract would usually endeavor to bring his wife over, under an "illegal" sponsorship if need be (that is to say if his salary did not entitle him to do so). The same was often true for Sri Lankan men. Once in Kuwait, the wife had to find herself a job to make ends meet. Usually, the only opening was in the domestic sector. Indians were particularly familiar with this strategy, with the result that family units were relatively numerous within this community. Not only spouses but also adult children and relatives gradually found their way to Kuwait. In fact, by the end of the 1980s, the Indian community showed many signs of following a development rather similar to that of the Arab population in terms of growth in size and kinship connectedness. Within such a community, the chances that young unmarried migrants could find marriage partners of their own ethnic and religious groups in Kuwait itself increased considerably, leading to increased stability.

Filipinos seldom attempted this strategy of family regrouping. Friends and sometimes relatives seemed to be the categories that these expatriates were most likely to help join them in Kuwait. Spouses, on the other hand, did not seem to enjoy any priority. The most common reason given was concern for the children. Antonio had told me that he could never think of asking Isabel to join him and leave their children behind with his, or her, mother. When I objected that many Filipino women worked abroad, he said: "Yes, but they come here as workers, to earn money, not just to follow their husbands."

Following her husband was precisely what Soma, a Sri Lankan, had done: she came to Kuwait in order that her husband would not be on his own and left behind four children aged between nineteen and ten. In Kuwait, she occasionally took part-time cleaning jobs. Although she missed her children, she said, she could not refuse when her husband John asked her to stay with him in Kuwait. He had experienced being alone for several years and he did not want to go through that ordeal again.

Since the history of all the well-settled expatriate communities in Kuwait, starting with the Palestinians (Brand 1988; Ghabra 1987), showed an evolution from single-worker migration to family migration, it is quite possible that it was only a matter of time before the Filipino community developed a similar pattern of family regrouping, especially among the young couples with no children at the time of out-migration. The latter was a rather common occurrence among Indians, as is illustrated by the case of Felicity, from Mangalore. She was a young bride when Mathew, her husband, came to Kuwait. After two years, he managed to buy her a sponsorship. She joined him in 1984 and had been working, since then, as a "non-live-in" maid. She had also given birth to her two children in Kuwait, although according to the Residence Law children born to domestic workers were not entitled to the residence permit as it was assumed—and the facts confirmed the assumption—that employers were usually unwilling to sponsor them. By means of an increased payment to her sponsor, who then took legal charge of both mother and children, Felicity and Mathew had solved this particular problem.

Awareness of *de facto* involvement with Kuwait could be brought about by other, more general relationships. In the case of Antonio, we have seen that the difficult decision he took to renew his contract in 1988 was a watershed: while he had previously overlooked his health problems, thinking that he would be able to slow his pace once he was home in the Philippines, in 1988 Antonio was reconciled to the idea that he might not be leaving Kuwait for some time. Suddenly it became important for him to take care of his health, and hence to stop doing overtime work, even if this meant earning less money. The fact that he also began attending church and socializing with other Filipinos was a natural consequence of this decision and may be taken as an indication that he had become resigned to his fate. On the other hand, Antonio's popularity within the Filipino sporting circles, coming as it did after years of social isolation, increasingly led him to settle into a pattern of life that seemed fairly common among Filipino male migrants.

My Filipino informants described this state as "the migration virus." By this, they were referring to a pattern of life in which migration had become an end in itself. The migrants' long absence from home has created a communication gap between them and their families, while their social networks in Kuwait, when they exist, become increasingly significant. The migrant finds it difficult to explain to his family what life in Kuwait is like, the loneliness, the sacrifices, the difficulties at the work place, the new friendships, and not infrequently, the extra-marital affairs. The more traumatic the initial experiences, the more difficult it is to speak about them. It is less arduous to communicate with people who have had the same experiences and who, therefore, understand almost without words being spoken. Sometimes, the "migration virus" can also have its complex origin in a question of the need to save face: as mentioned earlier, people expect all cases of labor migration to be success stories. For the migrants, to tell about the dark side of life abroad—and all migratory experiences, even the most successful ones, have their dark moments—is indirectly to admit failure. It seems that many avoid this step because it somehow tarnishes the heightened status migrants enjoy upon return. The price for silence is, not unexpectedly, loneliness. Once the migrant has mastered the pragmatics of migration, especially once he (less often she, it seems) has acquired a supportive social network in the host country, it becomes easier to go on working abroad, a decision with a ready explanation that makes sense to everyone. The men who are "'addicted' to migration," some of my informants said, "often fool themselves into believing that it is the continued need for remittances that keeps them on the road, while in reality, it is the difficulty of re-adapting among their families and friends." For such people, migration has simply become a way of life.

Whether this explanation fitted the case of Antonio, I cannot say. He personally never admitted to having "caught the migration virus." It was his friends, in their conversations with me, who had attempted this diagnosis of him. At the time, I tended to disagree with them. Antonio seemed too devoted to his wife and children. Given the choice, I thought, he would certainly prefer to go home and be with them. My chance encounter with him in Riyadh raised some doubts in my mind on the subject. He had signed up for a new job in Saudi Arabia after a mere three-and-a-half weeks in the Philippines following a period of more than three years during which he had not seen his family. Could he have exhausted all the possibilities of finding a job in Manila after three-and-a-half weeks? If not, why the rush? Was it only because he did not want to miss a good job opportunity?

Time, Space, and Migration

Whatever the answer may be in this particular case, *time*, by which I mean not just the temporal flow but also the sum of experiences that fills this flow, is a crucial dimension to be taken into consideration in the study of migration, in particular sustained migration. Beyond a certain threshold, it becomes unclear whether time spent abroad under migration is liminal time, that is to say time "stolen" as it were from "normal" life, or whether it is "normal" life itself, which the migrants, for personal or structural reasons, do not wish or are not allowed to consider as such (Sayad 1991). In Kuwait, the rules clearly stated that migrants were not here to stay. Expatriates knew that sooner or later everyone, including the long-time residents, would have to leave. In a way, life for them was, by definition, a place elsewhere. The problem is how to keep the connection with "elsewhere" alive throughout the years.

During fieldwork, I was struck by the way the topic of retirement was handled by my informants on the rare occasions it arose in the conversation. People who spoke willingly about it had a blissful and idyllic picture of it: Mervin, a Sri Lankan, dreamt of the farm he had bought outside Colombo with the money earned in Kuwait, and where he had built a house in which he had practically never lived. Safwat, an Egyptian, spoke enthusiastically of the piece of land he had bought in Asyut and on which he planned to build a small hotel that he would run with his two sons. "At last, I will be my own boss," he sighed with anticipated satisfaction. As a rule, however, the topic of retirement was systematically shunned. At first it did not surprise me, since most expatriates were young and one does not normally think about retirement at the age of thirty, thirty-five, or even forty. But I gradually found that, at least as far as the expatriates who had been in Kuwait for ten years or more were concerned, the topic was very much present on their minds, and that it was dreaded, not for the usual reasons (fear of idleness, boredom, and isolation, for instance) but because it meant that it was no longer possible for the migrant to "blind himself to the truth" of his migration, to borrow the phrase from Abdelmalek Sayad (1991).

Departure from Kuwait in most cases meant return to "durable" time, and to "normal" life. What many long-time residents in Kuwait feared, in a more or less precise manner, was to find that durability and normality for them had become identified with Kuwait rather than home. This was most obvious and explicit in the case of the Palestinians: even for those who carried a Jordanian passport and, therefore, had an official country to return to (unlike the Palestinians from Gaza, for instance, who had only a *laissez-passer* and had nowhere to go from Kuwait), "home" was often an unknown country since the majority were not from the East Bank, which is today Jordan proper (Brand 1988). While members of the other expatriate communities did not face such a specific and excruciating dilemma as the Palestinians, post-Kuwait life could still be perceived as problematic. A fifty-year-old Indian woman whose children, one son and two daughters, had grown up in Kuwait and were now working in the emirate, envisaged her husband's retirement with apprehension and sadness. After thirty years in the Gulf and with all their children and grandchildren in Kuwait, what were they to do in India, all on their own? And it was not as if they had the choice of remaining in Kuwait: retired people had to leave the country, even if they had children here who were willing to sponsor them.[18] How individual migrants actually experience their return is beyond the scope of this study. What interests us is the mediation between time (the years of migration) and space (Kuwait and the home country) through the production of social relationships *here,* and the reproduction of social relationships *there.*

Expatriate life in Kuwait was subject to the double contradiction of time and space: the expatriates lived in two lifeworlds, one related to Kuwait and the other to "elsewhere," usually their home country. The two could never be spatially and temporally reconciled. While in Kuwait, the *elsewhere-life-world,* that all migrants knew they would return to sooner or later, was far removed in terms of space; yet it was the only "legitimate" one in the long run. The *Kuwait-life-world,* on the other hand, might be a spatial reality, but it remained a temporal "unreality."

At the discursive level, each lifeworld was commonly identified by the actors as the matrix of a specific way of life, the one familiar since childhood and cherished, the other externally imposed by the circumstances of migration and more or less grudgingly submitted to out of purely pragmatic necessity. In reality, the borderline between the two lifeworlds could never be so clear. This was first of all because most migrants attempted in one way or another to turn their life in Kuwait into a replica of their life "elsewhere" through the creation of ethnic networks and the reproduction of at least some aspects of the various native ways of life. But most importantly, the two entities known as "Kuwait" and "homeland" became actualized through the agent's consciousness. Although they had a discrete existence in geographical space, the two places became lifeworlds only insofar as the actor attached a meaning to them that he or she derived from his or her experience in both places. Being brought into social existence by the praxis and consciousness of the agent, the two lifeworlds could not be dichotomous; they were at most two facets of the same life.

Time in Cultural Analysis

Anthropology has a history of an uneasy relationship with the concept of time. In the heyday of functionalist analysis, time was cavalierly dismissed as a non-existent entity, both in the small-scale societies we studied and in our theories. To the extent that a time dimension was involved, it was distinctively separated in two modes: one that was the anthropologist's time ("our time," as Fabian [1983] puts it), and another that was the natives' ("their time"). "Their time" was *synchronic* and static, timelessness really, since their social and cultural structures were replicated from generation to generation, or at least could be reconstructed by the anthropologist (Moore 1993); "our time," meanwhile, was *diachronic* and dynamic—"real" time.[19] This dichotomy was made explicit in structuralist theory, with the distinction drawn by Lévi-Strauss between "hot societies" that undergo rapid change and where time is "irreversible," and "cold societies," where change is slow and time is "reversible" (1966). Underlying this representation is the assumption that processes of social reproduction are interwoven with different forms of awareness of past, present, and future (Giddens 1979). In recent years, we have seen multiple attempts by scholars to reintroduce the time dimension into anthropological analysis, whether to account for cultural differences (Sahlins 1985), to explicate economic and political inequality and domination (Wolf 1982, and the Marxist-inspired school of political economy), or to carry out a critique of our epistemology and our ethnography (Colson 1984; Fabian 1983).

While we have come a long way from the days of functionalist "timeless snapshot" analysis written in the now infamous ethnographic present, we still tend often to treat time as a mere prop, a natural linear axis divided into (usually) two parts, the past and the present, along which change and cultural transmission take place. I suggest that there are two naturalisms we need to defeat here: first, the conceptualization of time as a *natural* variable of social life, and, second, the assumption that it is merely a linear axis along which social action unfolds.

To take the last point first: the idea of time as a linear axis external to social action must be discarded. The past, the present, *and* the future (we tend to forget the latter in our analysis, although it plays a disproportionate role in the lives of the people we study) do not only intermingle in human practice and consciousness; they are also mutually constitutive, and the agents' constant and simultaneous juggling with past, present, and future plays a major role in eliciting and shaping social action.

Indeed, if we define the present as a "here and now" point on the stream of time, how many of us live only in it? Whether we know it or not, our present is filled with echoes from our past in the form of patterns of habitualized actions, thoughts, and beliefs acquired through early socialization, while the future, our own, our children's, and our children's children's, is probably what we really live for. Decisions we make today spring from knowledge sedimented in a more or less distant past and from plans that we more or less consciously hold for tomorrow. The present thus makes sense only insofar as it serves as a mirror reflecting past memories and projects visions of the future. At the same time, the past is remembered through today's meaning, and the future can only be envisioned from the point of view of today's possibilities and constraints. Also, the interpretation of the past as well as the perception of the present are to a large extent colored by the hopes and fears we hold about the future that lies ahead of us. Social action and meaning arise from the complex and constant feedback of past, present, and future upon each other. Time, therefore, is not a discrete variable separable from social action, the backdrop for social life; it is an integral constitutive part of it (Rutz 1992), or, in the words of Fabian, "a constitutive dimension of social reality" (1983).

We must not only abandon the conceptualization of time as an independent linear axis; we must also stop thinking of it as a *natural* variable of life, as temporal flow, in other words, in terms of the natural succession of day and night, the return of the seasons, and the biological development and decay of human life. Time, in social theory as in social life, is always *social* time. Nowhere is this more clearly brought out than in Marx's analysis of labor-time in the economic order of capitalism and in the sociology of leisure (*i.a.*, Glasser 1970; Parker 1983). Migration, especially under the extreme conditions observed in Kuwait, also throws this social quality of time into clear focus. I have used the term "liminal time" to refer to the years the migrants spent working in Kuwait. Liminal time is not an analytic construct by the anthropologist; it is the native perception of the actors, both the expatriates, who knew that their stay in Kuwait could never become permanent, and the Kuwaitis, who were determined to keep the migrants' presence transient.

Why does temporal liminality seem to be a general property of labor migration? (see the epigraph by Sayad at the opening of this chapter). This question can be answered indirectly, through a recognition that time is not merely a natural phenomenon:

1. Unlike permanent migration, labor migration entails a series of temporary dislocations from a familiar environment. *Temporariness* and *familiarity* are not objective notions but subjective ones. They exist only in relation to their opposites, durability and unfamiliarity, just as liminality exists only in relation to normality. These are cultural categories, not natural ones; in other words, they are arbitrarily and contextually constructed. One could argue that natural time, that is to say, the temporal flow of hours, days, and seasons, plays an important role in shaping the perception of temporariness and familiarity. The adaptation by the body to the local climate and geography and the local rhythm of daily activities do indeed contribute to the process of habitualization. But human beings are first and foremost social beings and not mere organisms. Hence, it is the social content of natural time, rather than natural time itself, that most effectively affects the perception of temporariness and familiarity.

2. The social content of natural time varies widely. For the migrant, a crucial feature of this "social content" is his or her status vis-à-vis the host country. If migration time is so clearly perceived as limi-

nal, it is not least because liminality is given a concrete form in the legislation by the host society, which mobilizes a series of state institutions (the immigration department, the police, and so on) to make sure that the rules of limited residence are followed. This is clearest in the case of Kuwait and other non-immigration countries. No matter how long the residence, or how meaningful the relationships developed in the emirate, and no matter how reluctant the expatriates are to return home (as in the case of Nabil the Palestinian oil engineer), the law simply does not allow permanent immigration. Whether the time spent in migration is to be defined as durable or liminal is, therefore, the direct outcome of the power exercised by the host country over the migrants. This aptly illustrates Rutz's contention that time is "an object of power relations" (1992:1). Time in social relations, therefore, is anything but a natural phenomenon.

An "Ad Hoc" Way of Life

To the perception of migration as a liminal time, during which migrants were subjected to the Kuwaitis' dominance, corresponded a pattern of living shared by many expatriates that I try to characterize through the phrase "ad hoc." The term is used here as a metaphor. Something is said to be "ad hoc" when it is arranged or set up "for the end or purpose at hand and without reference to wider application or employment" (Webster's Dictionary). The essence of anything "ad hoc" is therefore its *instrumentality* and its *temporariness*.

Seen from the observer's viewpoint and in the perspective of *longue durée*, all products of human action, including culture, are instrumental and temporary, hence "ad hoc." The ambition of anthropologists, meanwhile, has always been to achieve an understanding from the actor's viewpoint and not merely from the observer's. Since Malinowski (1922), and increasingly within the past twenty years, we have been urged to take seriously the viewpoint of the acting subjects in order to understand how their thoughts and practices shape their situations. Such an approach also enables us to gain insights into the complex subjective knowledge that informs action. Representations and actions are not always perceived by the actor as being instrumental and temporary, although they may be so objectively and in the long-term perspective. Nor are the springs of meaning and action invariably to be found on the level of discursive consciousness, which is, I suggest, the level where instrumentality is identified.[20] They are also found on the level of representations internalized through socialization and past experiences, what Bourdieu calls "apprenticeship through familiarization" (Bourdieu 1977:88; see also Strauss and Quinn 1993). Theorists from Berger and Luckman (1981) to Bourdieu (1977) to Giddens (1979) have shown the important role routinization plays in our actions in everyday life. Routine action, whose instrumentality is at its least obvious in people's consciousness, is more common in relatively stable social contexts where one can assume a certain degree of durable cultural understanding. It is less common in unstable social settings where people are forced by ever-changing circumstances to be made aware of, legitimate, and defend, or alternatively, question their cultural premises. Even more significant are the conditions under which routinized action is internalized. Let me try to illustrate these points with an example.

Most of us behave politely in public life toward people whom we meet; although we may sometimes do so because we want to elicit a certain reward from our partners in the interaction, our politeness is more often than not merely the outcome of a life-long habitualization to which we hardly give any thought. In Kuwait, where expatriates were constantly reminded of the power asymmetry between themselves and the native population, politeness on the part of the former toward the latter was, if anything, even more readily observable. This form of behavior was also routinized, since expatriate politeness toward Kuwaitis was taken to be the "normal" state of affairs in Kuwait: it was "normal" to the Kuwaitis who took it for granted, but it was also "normal" to most foreigners after they had spent some time in the country. Yet, expatriate politeness toward Kuwaitis was perceived and experienced by many expatriates (and perhaps also by some Kuwaitis) as *studied deference* rather than spontaneous politeness. As such, it can be described as instrumental. What is the test of instrumentality in this case? I suggest that it is the following one: when I asked my expatriate informants why they, unrequested, went out of their way to please not only their employers but also Kuwaitis whom they did not know, or why they let them go first in a queue, most of them replied without hesitation, "Because we do not want any trouble," or "because this is their country." On the other hand, when I asked my colleagues in Oslo why they behave politely to people around them, they were at a loss to give me a concise answer.[21]

The reason why I choose to describe the non-Kuwaitis' behavior as instrumental and not that of my Norwegian colleagues does not simply lie in the fact that the migrants in Kuwait seemed to weigh the pros and cons of their most insignificant actions toward the Kuwaitis. It is rather that most people in Norway have, in their mutual interactions, the possibility of choosing among a relatively varied repertoire of roles: a person's employer can also be her friend, they may have attended the same school when they were children, they may be neighbors or meet in contexts outside work where their roles may be reversed; in other words, the relationships between the employer and the employee need not always be hierarchical, with A always in the role of inferior to B or vice versa. Routinized action in this case takes place within a continuous range of situations of multiplex relations, intricately built into one another and in which one instrumentality cannot easily be disentangled from the next one. The situation between a Kuwaiti and an expatriate did not present the same scope for variations. In a social context of heightened ethnic and class division, Kuwaitis and non-Kuwaitis did not commonly initiate and maintain multiplex relationships across group boundaries. The local population was divided into native employers and migrant employees, with a host of signs and symbols to express and sustain this division and a whole legal and administrative apparatus to ensure its reproduction. As I have argued earlier, the rules of exclusion and dominance had raised a protective wall around the Kuwaitis, with the result that interaction between natives and migrants did not flow freely and haphazardly, but in a highly regulated fashion. In this regulated interaction both natives and migrants had to choose from a narrow repertoire of roles assigned to them by the official immigration policy the premise of which was that expatriates were in Kuwait to work for the Kuwaitis. Therefore, in their mutual dealings the Kuwaiti was always an employer/sponsor, a client, and/or a representative of the authorities; and the non-Kuwaiti was invariably an employee, a worker, and/or a supplicant to the official system. These roles were tailor-made for instrumental interactions in the market (for labor, services, and commodities) and the bureaucracy. Actors in Kuwait, whether natives or expatriates, were thus not free to negotiate and create their roles vis-à-vis each other. Nor were they free to perceive and define their ties other than in terms of short-term business transactions between unequal partners. Since their relationship was by definition instrumental and specific, so too, were most individual aspects of their daily interaction, including politeness. Insofar as we can describe the pattern of living among the expatriates as "ad hoc," this dimension of short-term instrumentality that characterized the relations between Kuwaitis and non-Kuwaitis is a major justification for the use of the metaphor.

Even though all motivations underlying human actions and opinions are objectively instrumental, it is by no means certain that actors, under stable circumstances, perceive their own motivations as such. Most of us are willing to describe as instrumental some of the actions we perform, some of the statements we make, and, somewhat less frequently, some of the opinions and principles we hold. Other actions, statements, and principles we definitely do not view as such. For example, how many people in societies where the ideal of romantic love prevails view their decision to get married in terms of economic and practical purposes? It suffices to register the indignation with which most Westerners react to the practice of "negotiated marriages" to understand how some actions are classified as beyond instrumentality. In the same vein, religious faith, political allegiance, and all forms of ideological adherence in general are usually perceived by actors as matters of more or less uncompromising moral principles, not of pragmatic instrumentality. This state of affairs cannot be reduced to a question of actors' deliberate deviousness or false consciousness. Rather it is a fact that the line drawn between rational instrumentality and affect in real life is an entirely artificial one and that all human actions spring from a multiplicity of complexly related motivations, not all of which are equally clearly perceived by the actors themselves. Not all social situations, however, present the same degree of entangled multiplicity of meaning. While instrumentality is particularly difficult to delineate in the areas of kinship, friendship, ritual, ceremonial, and other forms of symbolic activities, it is much less so in the area of formal organization and contractual activities (Cohen 1976). Modern labor belongs to this sphere of life, especially when it is organized under conditions of ethnic stratification and political exclusion, as was the case in Kuwait. Here, the distinction between instrumentality and "expressiveness" is both easier to make and more readily acknowledged by the actors. Because expatriate life in Kuwait was organized along the lines of instrumentality rather than expressiveness, migrants were sharply aware of the purposiveness that steered their own and others' actions.

The above claims about instrumentality can also be made about temporariness. Even though we all know that most things in life are precarious, we embark upon many of our undertakings—for example starting a career, getting married, building a house—as if we are going to live forever. We often plan our lives for many years ahead, not just for twelve or twenty-four months at a time, which was the general pattern among the migrants in Kuwait, where there was a shared, implicit understanding that residence, jobs, wages, acquaintances, and non-kin relationships could come to an abrupt end, perhaps at any moment (remember the migrants' fear of deportation), or at least in the very near future. Cora, for instance, engaged in her relationship with Dennis fully aware that it was going to be transient, just as she, Dennis, Antonio, the Sharmas, and all the other expatriates *knew* that their jobs and their stay in Kuwait were for a limited period only. While life, relationships, possessions, and strategies everywhere and for everyone are perishable, there is a crucial difference in the way the variously positioned acting subjects view their own situations and approach their decision making. This difference not only colors their worldviews, it also has concrete, observable impacts on the way people organize their lives.

Awareness of temporariness had particularly important consequences for the organization of social relationships between expatriates and Kuwaitis, and among expatriates themselves. It provided a rationale for the expatriates' acceptance of exclusion and the structure of dominance under which they lived. Likewise, it led them to hold on to the status quo even though it was often blatantly in their disfavor. Thus the expatriates' acceptance of the power asymmetry between themselves and the Kuwaitis arose neither from false consciousness nor a fatalistic worldview but from the conviction that, given the temporary nature of their stay in Kuwait, submissiveness was the best strategy.

Temporariness was also the most important reason why expatriates practically always opted for individual action when confronted with the most diverse types of problem: collective action required lengthy organization; its outcome was, as a rule, protracted, so that by the time it materialized, even supposing that it was positive, the individual expatriate might no longer be in Kuwait to benefit from it. Finally, temporariness left the ethnic boundaries between the various expatriate communities more or less intact: because they perceived their interaction as chance encounters without lasting consequences, the members of the various ethnic groups usually showed indifference toward one another. No particular friendships were established across ethnic boundaries (except among the privileged middle class) but no explicit hostilities existed either (despite the latent animosities created by the ethnic-based differences in salaries). Especially as regards the imposition of Kuwaiti norms of public behavior, awareness of temporariness helped smooth the way for the expatriates' situational adaptation: submitting to the local norms was relatively easy when the migrants thought of it as a temporary measure, just one more compromise, a kind of tactical move required for a short while, the time it took for them to carry out their life-projects.

I do not claim that the recurrent patterns of meaning and action among expatriates existed *sui generis*, arising as it were by themselves out of some properties intrinsic to a uniform "migrant culture." I have suggested that the migrants in Kuwait shared a number of commonalities, most particularly life-projects and strategies. Although both life-projects and strategies were originally designed against the background of needs and wishes in the home country, they were usually modified along the way; strategies, in particular, were invariably reshaped by the opportunities and constraints that the migrants found in Kuwait itself. Commonality in this case and in others, such as the acute perception of temporal liminality, was the product of the Kuwaitis' rules and practices toward their migrants. If common patterns of meaning, action, and reaction were surprisingly widely distributed among this ethnically heterogeneous migrant population, it was because they (the patterns) existed in response to the peculiar local structure of dominance and the local politics of exclusion.

One could say that the expatriates responded to this politics by devising their own "politics" of acquiescence, compromise, and submissiveness. The use of the word "politics" in this context may seem inappropriate. Yet, it does help bring out the fact that expatriate acquiescence was not elicited by force alone, that it was not the result of a sort of "interactional terrorism" on the part of the Kuwaitis upon the expatriates. Although it was clearly dependent on the Kuwaiti structure of dominance, the expatriates' acquiescence was voluntary, the outcome of a thoughtful assessment in the light of the temporariness of their situations and against the background of their interests which were severely constrained by the interests of the Kuwaitis themselves.

Culture, according to Clifford (1986), is always "emergent." The conditions under which the emergence of any cultural pattern takes place are informative about its characteristics, its mechanism, and, not least, the purposes of its authors. Kuwaitis confronted their migrant workers from a position of dominance, whereas the latter labored under constraining

legal and social parameters set up by the Kuwaiti authorities and reproduced through the action of Kuwaiti citizens. These constraints called for
optimal strategies of compromise on the part of the expatriates. This was
the direct result of the Kuwaitis' strategies of dominance, but, in opting
for compromise, the migrants also participated in recreating and reinforcing the natives' dominance over them. The two cultural forms were thus
mutually dependent for their reproduction.

By using the metaphor "ad hoc" to describe the general outlook on
life, the choice of priorities and strategies, and the organization of social
relations among expatriates in Kuwait, I do not suggest that this cultural
form is qualitatively different from others observed elsewhere. Insofar as
there is a difference, it is a difference of degree—with the case of Kuwait
positioned at the most instrumental and temporary end of the continuum—and not of kind. Because this fundamental comparability combines with a sharp difference in degree, the situation found in Kuwait
allows us to explore issues common to anthropology in a way that can be
fruitfully thought-provoking. Before turning to a theoretical discussion
of a more general character, however, there is another task that needs to
be attended to.

We find a certain parallel between the situation of the expatriates and
that of the Kuwaitis: although they met each other "in the (labor) market," to use Furnivall's image (1948), with vastly different resources and
from diametrically opposed power positions, these were people who
were all undergoing disruptive experiences. To the disruptions and
dilemmas that the act of migrating wrought upon the lives of the non-
Kuwaitis corresponded the disruptions and dilemmas that the act of
opening up to the world as an oil-exporting country wrought upon the
lives of the Kuwaitis. Just as the migrants experienced migration overwhelmingly in terms of their interaction with the Kuwaitis, the latter
experienced modernity largely, though not exclusively, in terms of their
interaction with the expatriates. Their relations with, and their images of,
each other inevitably influenced the way both parties shaped their identities and self-perceptions as they went through the task of living under the
same overarching social structure. There was, nevertheless, a fundamental difference: while the migrants went through their experiences as
individuals or family units, the Kuwaitis went through theirs not only as
individuals or groups but also as a nation. This difference of scale and
approach is so crucial that the two experiences cannot be studied within
the same analytical framework.

Through their participation in the Kuwaitis' social world, the expatriates were pursuing a project of their own, that of individual life improvement through labor migration. I now wish to turn to the project of the Kuwaitis, which was that of building a modern national identity. From what precedes, it may not be difficult to see how the presence of the migrants contributed importantly to the process.

Notes

1. "Among the basic characteristics of immigration is the fact that, with the exception of very few situations, it contributes to blinding itself to its own truth. Because facts and the law cannot always be reconciled, immigration is condemned to produce a situation of double contradiction: we no longer know whether it is a temporary state that we choose to prolong indefinitely, or whether it is a more durable state that we choose to experience with an intense feeling of temporariness." (my translation)

2. The US residence and work permit.

3. The owner of the hotel had opened a seaside restaurant in Fahaheel, south of the capital city. For two years, Antonio was the electrician in both places and occasionally a waiter in the restaurant as well. Because he was an excellent electrician, the owner had agreed to remunerate his extra work financially.

4. For example: Al-Taher 1995; Bardawil 1988; Kanafani 1978; Khaled 1973; Al Shaykh 1989.

5. This is a pattern familiar from labor migration elsewhere in the world as well. See Castles and Kosack 1985, Kearney 1986, Wilson 1985.

6. Schools for expatriate children were known as community schools because they were created by the members of a national community to serve the educational needs of the children of that particular community. These schools taught the syllabi of their countries and in their national languages. Administratively, however, they were under the authority of the Kuwaiti Ministry of Education, Department of Private Education. Arabic was a compulsory subject for all students, and Islam was compulsory for Muslim children.

7. 50 percent of current expenses, teachers' salaries, and teaching materials were covered by the Kuwaiti state.

8. Statistics from the Ministry of Education for 1985–1988 show that throughout that period there were more expatriate students than Kuwaiti students in all the government secondary schools (Social Statistics 1989). At all levels (primary, intermediate, and secondary), the single largest expatriate nationalities attending the government schools were the Jordanians and the Palestinians (ibid.).

9. Roughly, the monthly salary scale can be divided into the following groups:

the lowest salaries (unskilled laborers, cleaners, domestic workers, etc.): KD 20 to KD 80; the low salaries (semi-skilled workers, technicians, clerks, etc.): KD 80 to KD 200; the middle-range salaries (skilled workers, junior employees in the public sector, some expatriate school teachers, nurses, etc.): KD 200 to KD 400; the high salaries (teachers, civil servants, etc.): KD 400 to KD 600; the executive salaries: from KD 600 upwards.

Apart from the Palestinians, who paid 3 percent in income tax to the Palestine Liberation Organization, no residents in Kuwait paid income taxes.

10. See Sayad 1991 for a similar observation among Algerian immigrants in France.

11. *Ramadan*, the holy month of fasting; *'id al fitr*, feast of the breaking of the fast; *'id al adha*, feast of the sacrifice that ends the *hajj* (pilgrimage) season; *mawlid al nabi*, birthday of the Prophet.

12. Literally, "markets," but in Kuwait they were, in reality, shopping malls.

13. According to the *Arab Times* in 1989, for example, 115 Egyptian *mullahs* and *imams* (officiating priests) were contracted to work in Kuwait. The Kuwaiti Ministry of Awqaf (Religious Endowments) and Islamic Affairs had often complained about the Kuwaitis' lukewarm interest in taking up preaching activities and regretted having to use foreigners, including non-Arabs, in the role of *muezzins* (callers to the prayers).

14. In fact, there are apartments and houses scattered across Kuwait that were used as minor chapels and churches. This was being done discreetly, and there were no external signs that could indicated the religious use of these places.

15. Because of the large number of cars in the emirate, it was decided in 1980 that the granting of Kuwaiti driving licences to expatriates would be suspended except to professionals in the public and private sectors (doctors, engineers, teachers, judges, journalists, etc.) and Arabs born in Kuwait. In reality, what this law excluded were the low-salaried migrants, in particular the Asians.

16. A classic case is money collected to pay the repatriation ticket of laborers or maids whose sponsors, for one reason or another, refused to shoulder this particular responsibility.

17. Typical marriage advertisements might read as follows: "Proposals are invited from Hindu doctors/engineers/executives/scientists below 29 years, well settled in USA, Canada or Kuwait. For an attractive, convent-educated girl from Bombay." "28-year-old engineeer, fair and good looking, in possession of US greencard, seeks bride, preferably nurse."

Although the other communities did not have this tradition of marriage advertisement, the "have-Green-Card-will-marry" approach was far from unknown. Among the Filipinos, for instance, the Green-Card argument seemed, according to my observations, at least as strong, if not stronger than among the Indians.

18. Expatriates could only sponsor spouses and children who were under age. The rule, however, did not apply to the Palestinians, who were allowed to sponsor their retired parents, especially widowed mothers.

19. It must be added that not all anthropologists of the classic period have been indifferent to time. We need only to think of the work of Kroeber, Steward, Evans-Pritchard, and Balandier to name a few (Moore 1993).

20. In his attempt to refine the polarity between conscious and unconscious, Giddens (1979) distinguishes between discursive consciousness and practical consciousness. He defines the first as "involving knowledge which actors are able to express on the level of discourse" (1979:5), or that which we can give account of through our discursive abilities, to use the language of Garfinkel (1967). Practical consciousness, on the other hand, is "tacit knowledge that is skillfully applied in the enactment of courses of conduct, but which the actor is not able to formulate discursively" (Giddens 1979:57). Unless we restrict instrumentality to the level of discursive consciousness, we run the risk of falling into the strong version of functionalism, which postulates that all institutions or behavioral patterns have a function that explains their presence. In other words, ultimately, all things are instrumental because all things serve a purpose.

21. Of course, what "polite behavior" means varies infinitely. I am, therefore, not comparing the conception of politeness in Kuwait and Norway but merely pointing out the fact that people in both places follow a pattern of demeanor that is viewed by the local population as acceptable and right.

7

Gender Relations, Ethnicity, and the National Project

Just as the role of migrant workers has commonly been underplayed in the analysis of social life in Kuwait, the role of Kuwaiti women in the building of Kuwaiti national identity has so far remained relatively unexplored. In a plural society of Kuwait's type, the collective identity of the minority elite and the ideology sustaining its rule over the other groups are closely connected with the position of the women on whom the elite depends for its biological and cultural reproduction. I will, therefore, approach the topic of nation-building from the point of view of gender relations among Kuwaitis, which are enacted within a context pervaded by modernization and ethnicity. Most studies of the condition of women in Kuwait ignore the fact of ethnic pluralism and demographic imbalance in Kuwaiti society. There is a total lack of communication between those conducting labor migration studies and gender studies in the Gulf, for these are routinely considered as two entirely separate fields of research: the one carried out by (usually male) economists and dealing with hard facts and figures in the sphere of policy-making, and the other by (usually female) cultural sociologists and dealing with ideology in the sphere of human relations. The fact that the two fields are viewed as unrelated and irrelevant to each other is symptomatic of the way experts, in their analyses, espouse the layman's view of the Kuwaiti and the expatriate populations as two entirely separate worlds; it also shows the way these same experts still define the role and place of Gulf women in their society—a point to which I shall return in more detail.

In the previous chapter I argued for the need to (re)introduce the human actor into the study of labor migration, in other words, to bring the study from the macro level of structural analysis down to the micro level of agency analysis. In this chapter I will argue for the need to move the discussion of gender relations among the Kuwaitis beyond the analytical confines of kinship patriarchy into the wider framework of ethnic pluralism and nation-building. In this context, Kuwaiti men and women do not only face each other in an asymmetrical confrontation, they also cooperate closely in a national project: not only men but also women are active in establishing the current pattern of gender relations.

Most discussions of the question of women in Kuwait are carried out without due consideration being given to the historical and material specificity of Kuwait's situation; thus, the analysis often runs somewhat mechanically along the familiar lines of "modernization versus tradition," with women caught in the middle as victims of an antiquated patriarchal system that fights for its own survival. This is the type of analysis being made of many Muslim societies, from Morocco to Pakistan. Although there are undoubtedly basic similarities between these societies, and although it is imperative not to overlook these similarities, we cannot be content with leaving the analysis at this. Few would dispute that the same processes of modernization are taking place in these societies which are all shaped by Islamic tradition, and that this has far-reaching social consequences. But the circumstances under which modernization is brought about, what people connote it with, and how they perceive their situations in this specific "modern" world order are not necessarily the same for all Muslims. The rationale behind social and sexual politics in Kuwait cannot be entirely equated with those in, for example, Egypt or Jordan, let alone Morocco or Pakistan. The crucial fact that the Kuwaitis are a privileged ethnic minority that feels beleaguered and threatened by a majority of foreigners, legally powerless but providing vital labor, cannot be without consequences for the relations between Kuwaiti men and women. Only through an understanding of this linkage can we understand what has been a constant source of puzzlement to outside observers, namely, that the truly substantial changes which have taken place in the lives of the Kuwaiti women since the end of World War II seem to have left many constraints on their condition practically intact. To account for this apparent contradiction we need to address the fact that Kuwait is a nation-in-the-making under the peculiar circumstances of oil prosperity and what one may describe as "exacerbated" ethnic pluralism.

Although Kuwait was ruled by the Kuwaitis, it was built and maintained by the migrants. The physical entity known as Kuwait (its roads, buildings, houses, and so on) was entirely the product of migrant labor. To what extent was Kuwait, the socio-political entity, dependent on the presence of the migrants? Posed in these terms, the question may surprise: Surely Kuwaiti political institutions and power structures were rooted in Kuwait's history and did not owe their existence to the migrants. The literature by historians and political scientists makes this point clear. Moreover, exclusion made any form of direct political participation by non-Kuwaitis simply impossible. The question becomes less surprising, however, if by "socio-political entity" we refer not to the body of formal institutions but to the community of feeling that connected the native population to the Kuwaiti state and the Kuwaiti nation. My contention is that the presence of the expatriates was a major factor which contributed, if not to making, at least to crystalizing, Kuwaiti national identity, built on the community of feeling. We saw in the previous chapters that "Kuwaitiness" was thrown into relief through contradistinction to "expatriateness," measured in terms of social and legal status and externalized through the dress code and demeanor. But "Kuwaitiness" itself needs to be broken down into finer categories: there is, for instance, "male" Kuwaitiness and "female" Kuwaitiness, as we saw in Chapter 5. One way in which the presence of the foreign workers influenced the shaping of Kuwaiti national identity was through the impact it had on the situation of Kuwaiti women.

Although most research on nations and nationalism tends to overlook the question of gender (Walby 1992), the literature on women in the Middle East has begun to address the linkage between woman and nation (Kandiyoti 1991; Yuval-Davis and Anthias 1989). To explore such a linkage in the case of the Arabian Peninsula may surprise. A common popular image of the Gulf oil-exporting countries is that of a dichotomy between change in the material sphere of life and continuity in the non-material one. In the non-material sphere, the status of women and gender relations figure most prominently in the outsiders' representation of the Arabian "Others." It has become accepted "knowledge" in the West that the Arabian Peninsula houses the richest (in terms of revenues and consumption) but most conservative societies in the Middle East, sexually discriminating and segregated, undemocratic, and generally impervious to a modern mode of thought. The French saying *"plus ça change, plus c'est la même chose"* has sometimes been used in this connection. There are many threads to unravel here, but I will pursue only those which fall directly within the concern of this study, namely, the relations between the Kuwaitis and their migrant workers.

"Change" and Kuwaiti Women

The notion of change is central to the present discussion. It is one of those multi-faceted concepts in anthropology that seem easy enough to capture empirically but often turn out to be extremely difficult to analyze, not least because there are no clear-cut criteria to help disentangle change from continuity at the level of analysis.

In Kuwait, everyone spoke of change as a fact of life. Usually, in the Kuwaitis' discourse, time was divided into a "before" and "after" period, with the advent of oil as the critical watershed event.[1] In the discourse of expatriates with a long history of residence in the emirate, "before" and "after" usually referred to the pre-oil boom and post-oil boom stages; here, the critical year was not 1938 (when oil was discovered) or 1946 (when the first shipment took place) but 1973, in the aftermath of which the politics of exclusion was more fully developed.[2]

The before–after mode of thinking pervaded the way Kuwaitis spoke of themselves and their country. At one level, nothing was easier to track down and describe in Kuwait than change, because so much of it consisted of external features—most significantly, material infrastructure and patterns of consumption.[3] At another level, continuity seemed to prevail. I would suggest that, as elsewhere in the world, what we see in Kuwait are, more often than not, situations of *changing continuity*, a claim I will illustrate by enquiring specifically into the conditions of Kuwaiti women. Let us begin by looking into the objective innovations that have had the greatest impact on the lives of most Kuwaiti women— keeping in mind that, due to variations in individual biographies, a wide spectrum of variations lies beneath the generalizations.

Umm Bader and her daughters
Umm Bader was a frail woman of approximately sixty-five (she was not certain of her date of birth). At puberty, when she was around twelve, she was given in marriage to her cousin, a man considerably older than her and who had been married twice before. "I knew nothing and was absolutely terrified on my wedding day," she recalled. But her cousin turned out to be a good man and a devoted husband. He never took another wife after he married her. When he died after thirty years of marriage, Umm Bader felt "like a lost child." As the son of a respected merchant family, which had produced many religious judges, her husband left her and their nine children in a secure material position. Today, Umm Bader lived comfortably in a villa, served by an Indian driver, an Indian cook, and two

Philippino maids. The old woman never spent a day without being visited by her children and grandchildren.

Umm Bader had two daughters, one a teacher and the other a lawyer. Both were married, the lawyer to a judge and the teacher to a Kuwaiti diplomat. Umm Bader had advised them in the choice of their husbands, who, incidentally, were the women's cousins. "But they decided on their careers themselves," she said. "Here, I could not help them: I have been to school for only one year before I got married." Umm Bader watched her daughters move in a world of learning and public responsibility that she herself had never experienced and about which she expressed an awed approval.

There was a striking difference between the two daughters. Mona, the teacher, wore Western dresses over which she negligently threw an *abaya* whenever she was out running errands or on her way to and from work. As a diplomat's wife, she had spent quite a number of years abroad and had developed a taste for cinemas and concerts. Maha, the lawyer, was strictly *muhajjiba* and never showed herself outside her home without the head-scarf and the *abaya*. She was the one who took her mother on the *hajj* to Mecca, while Mona vacationed in London with her husband and children.

Maha had three children and was not planning to have any more, she said, because her work took much of her time. Mona, on the other hand, was expecting her sixth child and was ready to have more if that was what her husband wanted. "Men like having children because it makes them feel young," she had confided one day as the two sisters and I sat together around coffee and cakes. "And it is always good for a marriage when the husband feels young." Maha dismissed her sister's view with some impatience. "You have enough children now," she told Mona firmly. "Tell your husband to find another way to stay young." After her sister left, Mona expressed her puzzlement and concern: "I can't understand that Maha is not afraid of losing her husband. Besides, she should also think of her country. This is not China or India. Kuwait needs many more babies."

The status of Kuwaiti women was by no means unambiguous. A foreign observer who comes to Kuwait expecting to find sexual segregation, veiling, and general female subordination, is often surprised by the diversity of female life circumstances as well as by the women's self-assured presence in public and private life. As the foreigner struggles to rectify her views, assuming on the basis of the newly acquired data that Kuwaiti women might, in fact, enjoy a status not markedly subordinate to that of Kuwaiti men, she would realize that the matter is not all that simple. How can one most accurately describe the position of Kuwaiti women nowadays?

In this, as in other areas of Kuwaiti life, the pre-oil/post-oil contrast was considerable. In pre-oil Kuwait, and well into the 1940s, Kuwaiti women lived under the constraining physical and social conditions often associated with orthodox Muslim female conditions of the past: secluded, veiled, and overwhelmingly illiterate, they were married at puberty to a male relative, and their social horizon was limited to the immediate neighborhood of their homes (Dickson 1978; Nath 1982). In 1957 the rate of illiteracy among women was around 90 percent (ASA 1989). By 1989 the situation had changed drastically: primary and intermediate education were compulsory and the university was coeducational. The number of women at Kuwait University was almost twice as high as that of men, many of whom went abroad to study, and women were found among deans, assistant under-secretaries, lawyers, doctors, and engineers. As for the private sector, women invested money, and some even managed companies and were on boards of directors of corporations. Kuwaiti women were known throughout the Gulf for their active presence in social life compared to most of their Arabian sisters. They were seen in public places, not walking meekly behind their male chaperons but often alone and at the wheels of their own cars. What's more, the state claimed to support their participation in the labor force, a claim that was substantiated by the national education policy and some declarations of intent: for instance, when the first development plan (for the period 1967–1968 to 1971–1972) was drawn up, one of the recommendations in it was to encourage women to enter the labor market to reduce the need for foreign workers (Tétreault and al-Mughni 1995). With the exception of cabinet and ambassadorial positions, there were, in the late 1980s and in principle, no secular jobs that were out of the reach of Kuwaiti women.[4]

Education in general, and female education in particular, were among the social achievements of which Kuwait was most proud. Official figures for 1985 showed that the percentage of Kuwaiti women with secondary and university education in the labor force was more than double that of Kuwaiti men (Table 3.5) and that the percentage of women in the labor force had increased from 2 percent in 1970 to 13.8 percent in 1985 (ASA 1989). Statistics on education and work are important as an indication of the state policy and general trend in development. But how they are arrived at depends on what particular concerns the statisticians have in mind. Therefore, we must treat the figures with caution and not expect to find in them a complete image of the situation, let alone insights into what the changes actually mean for the actors themselves. I propose to attempt to gain such insights by exploring the one dimension in the lives of Kuwaiti women that recurred again and again in all the accounts I have gathered, namely, *physical and social mobility*. Social mobility will be treated particularly in terms of work.

Subverting Spatial Confinement: The *Hijaab* and the Car

In the social context of Islam, mobility can be easily located in relation to its polar opposite, seclusion. "Seclusion" is customarily used in the literature to refer to the traditional state of affairs in which Muslim women lived before modernization occurred and brought in its wake sexual unsegregation (Mernissi 1983). Physical mobility and unsegregation may overlap, but they are not coterminous. Mobility means that women enjoy freedom of movement within a wider geographical space; this in turn may or may not entail a greater opportunity to live a genuinely unsegregated life in which they can expand their social networks to include not only men but also women from other classes than their own, and vary their role repertoires. The thesis presented here is that certain aspects of modernization (such as the introduction of the car and the telephone, especially the cellular telephone) had successfully defeated the physical confinement of Kuwaiti women's lives, whereas ethnic pluralization had contributed to the reproduction of their social confinement. In making the distinction between physical and social confinement, I do not dispute the fact that the significance of space is ultimately social and that space in Muslim societies derives its towering importance from the role it plays in the social organization of gender relations. There is, undeniably, a stark correspondence between sexuality and territoriality (Bouhdiba 1985; Mernissi 1983). This, however, does not mean that, under all circumstances, physical confinement necessarily coincides with social confinement, or that an opening of the physical space necessarily entails an equal degree of widening of the social networks, especially when work is posited—as it is here—as the primary mechanism that allows women to widen their social universe.

Traditionally, sexual segregation is the way in which Muslims ensure the social control of sexuality by restricting interaction between men and women who do not belong to the same kinship network. When interaction cannot be avoided, it is ritualized, and the major ritual is veiling. In Chapter 5 we discussed the ethnic meaning attached to the use of the *hijaab* in contemporary Kuwaiti society. The use of the *abaya* and head-scarf elicited ethnic recognition and deference by the migrants, and it conferred on the wearer a sense of protection against expatriate men. But prior to oil, a sense of protection and security was also associated with veiling, whose significance, seen from the viewpoint of most Kuwaiti women, has always lain more in its enabling than in its forbidding aspect. To outsiders the *hijaab* may appear as one of the most constraining impositions on Muslim women; it was not at all perceived in this way by most Kuwaiti women. As we have seen, the use of the *abaya* and headscarf were voluntary and spontaneous in Kuwait. It was not imposed by law, either by the government or by the religious authorities. For women who viewed veiling as a constraint on their freedom, there was always the possibility to opt for the Western dress code, which, in fact, was the choice of many upper-class Kuwaiti women. The majority, however, had chosen to retain the use of at least the *abaya*. My female informants seldom explained their choice with religious reasons. They all stressed the practical side of both *hijaab* and *abaya*. In addition to its being a guarantee of ethnic deference in public places, the use of these garments provided an anonymity which allowed the woman to go about her business without being readily recognized. A well-known public figure who wanted to shop undisturbed in the popular *souq*, a housewife who went for a lone afternoon stroll along the Gulf, a socialite who did not feel like dressing up for a quick visit to a friend's house, or a young girl who wanted to meet a man of whom her family disapproved, all gratefully made use of the *abaya* and headscarf, even when they would not do so under other circumstances. One could easily detect an undertone of feminine complicity in the way many Kuwaiti women made use of, and spoke about, the *abaya* in particular. In an unobtrusive but effective way, this garment counteracted the barrage of social norms that surrounded the women's lives. Its efficiency lay precisely in that it did so without challenging these norms. In a social setting where female social networks were severely constrained, by partly masking her identity, the *abaya* allowed the wearer a considerable degree of freedom.

The introduction of the car and car driving must be seen as an extension of this opportunity for women to accede to freedom of movement. It is curious that the literature on Kuwaiti women generally fails to point out the enormous impact of car driving on their lives. Perhaps analysts tend to take this activity for granted and do not, therefore, realize how revolutionary it is in societies where women's freedom of movement has been narrowly circumscribed for centuries. Many of us consider the fact that Saudi Arabia clings to its ban against women's driving as yet another quaint feature of Saudi conservatism, but we fail to ask what the absence of such a ban in the neighboring Gulf societies represents in terms of change in the female condition and gender relations in general. Unlike women in the other Gulf states, practically all urban Kuwaiti women under fifty were active car drivers.[5] Of the changes that had critically contributed to increasing the independence of women in Kuwait in the past decades, car driving must be among the most remarkable ones. Like the *hijaab*, the car combines the advantage of being at one and the same time an instrument of freedom and of protection. As Baudrillard (1976) remarks, the car has a protective quality that likens it to a home; it exudes both a sense of privacy and inaccessibility. As long as she is in the car, the Kuwaiti woman has not really left the protected sphere of the home. As is the case with the *hijaab*, only to a greater degree, the car sets a physical boundary between her and the outside world, while allowing her to move around freely. It is only when an accident or a mechanical failure occurs and she has to step out of it that the woman finally finds herself in the public sphere.[6] As a driver, the woman was very much in charge—of her own movements, of her timetable, and even of her social network, since it was difficult for her husband or anyone else to control whom she was seeing. Her responsibility over her own household was also more complete.[7] The relationship between physical mobility and the feeling of personal autonomy is a close one, as the following testimony by a fifty-three year old woman shows:

"I got my driving licence in 1968 when I was thirty-three years old. It made a big difference in my life. Before that, my husband had to take me shopping with him. Often he shopped alone too. He was the one who knew everything: where to find the best products, who to talk to, when it is best to go where. He also drove the children to school, collected them, talked to the teachers. I remember when our son Yaqoub was nine and was hit by a car outside school, Ahmed [her husband] went directly from his office to the hospital. I wanted to go with him, but it would have delayed Ahmed to drive home and pick me up, since his office was near the hospital . . . Today, my daughters know all about their children's schools. They don't depend on their husbands. And if they want to visit me or a friend, they just take their car and drive off. No one expects them to ask for their husbands' permission. I did not really have to ask for Ahmad's permission

either. But it was just as if I had to, because I always had to wait for him.
And if he was in a bad mood, he would simply refuse to drive me."

Car driving severely subverts the principle of female seclusion and
undermines the hegemony of men over women. When some Kuwaiti
men said, half-humorously, that "the car is the Kuwaiti woman's best
friend," they implicitly acknowledged that an important step had been
made toward a relationship between men and women that was *de facto*
more balanced. The fact that female driving had never been a big social
issue in Kuwait and was such a common practice was the best evidence
that change here was not simply cosmetic and restricted to the material
conditions of life, as many commentators have claimed. As far as I
know, no suggestions or attempts were ever made to circumscribe this
newly gained freedom enjoyed by women. Even after the war in 1991–
1992, when calls by conservative men for the return to a strict Muslim
dress code were heard everywhere, and conservative women demanded
the right to wear the *niqab* (face veil) while driving (which was against
the law), no one ever suggested that women should no longer be allowed
to drive. Such a move simply would not fit in with the Kuwaitis' positive
approach to modernity, especially to technology. Kuwaitis had a pragmatic, down-to-earth approach to material things: if they can help make
life easier and better and one can afford them, why not buy them and use
them? In this country of heat, dust, and distance (as a state Kuwait is
small, but as a city it is sprawling), the car was undoubtedly a good thing
to have, and no one (at least among the Kuwaitis) should be deprived of
its use. Like water, electricity, and air-conditioning, the car was too
much part of the Kuwaitis' representation of "the good life" for its use or
abuse to be questioned. And this concerned not only women. The country
had, for example, a horrific record of traffic accidents.[8] Interestingly
enough, the penalty for traffic violations consisted of fines, imprisonment, and/or deportation (in the case of expatriates). Withdrawal of the
driving licence, meanwhile, practically never occurred. This approach to
driving as a fundamental right for all Kuwaitis secured a large part of the
native female population its enjoyment of physical mobility. The same
legitimacy was not ensured when it came to female social mobility
through work.

Reproducing Social Confinement (I):
The Constraints of Ethnic Stratification

As already mentioned, official statistics indicate that there had been an increase in the Kuwaiti female participation in the labor force from 2 percent to 14 percent in the period between 1970 and 1985. On the basis of this computation, the total Kuwaiti participation in the labor force in 1985 was 36 percent. We have seen in Chapter 3 that in April 1989 the assistant-undersecretary of the Ministry of Planning personally refuted these statistics and announced at a press conference that the Kuwaitis represented only 14 percent of the labor force.[9] He did not give any breakdown by sex but, without denying that an increase had indeed occurred since the early 1970s, it is only natural to assume that the percentage of national female workers was lower than 14 percent. The official, Dr. Abdul Wahab Al Awadi, explained that the difference between the previous statistics and the present ones was due to the earlier inclusion of the *bidoons* (stateless) in the Kuwaiti category. This official rectification complicates the task of assessing the participation of national women in the labor force and calls for a reconsideration of some conclusions about their economic activity by social scientists.

One instance is the study by Shah and Al Qudsi (1990) of female work roles in Kuwait. Basing their account on official statistics collected before 1986, the year when the policy concerning the *bidoons* was radically changed, the authors quote a finding according to which, in 1983, the largest female Kuwaiti participation in the work force originated from the bottom income level (24.5 percent), while the equivalent participation in the upper income level was only 5 percent (Table 7.1). In the light of Dr. Al Awadi's rectification, we need to ask what the actual per-

TABLE 7.1 Proportion of Women in the Labor Force by Distribution of Household Income (private households only)

Households	Kuwaitis	Arabs	Asians
Bottom 40%	24.5	26.1	78.6
Middle 40%	16.3	19.2	39.2
Uppper 20%	5.2	4.8	10.8
Average	19.3	19.1	49.3

Source: Central Statistical Office, 1983, compiled from Shah and al Qudsi 1990.

centage of *Kuwaiti* workers was and to which income levels they belonged. It may not be incorrect to assume that the largest slice—the bottom income one—consisted mainly of *bidoon*, and not Kuwaiti, women. This claim cannot be formally substantiated, since no official information is available concerning the socio-economic situation of the *bidoons* as compared with the nationals. However, it is built on the following two observations:

1. As we have seen in Chapter 3, the *bidoons* did not have access to the same amount of financial and social support granted by the state to its citizens, nor were they involved in the major trade and business activities, which were the preserve of the citizens and the real sources of private wealth in Kuwait. Although these privileges were often held by the male heads of Kuwaiti families rather than by female citizens, the cumulative effect throughout the years was the enrichment of the national families, representing a definite economic guarantee for their daughters. Therefore, when a woman came from a rich family, she often enjoyed considerable material independence and security, not least in case of divorce. For women from ordinary families, on the other hand, such security was often lacking; divorce threatened to leave them economically stranded, hence the need for these women to take up salaried work. Compared to the citizens, the *bidoons* tended to aggregate toward this lower end of the economic continuum. Insofar as there were non-expatriate women who were engaged in the labor force for economic reasons, they were likely to be recruited from among this group rather than among the nationals. That *bidoon* women were skilled enough to enter the labor force made no doubt: until 1986 the stateless could not only attend government schools but also seemed to have had fairly easy access to the lower echelons of the public sector and even to higher positions in those occupations that Kuwaiti citizens shunned, such as the health professions.[10]

2. As regards occupational distribution, this approach to the data would elucidate a finding quoted in Shah and Al Qudsi (1990:218), which the authors themselves describe as "unorthodox": the concentration of Kuwaiti women in clerical work, which, they say, ran counter to "the traditional values concerning the segregation of the sexes." Shah and Al Qudsi are right in their claim that the custom

of segregating the sexes was deep-seated enough in Kuwait to lead Kuwaiti women to observe it, but only insofar as their economic situation allowed them to do so. Here, as elsewhere, people who choose "unorthodox" occupations are often those who simply cannot afford to respect orthodoxy. Skilled *bidoon* women were more likely to settle for clerical work in a mixed environment than skilled national women, who could easily find more "orthodox" jobs by virtue of their citizenship.

Even more striking, I would suggest, is another finding pointed out by the authors, namely, that the *Kuwaiti* service workers "were overrepresented in cooking and housekeeping jobs" (1990:225). Anyone with experience of life in the emirate is bound to feel puzzled by this finding since it contradicts the common knowledge that Kuwaiti nationals never opted for such low-status jobs, which, as we have seen, were shunned even by Arab female expatriates and were almost exclusively associated with Asian women. Insofar as there were indeed non-Kuwaiti women in cooking and housekeeping jobs—and there is no reason to doubt the authors' finding—these must have been women who did not enjoy the economic and social privileges of Kuwaiti citizenship, in other words, stateless women.

These peculiar features identified by Shah and Al Qudsi among the so-called "national" female labor force become more consistent with empirical observations if we, unlike the official statistics, make the distinction between the *bidoon* and the Kuwaiti components of this labor force and assume (in the absence of official confirmation) that the majority, or at least many, of the non-expatriate female workers were *bidoons* for whom salaried work was a necessity. It was a common unofficial assumption before the Iraqi invasion that the actual Kuwaiti female rate of labor participation was at most 6 percent (Ramazani 1988). This figure may be too low to be correct. According to recent statistical material published after the war in 1992, in which the *bidoons* are not taken into account (Russell and Al-Ramadhan 1994), the refined labor force participation rate for Kuwaiti women increased from 21.1 percent in 1985 to 25.4 percent in 1990, a percentage much higher than Ramazani's. But then again, these new statistics are based on the assumption that the total Kuwaiti labor force participation rate was 41 percent for 1985 and 43.9 percent for 1990—very high figures indeed, compared to the revised figures submitted by the under-assistant secretary of the

Ministry of Planning in 1989. On the other hand, if we revert to the 14 percent acknowledged by him then (for both Kuwaiti men and women), Ramazani's admittedly unsubstantiated 6 percent makes more sense. It would indicate that, in the late 1980s, there were almost as many Kuwaiti women as Kuwaiti men in the labor force, a fact that is interesting in itself.

The above discussion shows that making use of statistics on national labor participation in Kuwait is very much a matter of which interpretation one chooses to adopt. But independently of whether we opt for 6, 14, 21 or even 25 percent, the fact remains that the participation of the local citizens in the labor force by the late 1980s was exceptionally low, and this is what needs to be explained. Although it might not be unexpected in a country where the per capita income had been, for the past decades, among the world's highest,[11] this low participation cannot be entirely explained in terms of affluence. As far as women are concerned, tradition rather than affluence has been the most common explanation. The argument of tradition has been used so often in this regard that one tends almost to take it at face value. But what do we mean when we claim that tradition prevents Kuwaiti women from working?

We may be referring to the fact that in this part of the world the role of women has, for centuries, been confined to the organization of the private sphere, and the responsibility of earning the family's income has not rested on their shoulders but on those of their male relatives. As a result, being a salaried worker is a role that women do not primarily take into consideration when they grow up and decide what to do with their lives. Getting married, having children, and taking care of them are, on the other hand, real possibilities. The assumption that Kuwaiti (and Arabian) women never worked for money in the old days was true for the well-to-do women but not for the poorer women (Tétreault and al-Mughni 1995). As to the thesis that work was an alien thought to Kuwaiti women in the 1980s, it does not correspond to my field observations, at least as far as the generation under fifty was concerned. It is true that, for the overwhelming majority of Kuwaiti women, marriage and children remain the ultimate goal in life. This does not mean, however, that they do not consider combining this goal with having a job. All young female adults I have been in contact with contemplated salaried work as a natural part of their life-projects. That they may not remain in their jobs for a long period of time for lack of financial incentives and/or because they wanted to use more time to bring up their children, all the more so as the government's salary and leave policies did not encourage women to persist, may account for the women's low representation in the labor force. The question for them, therefore, was not whether or not they would work; it was rather whether they would be able to get the "right" kind of work. What was viewed as "right" is the crux of the matter here.

Considering that modernization came to Kuwait less than fifty years ago, it is impossible to ignore the role played by tradition regarding work. The task for us is to explain on what occasions and under what circumstances tradition was invoked to justify that a "modern" activity was deemed "unsuitable" for a Kuwaiti woman. Why, for example, did Kuwaiti women not worry about breaking the rules of tradition when they drove a car, attended unsegregated lectures at the university, or held high positions in government offices and corporations? To explain this situation by referring to tradition alone is clearly inadequate and begs the question. Tradition did indeed play a role here, not as "the dead-weight of an ossified past" (Barth 1984:80) but as an active element in the Kuwaiti politics of exclusion and ethnic stratification. In other words, insofar as tradition was involved, we are not witnessing its reproduction but its "reinvention," that is to say, the reenactment of a behavior and a discourse whose form was the same but whose content had changed considerably and was related to the novel circumstances. I suggest that the best way to understand the pattern of Kuwaiti female employment is to view it in the wider context of how work was conceived of in this society, how this conception had evolved, and the mutual stereotypical perception of Kuwaiti and non-Kuwaiti identities that underpinned its conceptualization.

In the early days of modernization, the 1950s and 1960s, expatriate female workers in Kuwait were mostly educated Palestinians, the majority of whom taught in the newly established girls schools (Brand 1988; Ghabra 1987; Khaled 1973). Teaching was then a highly regarded occupation, and working Palestinian women served as role models for a whole generation of young Kuwaiti girls. With the oil boom, this situation changed. Migrant women were now found in a variety of jobs, but most of these did not enjoy the prestige of teaching which, incidentally, was itself no longer so prestigious: in some Kuwaiti public schools the expatriate teachers from countries such as Egypt, Jordan, and Tunisia were granted little respect by their Kuwaiti pupils; Kuwaiti teachers were better off, but I noticed how most of the native women would stress to me that they were teaching out of pedagogical interest and not out of financial necessity.[12] The fact that they felt obliged to say so at all seems to indicate that the status attached to the teaching profession was in the process of being eroded. Not only female teaching but female work in general had come to be perceived differently. There is a direct parallel between this state of affairs and the growing diversification of the ethnic composition of the non-Kuwaiti population. Whereas the typical migrant woman was at first an educated Muslim Arab in a "respectable" job, she was now more likely to be a poorly educated Asian woman, employed in a menial job, ignorant of Islamic rules of conduct, and, last but not least, easy sexual prey to men, both Kuwaiti and expatriate. Meanwhile, the image of the Kuwaiti woman had evolved in the opposite direction. It was no longer that of an illiterate and secluded person, unable to work because she lacked the necessary skills, but of a rich and educated woman who could afford to remain idle and who, as a citizen, held the formidable power of sponsorship over migrant workers. Kuwaiti afflu-ence, leisure, and power now stood in stark contrast with expatriate eco-nomic need, dependence, and labor. The dichotomy of Kuwaiti leisure and non-Kuwaiti work became a central theme around which both com-ponents of the population, but especially the Kuwaitis, spun their ethnic stereotypes and built their social identities. To embrace these identities meant to embrace related values, norms, and expectations that inevitably impinged upon the role repertoire of actors and determined their choices.

As a direct result of these developments, work, which in the 1960s had seemed to many Kuwaiti women an exciting and liberating activity because it was then the symbol of education and modernity (Nath 1982), became more ambivalent in the 1980s. Most Kuwaitis conceived of their work as "employment," that is to say, remunerated activity, rather than "labor," defined as effort or non-rest. If it is correct to say that Kuwaiti women, like everyone else, have always made the distinction between which jobs are proper for a woman to do and which are not, by the end of the 1980s concerns about ethnic status were central to the choice of a "good" job. Working as a salesperson, a nurse, or an air stewardess was unthinkable for most Kuwaiti women. These jobs, which consist of offer-ing services to customers of various class and ethnic backgrounds, were associated with expatriates. It had also become crucial for working Kuwaiti women to dissociate their type of work from the ones carried out by expatriate women, hence the precautions with which Kuwaiti female work was hedged: most importantly, it had to take place in a "protected" environment (for instance, a school, a government agency, or a private company) and among socially acceptable people (preferably Kuwaitis). In cases where such precautions were not possible (ethnically mixed occupations, or low-level positions), extra care was taken by native women to mark themselves off from their expatriate colleagues, through, for example, the use the *abaya* and Islamic dress. Although education and greater freedom of movement had the potential of expanding substantially the social horizon of Kuwaiti women, the ethnic composition and the power structure of the society worked to obstruct such an expansion. Not all Kuwaiti women could, of course, get the jobs they dreamt of; nor were they all qualified for them. Those who found themselves in this situation did not, as a rule, orient themselves toward less prestigious occupations (nursing is a prime example, but also all the jobs in the service sector), because these were too closely identified with foreign migrant workers. Such ethnic constraints prevented them from entering the labor market and pushed them into a state of unemployment that was due neither to a lack of skills nor to an objective lack of opportunity.

To the women's own skeptical view of certain types of work as a possible source of "ethnic pollution" was added the view, held mostly by Kuwaiti men, of female work as a possible source of "moral pollution" as well.

Reproducing Social Confinement (II): The Discourse of Motherhood

Unlike women's car driving, women's work had been the object of frequent criticism, admittedly not directly as a reprehensible activity but indirectly as a development with unfortunate consequences for the women's ability to fulfill their role as mothers. In this, the Kuwaiti discourse did not differ much from those one finds in other societies around the world. The peculiarity here is that Kuwaiti society was exceptionally receptive to the discourse of motherhood because it built upon a set of arguments that, in the perspective of nation-building, were irrefutable, namely, Kuwait's demographic problems.

Kuwaiti men's view of their women's work was deeply ambivalent. On the one hand, most Kuwaitis, and not just the state policy, acknowledged the need to reduce the number of foreigners in the public sector, which inevitably meant replacing them with Kuwaitis, both men and women. It truly irritated the Kuwaitis to have to deal with Arab expatriate bureaucrats who, in subtle ways, sometimes took pleasure in seeing a native citizen fret under their deliberate administrative procrastinations. On the other hand, work outside the home broke open women's narrow social space in the same way as car driving opened up their geographical space. Work introduced the woman to a world of differentiated roles and statuses outside the kinship system, and it allowed her to meet and entertain relations with people whom social conventions would not have put in her path, such as men unrelated to her through blood or marriage. In a society where gender relations still took place mostly within the family, nuclear and extended, any interaction between mutually unrelated men and women constantly needed to be justified. Officially, work provided the main legitimating factor and the workplace one of the few legitimate public settings for face-to-face interaction between men and women. Similar legitimating devices and settings were also provided by higher studies and the university campuses, although there was much controversy and disagreement around the latter.[13] Unofficially, however, there was much resistance among men to the idea that anything other than kinship relationships could provide an acceptable frame of interaction between men and women. Beneath the official policy of "Kuwaitization" and development of human resources there was, therefore, a strong undercurrent of opinion that discouraged Kuwaiti women from working outside their homes. This was not formulated as a direct objection to female work: in a society where the size of the native work force was minute and the need for increasing it was so obvious, such a discourse would have carried little weight and would have had little chance of being embraced by the women. The discourse of motherhood, on the other hand, was a powerful one, considering the demographic deficiency and the imbalance of the ethnic composition that characterized Kuwaiti society. It was a discourse which the Kuwaiti women could not, and indeed, would not, refute, as I have had the opportunity to witness more than once. The view expressed by Mona, quoted earlier in this chapter, that it was a kind of civic duty for all the Kuwaiti citizens to increase the population by having large families was widely shared by Kuwaiti women. Discussing the topic of family planning with me, a male informant had energetically rejected the idea and suggested that the state should, instead, increase social security and public contributions to the bride-price to help people get married and "assume their national responsibility to produce more children" in order to "help build Kuwait." His wife said that "one need not, of course, have ten or fifteen children as in the old days," but that only one or two children were "definitely too few." Some young women want few children, nowadays, she added, and this she considered a "selfish attitude." As articulated by this woman and by many others, motherhood was the best testimony of Kuwaiti patriotism.

On the part of the state, lack of support for women's work, in spite of the official rhetoric, was given concrete expression in the measures aimed at encouraging women to retire early (at 40, if they had been working for a minimum of 15 years),[14] and through the quasi-neglect of social provisions to working women: maternity leave, for instance, consisted of only two months with full pay,[15] the social allowance paid to women was only half that paid to men, and women were not entitled to child allowance if their husbands worked in the public sector (Shah and Al Qudsi 1990). If this seems to run counter to the policy of equal pay for equal work followed by the government, it is because, according to the *shari`a*, the woman is the economic responsibility of her husband or father. If she is married and has children, it is not she but her husband who bears the economic burden for the maintenance of the family, even if she herself works. In theory, her income is strictly hers to be used for her own sake. In practice, however, all the working married women I have been in contact with contributed with their salaries to the family budget. In the case of divorced women who forsook their alimonies for one reason or another (for example, to obtain a divorce, or to retain the custody of their sons after these reach seven), their salaries were all the income they had for themselves and their children to live on. The state's unwillingness to take these realities into account hardly encouraged Kuwaiti women to enter the labor force.

More generally, the opinions against female work were unified in the discourse on motherhood. Its two main pillars were that work was detrimental to the children's upbringing and that Kuwait needed to expand its native population. Concern with motherhood is a typical feature of populations, in particular minorities, that feel acutely threatened (Gaitskell and Unterhalter 1989; Stoler 1989; Yuval-Davis 1989). The smaller the size of the ruling population in relation to the popular masses, the more important it is for it to adopt an aggressively natalist policy. In such a context, women play a central role as biological and cultural reproducers. Many Kuwaiti men claimed that Kuwaiti women, especially those who worked, were neglecting the latter task, a fact borne out by the presence of the large population of foreign housemaids brought in to replace the mother in the upbringing of Kuwaiti children (in saying this, they conveniently overlooked the fact that domestic servants served their masters as well as their mistresses).

Undeniably, Kuwaiti female work was predicated on the presence of foreign housemaids to carry out the domestic tasks that the national women no longer had the time to do. This argument is important because at its core lies the discussion on the upbringing of Kuwaiti children, which, in Kuwait, was still defined primarily as the duty of the mother. During the years I spent in Kuwait, there were numerous debates in the media and in society at large on the subject of the dangers of foreign maids becoming *ersatz* mothers in Kuwaiti families. In the first years of my stay, the focus of the public debates tended to be on the impact on children of growing up with a non-Arabic-speaking nanny, but experts have never been able to prove that this actually impaired the children's ability to develop their mother tongue later on.[16] More serious was the concern about children being mishandled by the maids, who might themselves have been mistreated, sometimes severely, by their employers. The young Kuwaiti working mothers whom I have interviewed were well aware of this danger; many never left their children in the care of the maid alone, but had their mothers, mothers-in-law, sisters, or aunts to keep an eye on the maids and the children. By the end of my stay in Kuwait, the discussion had shifted from linguistic handicaps and maids' bad behavior to the problem of the children becoming emotionally attached to these alien *ersatz* mothers and the need to somehow reduce the large population of housemaids for the sake of the country's demographic balance. The authorities issued draconian regulations restricting the number of maids each family was entitled to have, but they remained mostly unenforced. The most realistic among the Kuwaitis pointed out that, as long as the national citizens kept to their habit of living in over-sized houses, each with at least two kitchens,[17] and as long as the state provided no nursery facilities for children of pre-school age,[18] the maids would remain an absolute necessity. It is also important to bear in mind that Kuwaiti families were generally large,[19] and the only way a working mother could cope with both her outside job and her home was by using the services of maids.

Over and beyond the above arguments, the presence of foreign maids undermined the status of the Kuwaiti women due to the simple fact that the maids' services were being used in each and every Kuwaiti family, even when the mistress of the house was not working. It is, indeed, when Kuwaiti women employed servants to do all the domestic chores and to look after the children while they, themselves, contributed little to the labor force, that the native women became most vulnerable to the criticisms by those around them, in this case Kuwaiti men and expatriates. These criticisms centered around the theme of "bad parenting" by the "spoiled" women. Increased juvenile delinquency, drug abuse, and poor school performance among Kuwaiti youths reported in the 1980s were said to be symptoms of the crisis which the institution of the family was undergoing. The blame was practically always placed on the women, often portrayed as negligent mothers who left their children in the care of foreign maids. The role of the fathers, meanwhile, was seldom mentioned because, traditionally, it was the mother who raised the children. From this state of affairs there had emerged an image, particularly widespread among Kuwaiti men and among foreigners, of Kuwaiti women as idle, spoiled, and irresponsible. The following quote, found in the work of a male Kuwaiti sociologist, sums up the common male stereotype of the native female:

> Extravagance . . . has become a distinguishing feature of many Kuwaiti women. The trappings of luxury with which such women now surround themselves consume a great deal of both time and money, to an extent unknown in most countries of the developed world. (Nasif Abd al-Khaliq 1981, in Rumaihi 1986:109)

The various aspects of consumption in contemporary Kuwaiti society are a vast and important subject, which cannot be pursued here. What is of interest for our immediate concern is that many Kuwaiti women were aware of the above stereotype and reacted vigorously against it. Those with whom I discussed the topic agreed that the image of the spoiled, conspicuously consuming Kuwaiti woman was detrimental to the country's reputation. To the extent that it was true, they said—and here they were in agreement with many Kuwaiti men—it indicated that there was a need to return to Kuwaiti traditional values, which required, among other things, that women shoulder their traditional duties as mothers instead of delegating them to alien servants. Most Kuwaiti women, however, did not recognize themselves in the stereotype—certainly not Khalida, a thirty-five year old woman, married with three children. Khalida worked at the National Museum, her husband in the Ministry of Health. At home she had, like everyone else, a cook and a maid, both from India. Khalida was amazed by all the talk about "luxury." "What luxury?" she asked. "We live comfortably, that is true, but whatever extra expenditures we undertake, as for instance buying a new car or spending the summer in Cairo, we have to plan our budget carefully ahead like people everywhere." Khalida had a clear idea of why and how the stereotype of the spoiled Kuwaiti woman had arisen and spread:

"There are three types of people who speak of us [Kuwaiti women] as idle and luxury-loving.

There are first of all the Western mass media who know nothing about Kuwait. All they know are the rich sheikhs and sheikhas [members of the ruling family] who go to Europe to spend money. Such people exist in all societies and it is unfair to judge the rest of the country only by looking at them. Then there are our Arab neighbors who are spiteful and envious. Many of them live and work in Kuwait. They hate to see us rich, but they would not mind to get our nationality and become rich themselves. Finally, there are the Kuwaiti men who want to find an excuse to marry foreign women, you know, Egyptians, Jordanians, Iraqis. In reality, they marry them because they are cheap [i.e., they do not demand a high bride-price]. But then they realize after marriage that all these women ever wanted was to become Kuwaiti citizens. What interests them in the nationality is the money, of course, not our traditions. Therefore their children grow up with the Kuwaiti passport but, in their heart, they are foreigners."

It may be of interest to mention that Khalida, who had spent three years alone at the Arab University in Beirut on a government scholarship in the 1970s, decided to become *muhajjiba* in the mid-1980s. And although she occasionally traveled alone to Europe on assignment for the Museum, whenever in Kuwait, Khalida never went out in the evening unaccompanied by her husband, her brother, or, more recently, her fifteen-year-old son. This was a way of life that she had embraced of her own free will, she said. It was not imposed on her by anyone, least of all by her husband. To complete the picture, I must add that Khalida's own mother, Buthaina, had been among the first women to throw away the *abaya* in the early 1960s and to drive a car. Buthaina shocked many when she allowed Khalida to go and study in Lebanon.[20] (Khalida's father was dead, and her uncles did not succeed in convincing her mother to change her mind.) Buthaina was disappointed by her daughter's decision to become *muhajjiba*. She often said that it was a step backward. Khalida answered, "It is because you don't understand how things have changed nowadays compared with the 1960s."

There was a strong feeling among Kuwaiti women of Khalida's generation that the benefits of the modern age were, as far as they were concerned, a double-edged weapon that female expatriates, in particular, manipulated skillfully against Kuwaiti women in order to step in their place and marry Kuwaiti men, thus gaining access to Kuwaiti nationality. As they saw it, the best way to fight back was not to join the ranks of non-Kuwaiti women and compete with these on their own terms. On the contrary, it was to distance themselves, even at the expense of restricting their social space, to recover what they felt was the essence of Kuwaitiness, and to convince the men that Kuwaiti women were morally superior: as Khalida expressed it, they wanted Kuwaiti men to understand that "marrying Kuwaiti" was, in the long run, the best bargain, not least in terms of the reproduction of specifically Kuwaiti values and traditions.

The choice of this strategy can be better comprehended if we keep in mind the patriarchal legal structure under which Kuwaiti women lived and the resulting vulnerability of their position. I will address this topic presently. What the example of Khalida shows is that motherhood was not only a discourse used by men to keep women in line. It was also a strategy eagerly adopted by Kuwaiti women themselves to defend their own positions and interests, in the light of the legal parameters that constrained their lives as they faced the competition of alien women. In choosing to anchor their role repertoire mainly, though not exclusively, in motherhood, Kuwaiti women had actively endorsed the role of public emblem of Kuwaiti cultural tradition. In doing so, they had opted not to exploit fully the opportunities education and work offered to change their condition in relation to Kuwaiti men and to allow the maintenance and reproduction of the elements that constrained their condition.

"Citizenship" versus "Hareem"

The sparse social scientific literature on women in Kuwait, to say nothing of the popular literature on the region, usually depicts their situation as one of either female acquiescence to the patriarchal social structure or female opposition to this structure. Interestingly, the acquiescence model shows little else on the part of the women than a passive acceptance of the age-old religious injunctions and norms familiar in the Muslim world. From this static, ahistorical perspective, one gets the impression of Kuwaiti women as constituting a universe of their own, aimed primarily at the reproduction of Islamic precepts and divorced from the socio-political realities of their society. While Kuwaiti society at large was in the throes of vast changes, women are often portrayed as being absorbed in dilemmas and conflicts involving only their relations to their fathers and husbands. It is an undeniable fact that conflicts on these matters existed, as will be seen presently. But the premises of their perception, formulation, and not least the way they were dealt with reflected the specific social circumstances that prevailed in Kuwait at this particular moment of its history.

It is time we realize that the *hareem* paradigm—with *"hareem"* understood in the Western sense of the strict physical seclusion and sexual segregation that a patriarchal structure imposes on women—is no more valid for an analysis of the situation of women in Kuwait today than it is in many societies of Asia and Latin America, for instance. Although Kuwaiti women were indeed carrying on a critical dialogue with their men, this dialogue took place within a context that impinged upon the lives of men and women alike, and in which both participated. In other words, Kuwaiti actors do not define their identities and positions vis-à-vis each other exclusively in terms of their internal kinship politics, but also in terms of the heightened perspectives or the threatening shadows cast by extrinsic factors on the context in which their relationship unfold. Among the main extrinsic factors were the common feeling of being under siege and the need to build a strong national community to avoid being overrun by the expatriate majority.

To understand the situation of women in Kuwait and to grasp the nature of their relationship to men today, we have no alternative but to place the women squarely in the context of the society at large and to acknowledge the fact that the parameters of their decision making were also shaped by non-religious, non-traditional dimensions, such as modern affluence and cultural pluralism. We need, in other words, to look at them as female *and* Kuwaiti actors. Not only gender but also citizenship must, therefore, be an integral part of the analysis.

Gendered Citizenship, Ethnicity, and Class

In the Western liberal discourse on citizenship, the citizen is invariably thought of as male. The "masculinized construct" (Joseph 1993) of the citizenry is not only a result of the gender-boundedness of many, including Western, languages. It also has its roots in the history of the differential achievement of citizenship rights by men and women in several countries of the First World, where men often won the suffrage several decades ahead of women (Walby 1992). In the USA, for example, men got the vote in the 1840s, but women had to wait until 1920. The situation was quite different in most countries in the Third World, where the franchise was granted to men and women indiscriminately upon independence. Kuwait and the other Arabian countries are notable exceptions. In the USA, not only women but also ethnic minorities were admitted into the fold of the civic community later than white men. Black men technically got the vote some forty years later than white men, but it was only in the late 1960s, after the civil rights movement, that they exercised their right in practice (Walby 1992). Likewise, black women may have been granted the suffrage officially in 1920, together with white women, but they did not become full-fledged participants in elections before the late 1960s. Again Kuwait presents a pattern of discrimination that evokes the one observed in the USA in the earlier phase of its nation-building: among Kuwaiti citizens, only first-category Kuwaitis have the suffrage, the others enjoy all the benefits of citizenship but have no access to the decision-making process. Finally, there is the large migrant population for whom access to Kuwaiti citizenship, let alone the exercise of political rights, is, for all practical purposes, beyond their reach.

As can be expected, the Kuwaitis' reaction to these various forms of discrimination was not uniform. As regards the exclusion of non-Kuwaitis, the word "discrimination" was practically never used publicly, neither by natives nor by migrants. It is important to remember that the overwhelming majority of the migrants came from countries without a strong tradition of the universal exercise of political and civil rights, hence their predisposition to accept the situation in Kuwait as "normal." As for the Kuwaitis, the exclusion of non-Kuwaitis from political rights, justified by their being non-citizens, was the topic that enjoyed the most unanimous support among them.

When it comes to discrimination against Kuwaiti women, before the Iraqi invasion, denial of suffrage to women had been an issue only among a tiny group of upper-class merchant women who could see their fathers, brothers, husbands, and sons exercise a right that was denied to them. Even in these circles, a majority of Kuwaiti women supported political discrimination for fear that universal suffrage might result in the predominance of Bedouin and conservative forces in parliamentary politics. Among the less privileged women, in particular those whose male relatives were themselves not entitled to the suffrage, political discrimination based on sex was less important than general discrimination based on sectarian (Sunni-Shia) and ethnic criteria (urban-tribal). The daily preoccupations of the less-affluent women were likely to center around questions of personal status rights (to decide on their own marriages, to divorce, and so on) rather than political rights. Interestingly, with a few exceptions, the upper-class women who demanded equal political rights had been silent on women's subordinate status under the Family Law. Parallel to the progress in educational opportunities, we find a body of family and personal status laws directly based on the *shari`a* that have remained largely unaffected by change. Although Kuwaiti women were free, and even officially encouraged, to acquire higher education and seek prominent jobs in public life, they were at the same time still expected to acquiesce to their husbands having other wives or to being repudiated (Al Awadi 1985). Many women lived in the constant fear of "losing their husbands," as Mona, quoted above, put it. This was true not only for the less-educated, less-well-off women but also for some highly educated women of rich families. Mona was a typical example. Nadia was another. A laboratory researcher with a degree in sciences, she was 44 years old and had three children. She suffered from diabetes and was going to have her fourth cesarean delivery. The doctor had warned her not to become pregnant again and had advised Nadia to have herself sterilized after her third child. She had chosen to ignore his advice then, although she was fully aware of the hazard to her health a diabetes pregnancy represented. But, in her own words, Nadia thought "sterilization such an irreversible thing." By undergoing this operation she felt that she would be explicitly admitting her inability—which could also be interpreted as her unwillingness—to bear any more children; this, she felt, was like presenting her husband with a good reason to take another wife. Polygamy among ordinary state-employed citizens often meant that the wife had to share the family home with the new woman; among the wealthy people, the husband had, for the sake of his own reputation, to provide each wife with her own dwelling. As for divorce, it often meant that the woman had to return to live in her parents' home, since local norms disapproved of unmarried women living on their own. Although polygamy was relatively rare among the well-educated urban Kuwaitis, there were indications that it had increased with affluence among the less-educated non-urban Kuwaitis.[21] The trend here was for men to marry foreign (mostly Arab) women and to bring them back to live in Kuwait. The 1989 proposal by the immigration authorities to curtail the delivery of entry visas to foreign wives was an attempt to curb this development.

Legally, the Kuwaiti woman was under the tutelage of her father or husband, who often had the practical guardianship of her worldly possessions (Rumaihi 1986). Mohammed Rumaihi, a Kuwaiti sociologist, claims that "generally speaking, women are still considered the private property of men" (Rumaihi 1986:114). Not all Kuwaiti women viewed the problems arising in connection with polygamy and divorce in the same way. Typically, the fear of polygamy and divorce was more explicit among the less-affluent women, on whom economic constraints were greatest. Upper-class women enjoyed the protection of their families. As mentioned, polygamy was relatively rare among this class and so was divorce. It was also here that the practice of endogamy (especially marriage between cousins) had been most resilient. In such marriages, women usually enjoyed a greater security: kinship relationships and the pressure of the kin group constituted a guarantee that the husband would carry out his duties vis-à-vis his wife and children. Among the upper class, concern for the name of the family usually led the husbands to act correctly and even generously toward their wives, regardless of whether they were related to them through blood or not. The same concerns usually also led these men to "marry Kuwaiti," unlike men with less prominent backgrounds. Even when she married outside her kin group, and especially if she married below her rank, the status of the wealthy woman's family often provided her with considerable respect and protection. In case of divorce, an upper-class woman had her family to return to, and usually her own personal fortune to support her. In fact it seldom took long before these more privileged women remarried.

For these reasons, the politically minded women of the upper class had seldom bothered to challenge the content of the Family Law and the current state of affairs. The "inconveniences" of the present legal system seemed as irrelevant to their lives as the suffrage did to the less privileged women. Yet, even though they were separated by different class positions and different life experiences, Kuwaiti women shared the privilege of citizenship, which both groups exercised over the expatriates. Deference, the material and non-material benefits of the right to sponsorship and, generally speaking, access to all that was withheld by law or custom from the non-Kuwaitis created a bond not so much *between* them as *in contradistinction to* the expatriates. This was a fragile bond inasmuch as it glossed over the cracks and differences rather than narrowing and solving them. But within the Kuwaiti context, and as long as the politics of citizenship remained firmly associated with ethnic stratification, the class dimension was subordinated to that of national identity.

Women as Nation-Builders

Given the differential distribution of political rights between the sexes, one can raise the questions of whether women and men participated equally in the national project and whether ethnic consciousness impinged differently on their participation. Sylvia Walby writes:

> Different genders (and classes) may . . . be differentially enthusiastic about "the" ostensible ethnic/national project, depending upon the extent to which they agree with the priorities of "their" political "leaders." It may be that there is unanimity on "the" ethnic/national project by members of both genders and all social classes, but this is unlikely, and at least it is a question to be investigated. (1992:84)

Walby's own answer to this query is that, considering the varying positions of women and men, one may have to think not in terms of different participation in one project but in terms of different projects altogether. Yuval-Davis and Anthias (1989) have a more cautious answer: women and men are engaged in the common national project, but women's engagement is sometimes voluntary, sometimes coerced, and sometimes passive.

In the case at hand, the national project was the building of a modern national identity. As with most other new states in the Third World, the Kuwaitis were faced with a pressing dual task: first, to build an image of Kuwait and its people for the benefit of the international community, or what one could call "flag-waving" nation-building; and, secondly, to instill in the citizens a feeling of loyalty to the state and a sense of shared commonality, what one could call "heart-and-mind" nation-building. These were distinct but related processes, which relied equally, although in different ways, on affluence and the presence of the migrant workers.

Of the two, "flag-waving" nation-building was the easiest to achieve: its main ingredients, here as elsewhere, were the three institutions of census, map, and museum (Anderson 1993), whereby the Kuwaitis classified their population, delimited the territory under their rule, and substantiated their cultural legitimacy. As can be seen from the discussion about the *bidoons* in Chapter 3 and their inclusion, until 1986, in the category

"Kuwaiti" both for population and labor force purposes, censuses played a particularly crucial role in Kuwait's self-presentation to the outside world. Another important instrument was the selection of facts and events to be officially recorded as the history of the country. Until the early 1960s, for instance, the contribution of Palestinians to the building of Kuwait was officially and gratefully acknowledged by the authorities (Ghabra 1987). After the 1973 oil boom, however, this public recognition became much less frequent, and, by the late 1980s, the ordinary Kuwaiti men and women had an understanding of labor importation by their country as a much needed boon for the workers rather than anything else. The expatriate presence in Kuwait was consistently recorded as a problem rather than a positive contribution, or it was not recorded at all. The purpose was to present an image of Kuwait as a truly Kuwaiti country. The task of "flag-waving" nation-building was much facilitated in Kuwait by the presence of a modern and affluent society, the jewel in its crown being its welfare system. The country was also known for the judicious use of its oil money, featuring, in particular, wise financial investments, a willingness to emphasize health and education at the expense of armaments,[22] the creation of a Fund for Future Generations in preparation for the days when the oil wells run dry,[23] and a generous commitment to foreign aid in the Middle East, Africa, and Asia.[24] These features contributed to projecting a positive image of the country abroad, which encouraged the Kuwaitis to identify with it.

"Heart-and-mind" nation-building is generally a more difficult and subtle task than "flag-waving" nation-building, although strategies to achieve the latter to a certain extent also achieve the former. Experts on nation and nationalism have stressed the importance of the institutions through which the body of orthodox knowledge is instilled in the young members of the nation, thereby laying the foundation for deep-seated cultural and national identification. Among these institutions are the family (Gaitskell and Unterhalter 1989) and the standardized public education system (A. Smith 1991). In Kuwait, the school was considered a weak link in the institutional chain of socialization owing to the predominance of expatriates among the teachers.[25] Many Kuwaitis were realistically aware that there was no reason for Palestinian, Egyptian, and other Arab expatriate teachers to be motivated to instill nationalist feelings in their Kuwaiti pupils. This left most of the burden of socializing the young citizens on the family, in particular on the mother. She was greatly helped in her task by the plural situation in the country. At the same time as affluence and the state's protective paternalism discouraged the Kuwaitis from seeking other forms of large-scale identification than national identification—tribal identity, for instance, had been systematically undermined for the benefit of family and national identification (Al Haddad 1981)—the pervasiveness of practices reflecting strict ethnic stratification convinced Kuwaiti children of their natural superiority. The combined effect of growing up at the top of the hierarchy and being an ethnic minority considerably sharpened the young citizens' allegiance to the national project, especially if they had been brought up at home to value their cultural tradition.

The stakes in this ethnic/national project were as high for Kuwaiti women as they were for Kuwaiti men, if not higher. Indeed, while a Kuwaiti man could marry a foreign woman without losing any of his citizenship rights and privileges, a Kuwaiti woman who married a non-Kuwaiti man immediately lost her right to housing and, if she was poor, to social assistance. Prior to 1980 she was also required to take her husband's nationality if the law of his country permitted. This decision, however, was reversed in 1980 by an amendment allowing her to retain her citizenship and even providing for women who had previously lost their citizenship through marriage to have it restored if they lived in Kuwait.[26] A woman's non-Kuwaiti husband and their children always remained foreigners, whereas the non-Kuwaiti wife of a man could become naturalized and their children had the right to citizenship by birth. The notion of citizenship and, by implication, of the nation in Kuwait rested on a patriarchal definition of the relations between men and women. According to this definition, men could, if they would, enlarge the Kuwaiti nation by incorporating into it foreign women through marriage and by fathering these women's children. Women, on the other hand, could only do so through having children with Kuwaiti men. While the majority of Kuwaiti men rejected the liberalization of the Nationality Law for fear of having to share their exclusive political, social, and economic privileges, it was first and foremost the male foreign candidates they had in mind, not the female ones. In most cases, naturalization of foreign men was a theoretical notion, whereas that of foreign women had always been a reality. Statistics show that the number of marriages contracted between Kuwaiti men and foreign women has been increasing slowly but steadily throughout the 1980s, reaching the number of 1034 in 1988 (Table 7.2), while there were only 550 registered marriages between Kuwaiti women and foreign men (most of

TABLE 7.2 Number of Marriages Between Kuwaiti Men and Foreign
Women, by Wife's Nationality

Wife's Nationality	1984	1988
Arab	786	900
Asian	120	97
African	-	3
European	18	17
American	8	17
Total	932	1034

Source: Kuwait, *Annual Statistical Abstract,* 1989.

them *bidoons*) in the same year. The bias in favor of Kuwaiti men compared to Kuwaiti women in the Family Law and the Nationality Law
contributed to making ethnic pluralism particularly threatening to
women. To the extent that nation-building was a project that aimed at
keeping "Kuwait to the Kuwaitis,"[27] women were the most committed
participants in it.

Motherhood had been the unanimous rallying cry since the 1970s. Its
appeal to men lay in its instrumentality in curbing the effects of modernization upon women's lives (freedom of movement, education, work). Its
appeal to women lay in its ability to reinforce the legitimacy of their
position within Kuwaiti society, against the intrusion of alien elements.
In other words, the discourse of motherhood regulated the impact of both
change (in the women's opportunities) and continuity (in the men's
prerogatives), while, at the same time, it served the demographic needs
of the country.

Change and Continuity: The Shifting Sands of Modernity

Obviously, to claim that the material and cultural spheres of social life
in Kuwait (or anywhere for that matter) were so dichotomous that the
one could undergo change while the other remained unperturbed (the
plus-ça-change-plus-c'est-la-même-chose approach) is theoretically un-
tenable and, in the light of empirical data, plainly wrong. The question is,
therefore, not whether or not change in the material living conditions had
affected social relations and cultural meaning. Rather the question is:

what is the dialectic between change and continuity in a social context such as Kuwait's, where modernization unfolded under conditions of affluence and ethnic imbalance? The focus of the discussion in this chapter has been gender relations between Kuwaiti women and Kuwaiti men. Naturally, these relations cannot be divorced from those between Kuwaitis and non-Kuwaitis. Given the rapidity and pervasiveness of modernization in Kuwait and the relatively liberal policy of the state in matters of female education and physical mobility, one could have expected the eruption of sharp conflicts between men and women.[28] I have tried to show that any disruptive consequences had so far been relatively limited for two main reasons.

First of all, in the very process of modernization, achieved through importation of migrant labor, was an in-built mechanism that prevented its spread beyond a certain danger threshold, namely, where female actors begin to question the basis of the hegemony of their men over them. This mechanism was the cultural awareness that went hand in hand with ethnic pluralization. The larger the presence of the migrants, the more acute the Kuwaitis', in particular the women's, awareness of their cultural identity and social position. One can also add: the more they embraced and internalized their cultural identity and social position as these were reflected through interaction with the expatriates, the more the Kuwaitis needed these expatriates in order to reproduce both identity and position. Ethnic imbalance and minority position inevitably colored and shaped the Kuwaitis' experience of change, leading them to assess each turn of events in terms of their position relative to that of the expatriates. Thus the increasing presence of the expatriates and their depreciated status relative to the Kuwaitis caused native women to distance themselves from the opportunities that modernity offered in order to crystalize their own ethnic identification.

The other factor that motivated a retreat back into the fold of tradition and away from potentially disruptive innovations must be analyzed against the backdrop of the state's circumscription of female sexuality through the legislation on family and citizenship. As far as Kuwaiti women are concerned, the enjoyment of the social rights attached to Kuwaiti citizenship was contingent not only upon their ethnic origin but also on their sexual allegiance. Whom they married and whose children they bore were essential elements in their continued full-fledged membership in the Kuwaiti community. Insofar as the native minority perceived the non-Kuwaiti majority as a threat, this perception was particularly sharp among Kuwaiti women whose position depended on the continued existence of an ethnically bounded Kuwaiti nation with themselves as gatekeepers. We are not witnessing the mere replication of the old traditional pattern of social confinement and motherhood. Besides being voluntarily embraced, the return to tradition unfolded within a context of greater education, information, and social participation. One can assume that, under these circumstances, women's consciousness was also undergoing gradual change.

Objectively, motherhood still ensured the reproduction of patriarchy, both in its private and its public form.[29] If a great many women, including those with higher education, were quick to respond to its discourse, it was because "motherhood" in the present Kuwaiti context had developed well beyond the traditional understanding of the concept. It implied much more than the mere biological reproduction of a new generation. Even though giving birth to children was important (but we have seen that Kuwaiti women were replaceable here), a much more important task, it was often said, was bringring them up to be *real* Kuwaitis. It was felt by many that, with their education and their other newly acquired skills, today's young women were well groomed to be the enlightened vessels of a morality centered around values and practices associated with contemporary Kuwaiti culture as opposed to expatriate cultures. At stake was the reproduction not only of a population but a nation and its tradition. In this light, motherhood had an unmistakably political character, and Kuwaiti women were called upon to act as nation-builders. Here, it is not a case of *"plus ça change, plus c'est la même chose."* Rather, it is a case of "the more things remained the same, the more they changed" (Sahlins 1985:144). As vessels of morality and nation-builders, however, the Kuwaiti women's room for maneuver to achieve greater equality with Kuwaiti men was severely restricted. They could not be good mothers and upholders of tradition and morality *and* at the same time openly question the family and personal status laws, the sole area in which the *shari`a* was implemented, in the otherwise secularized national legislation (inspired, as in Egypt and Iraq, by the Code Napoléon). It was one thing, for example, to challenge the Election Law, a man-made code, but quite another to question the *shari`a*. Such an act would have been tantamount to denial of Kuwaiti identity and betrayal of Kuwait's efforts at nation-building.

For the Kuwaitis, modernization, indeed, held promises of "adventure, power, joy and growth" (Berman 1988). But it also contained seeds of cultural disruption in the form of massive labor immigration and rapid modernization. Paradoxically, it was the same massive expatriate presence that had contributed most to the preservation of Kuwaiti tradition: in their attempt to shield themselves from the alien influence and protect their national privileges, the Kuwaitis had systematically worked at maintaining and refining all that could serve as distinctive ethnic markers in contrast to the non-Kuwaitis. In coping with the vast change entailed by the modern oil economy, they had turned national identity into a unifying ideology, thereby recuperating, (re)inventing, and (re)interpreting their tradition, and thus precipitating the process that I have called "heart-and-mind" nation-building. In this process, Kuwaiti women played a central role.

Notes

1. Since 1991, there has been another watershed event between "before" and "after", namely *al ghazu* or the invasion (by Iraq).

2. What these expatriates used to say was that "before, the Kuwaitis were not so distant," or "in the good old days, my sponsor and I had a more relaxed relationship." Another major difference between "before" and "now" (the late 1980s) was that the level of earnings for practically all non-Kuwaitis had decreased considerably: a job in Kuwait no longer meant a guaranteed way of becoming rich.

3. In the wake of oil, the outlook of the emirate had changed beyond recognition. In the 1950s, practically the whole town was torn down and rebuilt. The modern houses and large avenues that one can see today throughout the Gulf region strike any observer familiar with the Middle East as being peculiarly Western. In Kuwait today, only a few houses and mosques are left that give the population an idea of what Kuwait must have been once.

4. After the war, in 1991, Kuwait appointed its first woman ambassador.

5. Although women are allowed to drive in all the Gulf countries, except Saudi Arabia, it is in Kuwait and Bahrain that the practice seems to be most widespread.

6. In such situations, female drivers in Kuwait merely remained seated in their cars, knowing that help would be immediately forthcoming. Male drivers never let a female driver remain stranded and would do anything to save her from the embarrassment of having to stand on the roadside.

7. When Iraq invaded Kuwait, women whose husbands had been arrested or killed took the decision and the responsibility on their own to drive to Saudi Arabia with their children and household. The Saudi border authorities, as an exception, allowed them to drive to their destination in Saudi Arabia. It was,

among other things, the sight of these female drivers on their television screens that sparked the (unsuccessful) campaign by some Saudi women for the abolition of the ban against female driving in their country.

8. Picking at random an issue of the *Arab Times* dated November 24, 1988, one can read that 244 persons were killed and 91 hurt in traffic accidents in the emirate during the first eight months of the same year.

9. *Arab Times*, April 8, 1989.

10. Interview with the head of the Zakat House in Kuwait November 19, 1988. In addition, I refer to the information sheet of the Committee for the Support of the Stateless. According to the Committee, prior to 1986 *bidoons* were treated practically as nationals (as regards the basic rights to education, healthcare, and work), although, whenever there was the choice between a Kuwaiti and a *bidoon*, priority was, as a matter of course, given to the former. The *bidoons* I have spoken to used to feel a close identity with the Kuwaitis, and, before the war, would only in exceptional occasions publicly acknowledge their status as stateless.

11. In 1989, for example, Kuwait's per capita income was US$16,150.

12. I have never heard medical doctors, lawyers, high-level bureaucrats, or businesswomen make a similar comment about their jobs.

13. Ever since Kuwait University was opened in the early 1970s, its unsegregated campuses have been the object of a bitter social battle in which conservative forces, not least among the students themselves, were deeply engaged. If the liberals have had the upper hand so far, it was not because they were in the majority but because coeducation was the policy adhered to by the government. Demands for sexual segregation on the campuses grew stronger after the war. In late 1994, a motion to that effect by the Islamists was narrowly defeated in parliament by only one vote. This defeat was obtained thanks to the fact that cabinet ministers are also *ex officio* members of parliament; as such, their votes reflect the view of the government, not the opinion of the electorate, which, in any rate, had, until then, been restricted to first-category male Kuwaitis.

14. I have not had access to statistics on women's retirement for the period covered by this study. Data gathered after the war by the Women's Socio-Cultural Society indicate that in the early 1990s, Kuwaiti working women do tend to retire early: 30 percent do so as the result of pressure by their husbands while 20 percent retire because they are unhappy with the conditions at work, primarily discriminatory promotion practices in the system. Among those who do not retire early, there is a predominance of divorced and widowed women. Whether the absence of a husband means absence of pressure to retire or greater financial need is unclear. Personal communication by Ferial Al Fereh of the Society, May 1995.

15. In 1994, four months of leave with half pay were added to the two months with full pay.

16. Although it did often instill in many of them the habit of picking up in addition the "creolized" language consisting of elements of English, Arabic, and another Asian language, which the expatriate domestic workers developed in Kuwait.

17. Some villas may have up to three kitchens: one "tea kitchen" on the upper floor near the bedrooms, one so-called "breakfast" kitchen on the ground floor, and an "outside" kitchen near the maids' annex. It is this last kitchen that is used for cooking hot meals, in order to avoid food smell in the main house.

18. This latter argument, however, never carried much weight, as most Kuwaiti women disliked the idea of sending their toddlers to nursery schools, saying that if they had not had a nannie, they would have preferred to send them to a relative. The creation of nurseries to help working mothers has never enjoyed any priority in this otherwise welfare-minded society.

19. A population study by the Ministry of Planning (*Arab Times*, September 19, 1989) reported that 35.3 percent of Kuwaiti families consisted of more than ten members.

20. Even in the late 1980s, few Kuwaiti women attended university abroad. Those who did were practically always married and were accompanied by their husbands, who were usually students themselves.

21. Official statistics are, unfortunately, not available.

22. Since the Iraqi invasion, this priority seems to have changed.

23. Almost 70 percent of the country's income derived from its financial investments around the world went to the Fund. The Fund was practically exhausted in the war efforts of 1990–1992.

24. At its highest, an average of 6 percent of GNP yearly was earmarked for development aid.

25. According to the dean of the Faculty of Education, Kuwait University, in 1990 the teaching staffs of the government schools comprised a total of 11,859 Kuwaitis and 27,834 non-Kuwaitis (*Arab Times*, February 20, 1990).

26. I am grateful to Sharon Stanton Russell, who brought this information to my attention.

27. "*Al Kuwait li'l kuwaitiyyin*" is a popular slogan in Kuwait, used by various political groupings especially during electoral campaigns.

28. And between generations, social classes, etc., as well. Gender relations are but one of the many social cleavages affected by the turbulance of affluence, modernization, and ethnic pluralization.

29. For a detailed theoretical treatment of the two forms of patriarchy, see Walby 1990.

8

Pluralism and Integration

> *[E]ach historical system is some kind of* Gesellschaft *which gives rise to its own particular kinds of* Gemeinschaften . . .
> Immanuel Wallerstein

In his book *Disorientations* (1993), Peter Lienhardt wrote that he "had set out for Kuwait with the idea of studying a society that was changing, but it proved quite unexpectedly difficult to think of the local population of Kuwait, indigenous and immigrant, as anything coherent enough to be called a society." Lienhardt first visited the emirate in 1953, when Kuwait bore all the marks of a boom town, and the new oil industry attracted a mixed crowd of exiles and adventurers. More than thirty years later, an independent country with a strict immigration policy, Kuwait still puzzles, and the question of what kind of society natives and migrants form is still relevant.

When the news of the Iraqi invasion broke on August 2, 1990, some Western observers saw in the event the end of what had been known, rather euphemistically, they thought, as "Kuwaiti society." They predicted that the non-Kuwaiti population was going to side with the Iraqis: considering the way the Kuwaitis had been treating their migrant workers, it was claimed, the migrants were bound to see the Iraqis as liberators. This contention betrayed a tendency among analysts to fail to regard migrant workers as active and conscious agents for whom migration was a planned, rational project and whose major purpose in life was to see it through. They seemed, rather, to picture them as hapless men and women who had, unknowingly, gotten themselves into a predicament from which the only exit was through the benevolent intervention of external powers. As it turned out, the invasion did not give rise to outbursts of relief among the rightless, "alienated" migrants, as many had expected.

223

On the contrary, it was viewed by the majority of them as a personal dis-aster—a view also shared by the Kuwaitis, but for different reasons. Far from siding with the Iraqis, many non-Kuwaitis showed solidarity with the besieged Kuwaitis and helped them survive under the occupation; some of them, like Nabil, even incurred risks to help the natives resist the occupying power. For the first time, natives and migrants seemed clearly united in a common project: to return the country to its *status quo ante*.

The present study has been an attempt to understand how this plural society, built on exclusion and dominance, had come to acquire a social viability in which not only the dominant groups but also the subordinate ones actively participated. What happened during the war in Kuwait lay bare the complexities of such phenomena as migration, social change, and identity-building. The case of Kuwait seems to indicate that, in our traditional ways of thinking about relations of power and subordination, we may have neglected to explore certain facets of the interplay between human agency and the prevailing structures of constraints and opportunities.

Considering explanations formulated in purely economic terms to be unsatisfactory, I have sought to illuminate the case at hand with data of a cultural character. "Cultural" is to be understood as "related to meaning." Meaning arises partly from the tradition in which actors have been brought up, the set of prior understandings with which they come to their action, and partly from their daily encounter with material circumstances and concrete life situations in the real world "out there" (Roseberry 1992). There is a constant dialectic between prior understandings and daily encounters with reality, the former informing the latter, and the latter feeding back into the former. Sometimes these encounters conform to, and confirm, prior understandings. More often than not, the two con-flict with each other, and life circumstances usually force actors to recon-sider their prior understandings. Sometimes again, instead of correcting or redefining these understandings, actors pragmatically "bracket" them and adopt a situational behavior that suits the prevailing circumstances. This situation is most commonly found among subordinate ethnic groups, especially in plural societies of the Kuwaiti type, where exclu-sion is accompanied by the complete dominance of one ethnic commun-ity over the others.

Integration in Plural Societies

In Chapter 1, I stated that my use of pluralism is more narrow and specific than the ones found in the works of Furnivall (1942, 1948) and M. G. Smith (1960; 1969a; 1969b). My redefinition of the plural society arises from the view that all societies are more or less differentiated. I have, therefore, suggested that the term be kept for situations in which ethnic differentiation results from the connection between actors' practice and an official ideology. Granted that differentiation will always be present in any social aggregates, the question is how the power elite deals with it, why it chooses one strategy (for instance, exclusion) rather than another (for instance, inclusion), and what consequences the decision has on the dynamics of social life. My working hypothesis, inspired by the literature on the controversy over the concept of the plural society (Kuper and Smith 1969; Rubin 1960), and particularly by Zubaida's work (1989), has been that daily social interaction everywhere gives rise to a degree of cultural commonality across ethnic and other boundaries. What needs to be identified is the type and level of commonality and how it relates to the state of pluralism.

As it is used here, the notion of integration refers primarily to the production and reproduction of cultural (i.e., meaning-related) commonality in the face of initial material and/or structural impediments. It is clear from this definition and from the above reference to Zubaida's work that my interest is in the *diachronic* rather than the *synchronic* approach to integration. While the synchronic perspective is mainly concerned with the mutual fitting of the society's constitutive parts and their interplay here and now, the diachronic perspective is concerned with the effect of interaction through time on the state of actors' social relations and worldviews and on the system as a whole. Although this perspective takes into account the organizational framework of social action, it is not content to do just that. For my purposes, the advantage of the diachronic perspective is that it also necessarily addresses issues lying *outside* this framework, more directly related to the interplay between agency and structure. A society may be organized according to a given pattern (for instance, exclusion) here and now, but this pattern is never fixed; it is always open to diverse contingencies, the most important of them being human action. Only through a diachronic perspective can we fully assess the variations engendered by human action. I will return to this important point in more detail later.

Socio-cultural integration in rigidly stratified and differentiated societies is an intellectual challenge to social scientists because of our conceptualization of society as an essentially cohesive phenomenon. Whether
cohesion is consensual (liberal sociology) or imposed (Marxist sociology) depends on the theoretical inclination of the individual scientist,
but the general assumption is that members of a society share, in various
degrees, a minimum number of common values and a common discourse
(Aberle et al. 1950; Durkheim 1985; Parsons 1967; Simmel 1971). How
justified we are in speaking of societal cohesion as a form of integration
remains a subject of controversy. Considering the positive connotation
attached to the concept of integration, the connection between the two
seems to depend mainly on what we posit as the source of cohesion: succinctly, and pending further discussion below, we may say that it is consensual cohesion rather than imposed cohesion that entitles us to speak of
integration.

The skepticism with which M. G. Smith's theory of pluralism was
received in the 1960s is due precisely to his claim that cultural commonality does not exist in the so-called plural societies whose various
components, he contended, were held together through force. Such a
claim seriously questions one of the most widely accepted postulates in
the social sciences, in the light of which integration in a plural society
seems to be a contradiction in terms. Leo Kuper (1969:462) adequately
sums up the problem with the following question: "Indeed, if [these
societies] are plural, can they be societies?"

Integration, Coercion, and Material Interests

When we speak of integration in the context of migration and ethnic
and minority relations, the term carries a positive moral undertone. It is
commonly opposed to "assimilation" which is often negatively loaded.
Assimilation, at best, means the slow absorption of the minority into the
majority and, at worst, its elimination as a minority (Simpson and Yinger
1986): it is an event that unambiguously takes place on the terms of the
dominant population. An "assimilationist policy," for example, implies
the use of coercive action. "Integration," on the other hand, is a more
subtle term. It is understood to involve the idea of a willing communal
inclusion, a mutual *rapprochement* between majority and minority. As a
condition for harmonious social balance, integration, in theory, rests on
the spontaneous embrace of shared values and beliefs, translated

through the adoption of common behavior and the use of common symbols. In other words, it is ideally assumed that integration can neither be brought about by coercion, nor rest exclusively on material interests; hence Furnivall's and Smith's efforts at elaborating an analytical model specific to their "plural societies"—since what made the components of these societies cohere was, according to the former, material interests, or, according to the latter, coercion.

If the ideal assumptions about the nature of integration are never perfectly realized anywhere, they seem to fare particularly badly in the case of Kuwait. The emirate's skewed demographic structure and the politics of dominance and exclusion carried out towards the migrants have led many observers to predict the imminent breakdown of Kuwaiti society ever since the country's independence in 1961. Yet, until August 1990, Kuwait had shown a remarkable stability, and two years after the devastation of the Iraqi invasion, it seemed to have gone back to being its old self.

Stability, in this case, has often and widely been explained by reference to the combination of use of force and material interests, an explanation that can hardly be disputed. Through the scrutiny of the politics of exclusion and the structure of dominance, this study is yet another confirmation of this viewpoint and of the contentions by Furnivall and Smith. Where I depart from the coercion-and-material-interests approach is in my argument that, although these variables were undoubtedly instrumental in holding the various segments of the population in Kuwait together and achieving societal cohesion of a sort, to claim that nothing but coercion and material interests were involved would be more to beg the question than to illuminate. It would mean that the analysis is built on the assumption that human actors are automatons steered by fear and material needs, and, more important still, it ignores the indisputable fact that, for several decades, labor migration to Kuwait had been a phenomenon consciously willed and planned by the migrants. My data on social life in Kuwait have convinced me that not to bring the analysis beyond the argument of external constraints would be to fail to capture the situation in all its complexity. As a result, the picture might correspond more to a construction by the observer than to the situation as experienced by most actors. The question is: what other factors function as "social cement" in this plural society?

What Kind of Commonality?

Many anthropologists start their fieldwork expecting to find a more or less unified configuration called "Samoan culture," "Javanese culture," or whatever "culture" they have set out to study. It is usually during fieldwork that they discover how tenuous cultural unity can turn out to be at close quarters. In Kuwait diversity was the starting point, both for actors and for observers. As a student of this society, I had been warned by the literature and population statistics about the serious demographic imbalance of the emirate; cultural unity, beyond the small circle of Kuwaiti citizens, was the last thing I had expected to find. And indeed, diversity was what one could see, hear, and experience everywhere, all the more so as difference, not only between Kuwaitis and non-Kuwaitis but also among the expatriates themselves, was freely emphasized rather than glossed over in official discourse as well as private practice. Yet, the more I came to know Kuwait, the more I became aware of certain recurrent patterns of meaning and action among the population that gave a distinctive character to social life in the emirate.[1] The reason this commonality was difficult to capture was because its form and content differed from what one usually finds in less diversified, more conventional societies.

It is a commonly accepted view that what binds the members of a society together is a set of elements that Marxists subsume under the term "ideology" and anthropologists, in general, under the term "culture": values and beliefs that inform action and are related, in a causative or consequence-like manner (depending on the theoretical orientations of the researcher), to the surrounding material conditions. A major difficulty with this assumption is how to explain that people who are differently positioned subscribe to the same set of values and beliefs. This is a problem that has greatly preoccupied anthropologists confronted with social systems where inequality and stratification are pronounced features.

Among India experts, for example, a familiar discussion concerns the degree to which Untouchables espouse the view that the high castes have of them as ritually inferior and polluted. Some scholars claim that Untouchables fully share the values and beliefs of the other castes and do not have a separate subculture:

> The view "from the bottom" is based on the same principles and evaluations as "the view from the middle" or "the view from the top." The cultural system of Indian Untouchables does not distinctively question or revalue

the dominant social order. Rather, it continuously recreates among Untouchables a microcosm of the larger system. (Moffat 1979:3)

Moffat's argument rests on his observation of the "replicatory" principle, or the constant tendency for the Untouchables whom he studied to reproduce among themselves the same hierarchies and the same cults common in Indian society at large. Whenever they were not allowed to participate in a ritual with the other villagers, they would carry out a parallel ritual among themselves. Moffat concludes that the response of his Untouchable villagers to exclusion is replication, which he takes as evidence of cultural consensus.

From the point of view of exclusion as a social ideology, one could trace a parallel between these Untouchables and non-Kuwaiti migrants in Kuwait. Keeping in mind all the reservations such a parallel calls for, we may raise the question of whether replication also existed in Kuwait, and, if so, whether it was evidence of cultural consensus or of "integration."

In Kuwait, ethnic relations were the area where explicit standards for social discrimination were produced and enacted; as such, they played the role that ritual life plays in India. It is, therefore, to relations between ethnic categories that we must turn to see whether non-Kuwaitis replicated the Kuwaitis' conceptualizations, discourses, and behaviors. We have seen that Kuwaitis classified the population roughly into three categories, expressed in the form of dichotomies: Kuwaiti–non-Kuwaiti, Arab–non-Arab, and Muslim–non-Muslim. This classificatory scheme was common knowledge, and the expatriates, likewise, made use of it in their mutual interaction. Can we claim that this is an example of replication? If so, can it be taken as evidence of consensus? and consensus of what?

Let us consider the Kuwaiti–non-Kuwaiti dichotomy. The official Kuwaiti discourse and much of daily practice stressed the social superiority of the natives over the migrants. As we have seen, not only Kuwaitis, but also non-Kuwaitis actively contributed to upholding this stratification through their docile and deferential attitude. Likewise, Kuwaitis operated an informal classification of the expatriates: Arabs were "better" than Asians, Palestinians had a higher status than Egyptians, and so on. We could find the same attitude among the expatriates themselves, and while the "lower" ethnic categories certainly did not agree with the way they were characterized by the others, they often admitted that, objectively speaking, they were the underdogs in the social hierarchy. There is little doubt that non-Kuwaitis subscribed to the native ranking pattern. If we admit that there was "replication" of a kind at this level, and that underlying this replication was a general consensus, we have to ask what exactly it was that people were agreed upon. The answer is obvious: the only point of agreement between the various ethnic groups was the objective state of the labor market. Indeed, it was a matter of common knowledge that Arabs were better paid than Asians and that Palestinians, as a rule, held better jobs than Egyptians; if they did the same work, it was well-known that Palestinians were often paid higher salaries. As a result, Palestinians enjoyed a higher social status, which they carefully nurtured through a narrowing down of their social networks and by strictly holding on to group endogamy, two strategies that were the hallmarks of the Kuwaitis themselves.

In this light, it is appropriate to ask whether the ethnic communities that were positioned closer to the Kuwaitis on the social ladder tended to replicate the native pattern of behavior. Indeed, the middle-class expatriates, whether Arabs or South Asians, not only adopted the same exclusionary attitude toward all those whom they considered to be socially inferior to themselves but also held closely to the traditional distribution of gender roles. This was particularly evident among the Arabs. We have seen, for instance, that Asian women in Kuwait generally participated more actively in the work force than Arab women, many of whom were in the emirate as dependents. However, it is difficult to claim that what the middle-class expatriates, Arabs and non-Arabs, did was to reproduce the Kuwaitis' system of moral values. It may be more correct to interpret their behavior in terms of a class culture, common to many parts of the world, and certainly widespread in the Middle East and Asia, according to which higher social status, as a rule, entails a more severe circumscription of the women's lives, and their productive and reproductive activities.[2] If this circumscription seemed particularly developed in Kuwait, it was because of the exceptionally close connection between a person's ethnic, social, and moral identity and the position he or she occupied on either side of the line that separated the population into a closed ruling class and an open working class. Inasmuch as there were unified patterns of behavior between natives and migrants, they were more likely to be inspired by class concerns commonly articulated around the concrete situation prevailing in the labor market than by attempts by the subordinate migrant groups to reproduce the culture of the dominant native group.

The (labor) market played a crucial role in this plural society—as Furnivall rightly insists that it did in the European tropical colonies. But because he assumes (with much distaste) that social life under such conditions was bound to be "uncivilized" (1948:310), Furnivall does not pay attention to the cultural commonality that arose among the inhabitants from their involvement in the same market. In Kuwait there was not, strictly speaking, replication in the way Moffat (1979) claims there was among Untouchables in Southern India. As a matter of fact, each group was indifferent to the social worldviews of the others. Since they did not share a common language, each ethnic group was usually incompletely informed about, or ignorant of, the others' representations. If the expatriates subscribed to the Kuwaitis' dichotomies, it was because these affected them directly, in pragmatic terms of jobs, salaries, and adaptation. They were not interested in them as ideas and beliefs to be replicated because of their intrinsic value, but as a guide to a local social organization into which they had to fit and in terms of which they had to function.

It was not Kuwaiti cultural hegemony but the objective configurations of the labor market and the actual ethnic division of labor in the public, private, and "domestic" sectors that were instrumental in instilling in the expatriate population stereotypical characterizations of the various ethnic communities. Through daily repetition, this pragmatically acquired knowledge engendered a discourse that was accessible to, and shared by, all those who participated in social life in Kuwait, regardless of their ethnic and class origins. Like the practice of the *kafala* (sponsorship system) and its implications, the details of ethnic stratification had become an integral element in the social knowledge shared by the inhabitants of the emirate, a knowledge that was neither purely Kuwaiti nor purely imported, but a genuine product of Kuwait's prevailing plural situation.

I have argued that, between the non-Kuwaitis themselves, this commonality, in the light of which national and ethnic particularities seemed to be variables with no major consequences, existed at the level of dispositions, hopes, aspirations, concerns, and life-strategies. Inspired, strengthened, and reproduced by the dynamics of migration, it formed the basis for distinct patterns of behavior and meaning that facilitated the actors' practical purposes of communication and interaction across the many cultural divides. A typical feature of this commonality was its expression at the level of action rather than of discourse. Work and consumption were two cases in point.

In any "conventional" society, for example Norway, people view work in various ways: for some, work has an intrinsic value, as a means of human and moral advancement; for others, it is merely a way of making a living, sometimes drudgery, or it is a status marker and an instrument for social mobility; for yet others, it may be a combination of all these. We find the same variation regarding consumption patterns: some Norwegians save scrupulously for retirement; others spend on cars, boats, and trips abroad; others again prefer to buy shares or give to charity. Objectively speaking, what make these different individuals with their diverse outlooks on life and different behaviors fall under the unifying category of "Norwegians" are mainly a common language, common social and political institutions, and an official history attached to a common territory.

The various expatriate communities in Kuwait shared no such "codified" commonalities. What they shared were the *other* things that Norwegians do not share: a common view of work not as a means of human development but as a means to achieve a specific goal; a will to earn and save money for remittances and delayed gratification; an almost desperate search for stability, without which their life-projects could not be realized; a belief in individual strategies, and, last but not least, a spatially and temporally based diversity of life-worlds. They also shared the fact that the meaning of the present, springing as it did from material constraints, or what Bhabha (1991) calls "memories of underdevelopment," was a function of their dreams about the future. There was undoubtedly a commonality of experiences among the non-Kuwaitis that, in a cumulative way, engendered mutually recognizable habitual dispositions.

If the cultural commonality among non-Kuwaitis found expression more in actors' practice than in their discourse, it was because of what one may describe as its quasi-illegitimate nature. With very few exceptions, this commonality was not acknowledged by the actors themselves and was veiled under a prevailing discourse of ethnic diversity and class differences. It was a tacit and unacknowledged "culture" based on situational and dispositional comparability rather than the conscious reproduction, through socialization and systematic education, of generally accepted norms and values. Because of the structural impediments imposed by migration and exclusion, the actors who participated in this "culture" did not have at their disposal an idiom, such as an accepted body of myths and rituals and an official history, through which to express and further develop their commonality. In other words, they lacked the ideological and rhetorical apparatus that accompanies the status of legitimate members in a social space where cultural commonality unfolds and that plays such a central role in reenforcing and accelerating the process of socio-cultural identification.

As a device to cement all the various societal components together, culture/ideology generally plays a limited role in a plural society. As I have argued in connection with my analysis of power, a society that openly builds on exclusion gives up recourse to symbolic constructions and cultural hegemony as instruments of generalized social action. Fragmentation in terms of languages, religions, private social practices, and the confinement of relations within separate social worlds, render practically impossible the establishment of a dominant ideology imposed on, or embraced by, the majority, let alone the whole population. Ideological elaborations are most likely to take place within, rather than across, ethnic communities, even if they often draw their most important raw material from the presence of the other segments of the population. The clearest example in the case at hand was the intense process of national identity-building among the Kuwaitis, in which the expatriate population represented the most important source of inspiration.

Subjective Integration: The Role of Experience

What the case of Kuwait shows is that while elaboration of commonality is a property of human action that even the most rigorous politics of exclusion cannot prevent from arising, it does not take on the same expression, nor is it perceived by actors in the same way, everywhere. There is a close interconnectedness between the nature of commonality, its perception by actors, and the organizational structure under which commonality arises. It is in this sense that I understand Wallerstein's argument for thinking of *Gemeinschaft* and *Gesellschaft* in more nuanced terms and not as opposite societal forms. As he formulates it:

> The premise of the vector of change was that we were going from *Gemeinschaft* to *Gesellschaft*. But perhaps it is rather that each historical system is some kind of *Gesellschaft* which gives rise to its own particular kinds of *Gemeinschaften*, and that the definition of *Gesellschaft*, that is, of the structure of an historical system, includes what kinds of cathectic groups, or *Gemeinschaften*, it permits, encourages, requires, creates. (1988:530–31)

In Kuwait, in accordance with the politics of exclusion, subjective integration could not proceed beyond the stage of implicitness: cultural commonality could be apprehended and expressed only along lines permitted by the politics of exclusion. In the context of a plural society based on an ideology of ethnic differentiation and ruled by a cultural minority that perceived itself to be threatened, integration is, by definition, a nontopic. The only way actors can be informed of its existence is through their own experience. "Experience," by which I mean the conscious engagement by actors with the material world and with events contextualized in time and space, is not a term commonly used in studies on integration. It refers to a different order of reality than, for instance, "consensus." Whereas consensus implies the notion of public collectivity, experience is conceived as something deeply personal. Whereas consensus is objective, or so it is commonly claimed, experience is subjective. Let us take a closer look at the two concepts.

In sociology/anthropology, consensus often refers to the fact that those who participate in a culture hold common values, beliefs, and attitudes. Unlike political consensus, the outcome of which is the delineation of an area of agreement, cultural consensus does not occur through a dialogical process between individuals and groups. To the extent that it results from a process, cultural consensus results from socialization, the complex succession of practices and events in which the individual is engaged and from which he or she emerges as a social person. The consensus that results from the process is, therefore, one internalized by actors around an area or set of items conceived to be part of the common-sense or "natural" world, what Bourdieu (1977) calls *doxa*. The wider the doxic field, the stronger consensus is, and the closer we come to socio-cultural integration.

It is difficult to contend that this type of consensus can be widespread in any large-scale, differentiated modern society, let alone a plural society. Here, the doxic field of unquestioned truth is drastically reduced, mainly because individuals and groups live in fragmented life-worlds. The notion of "life-world" is credited to Alfred Schutz and refers to "the total sphere of experience circumscribed by a natural environment, man-made objects, events, and other individuals" (Wuthnow et al. 1984:30). When people engage in interaction with one another, they do so as social persons or "inhabitants of life-worlds," with a cultural knowledge gathered through, and derived from, their unique experiences. Differentiation causes people to ask different questions and to hold to different truths.

On the other hand, as is clear from Wuthnow et al.'s definition of life-worlds, experience, however much a private construction, is communicable, since it does not arise in individual isolation but in the direct or indirect interface between conscious actors within a context of shared materiality. Experience is what makes actors feel that they "belong" or "do not belong" in a society, because only through experience can they grasp the meaning of sharing, which is a prerequisite for belonging. The subjective perception of social belonging is central to the way actors conceptualize integration. In both plural and other modern societies, to use the term "integration" in the sense of institutional homogenization and structural incorporation without taking into consideration the agency of the people to be integrated leads to a serious impoverishment of the concept. "Integration" is usually appropriated by the discourse of the power-holders—whether these are the state in relation to civil society, the "center" in relation to the "periphery," or the dominant ethnic group in relation to the subordinate ones. In most policy-oriented research on ethnic and majority/minority relations, "integration" is usually approached from the *insiders'* viewpoint, with the *outsiders* in the role of the entity to be integrated. Seen from the perspective of the authorities, integration is commonly understood as structural incorporation (granting of formal rights, attribution of collective duties, and so on), a political process connected with decisions that rest with the state, not the ordinary actors. This is not to say that structural incorporation in plural situations is of little significance. Structural incorporation, however, should be studied alongside another form of integration, one in which the initiative rests with groups and individuals. To explore this form, we need to ask what the concept of integration means to the men and women who belong among the outsiders. Seen from their viewpoint, integration implies the experience of being part of a common social space and a common public discourse that encompass and, in varying degrees, affect their life-worlds. Unlike structural incorporation, integration is thus actively mediated by the subject himself or herself: for instance, suffrage can be granted to a person or a group through structural incorporation, but without the contextualized performance of the act of voting it is unlikely that the new voters experience any real feeling of having become part of the social category known as enfranchised citizens. The feeling of belonging somewhere arises through activities performed, people encountered, events witnessed. One can claim that at the center of integration is the subjectivity of the active agent. This statement can be illustrated by a case reviewed in Chapter 5: when Nabil, the Palestian oil engineer, said about Kuwait that "this place means more to me than anywhere else," he was expressing a feeling that at the same time summed up his biography: he was born in Kuwait, grew up, and went to school there; key events of his life, such as his friendship with Fahad, his first job, his meeting with the woman who was to become his wife, the birth of his children, all took place within a social context identifiable with Kuwait. Events and contexts were thus inextricably related in Nabil's consciousness; by instilling in him a sense of belonging, lived and embodied in daily practice, they contributed to transforming his perception of Kuwait from being a geographical space to being a social place. Subjective integration does not mean that actors go through their experience as isolated individuals; external circumstances and their interpretation are constitutive elements in human experience. Thus Nabil's feeling of belonging vis-à-vis Kuwait developed not only in spite of the exclusion that characterized his situation as a Palestinian; rather, exclusion was an integral part of this feeling, which, as we have seen, was as ambivalent[3] as it was deep. Many expatriates lived and spoke of their situation in the emirate in a way that indicated that Kuwait was an integral part of their lives. Only a few, like Nabil, said so explicitly; the majority indicated this view through their action and implicit discourse, as when they dreaded the time of retirement, which meant that they would have to leave the emirate, or when Cora unexpectedly declared that she would have gladly stayed in Kuwait if she could, and when a host of others spoke of their impending departure but kept postponing it year after year.

What is unexpected in the case of Kuwait is that subjective integration among expatriates clearly took place in spite of their structural marginality and exclusion: they were virtually rightless, and had no access to real estate ownership and citizenship, or even to claims to more or less secured residence permits. Officially, their relationship with Kuwait was strictly contractual, based on the exchange of labor for wages. Any non-contractual ties were frowned upon; as proof of long-time residence, these ran counter to the principle of migrant transience, which was a cornerstone in the country's policy. In Kuwaiti eyes, therefore, expatriate non-contractual ties with the country were unwelcome and had, thus, to remain subdued and undercommunicated. Most unwanted, naturally, was integration between Kuwaitis and expatriates. It was feared that such an integration might be read as a signal of the dependence of the former on the latter and, through its potentially devastating consequences on the politics of exclusion, could directly threaten the cultural survival of the Kuwaiti nation.

Subjective integration was viewed no more positively by the migrants themselves; in fact, if they developed a sense of belonging in Kuwait it was more often than not reluctantly, as part of an unplanned twist in their lives. Both natives and migrants, therefore, held firmly to the common official discourse that stressed the economic reasons for the expatriates' presence in the emirate and undercommunicated any other reasons. Insofar as we look upon the subjective integration of non-Kuwaitis as a form of *Gemeinschaft*, as I think we are justified in doing, it was an unwilling *Gemeinschaft* that could only arise out of the historical system that was the Kuwaiti *Gesellschaft*, as Wallerstein rightly presumes.

What this *Gesellschaft* elicited and facilitated was subjective integration among the Kuwaiti citizens. The Kuwaitis derive their feeling of being a community from a common history in which the sense of being threatened—previously by desert raids, nowadays by alien migrants and predatory neighbors—has always been one of the major recurring themes. The overt politics of exclusion against the migrants, implemented through the rigid division of labor (Kuwaiti employers versus non-Kuwaiti employees) and the rhetoric of nationalism in the post-oil era, considerably strengthened this feeling. Whatever discontent arose from the perception of social discrepancies among Kuwaitis was held in check by the parallel perception of differentiation from the migrant workers.

The state, with its power of regulation and administration, plays, directly or indirectly, an important role in the emergence of subjective integration. I am not, therefore, claiming that structural incorporation (in which state initiatives are crucial) and subjective integration (most intimately related to individual experience) do not overlap empirically. We cannot, nevertheless, posit a one-to-one relationship between the two. If, in some cases, structural processes and subjective integration coincide, in others they show discrepancies: under specific conditions, we can have societies with advanced structural incorporation but relatively weak subjective integration and societies with advanced structural exclusion but a relatively strong subjective integration.

With their implicit claim to belonging in Kuwait, despite the ruthless official politics of exclusion, Nabil and the other expatriates seem to vindicate a postulate central to holistic theory, according to which human beings build their identities as they build society, and vice versa. What is interesting with the present case study is that this vindication has not been brought about in the way presumed in classic theory, namely, through the integration of parts into a whole, and the internalization by all members of dominant values and beliefs. It came about through many detours, some of them unabashedly individualistic. If society-making is the most essential human property, the case of Kuwait is an indication that, for an increasing number of people around the world, the circumstances under which society-making and identity-building take place have been undergoing dramatic changes in recent years as a result of increased physical mobility and the accelerated pace of change. We need to elaborate approaches that allow us to identify and analyze the problems this entails. I will conclude this study by pointing to what I consider to be an area of research in need of anthropological attention in the years ahead.

Toward an Anthropology of Deterritorialization

According to Appadurai (1991:191), there are "some brute facts about the world of the twentieth century that any ethnography must confront," the major one being the changing "landscapes of group identity." Increasingly, we are dealing with groups that are no longer "tightly territorialized, spatially bounded, historically unselfconscious, or culturally homogeneous." This situation has produced a type of cosmopolitanism that can be understood only through the study of "transnational cultural flows," which "defeat and confound many verities of the human sciences" (192).

The problems that Appadurai has identified are aptly illustrated by the data from Kuwait presented in this study. The case at hand brings into focus the need to rethink some basic assumptions in the discipline. Unlike most societies described in the classic literature, Kuwait presents us with a profoundly *disembedded* world, in which most of the population were migrants who refused to stay put, and blue-prints for living seemed to be curiously ad hoc, where the cultural construction of identity and belonging constantly challenged the logic of space and territoriality, and where all that was not affected by physical displacement seemed to be affected by the rush of time, through modernization. The order of this world does not impress us as *natural* and immutable; on the contrary, it strikes us as being essentially *constructed* and held together through the working of human devices—which, of course, all societies basically are.

I suggest that what Kuwait calls to mind is Benedict Anderson's (1993) phrase "imagined communities." Anderson uses "imagined communities" to describe nations because their members "will never know most of their fellow-members, meet them, or even hear of them, yet in the mind of each lives the image of their communities" (1993:6). Anderson's statement can be fruitfully extended beyond the context of nationalism and used to describe the kind of group-identity formation observed in Kuwait and elsewhere today.

In Kuwait, there are several ways in which we find ourselves dealing with "imagined communities." We can use the phrase, as Anderson does, to describe the process in which the Kuwaiti population was engaged as it tried to gather the various native elements together in an effort at nation-building. However, in this case, we need to stress the role of exclusion as much as inclusion in the emergence of the Kuwaiti "imagined community": by limiting the community to Kuwaitis only, the citizens overlooked the social presence of non-Kuwaitis and the product of their labor; they also denied that there was a fund of common experiences gathered by natives and migrants throughout the years. There were, for instance, few expatriate individuals or groups named in Kuwaiti history books and other records of Kuwaiti collective memory, such as songs, literature, or paintings. Such documents had only one message, namely, that Kuwait was a Kuwaiti country. When combined with the daily practice of ethnic distance and stratification, the omission of recording non-Kuwaiti presence at the level of public discourse contributed to making the migrants' social existence a blind spot in the Kuwaitis' perception of their history. Thus, if the image of the Kuwaiti community in the Kuwaitis' mind was more inclusive than the individual Kuwaiti would ever know, it was also more exclusive than he or she would ever be willing to acknowledge.

In the case of the migrants, "imagined communities" can be used in a different sense, more related to displacement and the notion of deterritorialization. Although it has been a constant feature of society throughout the ages, migration today seems to be taking on a new character: never have so many people traveled so far away from their homelands and at such an accelerated tempo. At the same time, never has the world in its entirety been so neatly divided into nation-states, the key to whose formal membership everywhere is citizenship. The fact that the simultaneous occurrence of international migration and nation-states gives rise to problems of ethnic and political character is becoming increasingly obvious. The potential for disruptions, meanwhile, is perhaps greatest in the nation-states created after World War II. Although relatively limited until recently, international labor migration to such countries has grown substantially in the past decades, triggered first by the oil boom in the Middle East, Nigeria, and Venezuela, then by economic development in the new industrializing countries of East Asia. Today, large movements of labor migration are likely to follow a South–South trajectory as much as a South–North one (Appleyard 1989). By introducing alien elements into the boundaries of the young nation-states, international migration seems set to disturb their fragile national identity—unless the alien presence is deliberately used to enhance internal fusion, which in practice means that, as in Kuwait, the native population opts for a plural society model based on an exclusionary ideology. If this scenario does gain momentum, we may witness not the disappearance but the reemergence of something akin to the old situation of pluralism, in which one community rules over the others, and ethnic groups "mix but do not combine."

Of particular interest for anthropologists is the question of the formation of group identity under conditions of migratory flux from one "imagined community" to another. We can no longer be content with treating international migration within the narrow synchronic framework of relations between ethnic groups and the struggle for scarce resources (jobs, social status, moral prestige). We must also be prepared to ask large questions about this large phenomenon, which encompasses people from a whole range of cultural traditions, and which gives rise to problems of identity and primordial loyalty. We need, above all, to recognize contemporary international migration for what it is: a process of deterritorialization in a world of nation-states and "mapped" societies (Gupta and Ferguson 1992). Such a recognition will allow us better to identify the problems that are peculiar to contemporary international migration compared to similar population movements in previous periods.

Most commonly found in the literature on globalization (Appadurai 1991; Robertson 1992), deterritorialization, when applied to human beings (rather than consumption, information, and investments, for instance) denotes more than physical disembeddedness. It also refers to what Michael Watts (1992:122) describes as problems arising from the existence of "multidimensional set(s) of radically discontinuous realities [where the] truth of the experience no longer coincides with the place in which it takes place." Prime instances of deterritorialization are found among people "out of place": immigrant minorities, labor migrants, refugees, and displaced persons of various diasporas, who gather at the margins and in the interstices of national societies. In their efforts at identity formation, these groups do not benefit from claims to a legitimate territory or an officially codified history. Confronted at every turn of life with dilemmas, contradictions, dissonance, and, possibly, exclusion, their social survival depends on their ability to *invent* "ad hoc" cultures. Being "out of place," they often develop a group identity the components of which are drawn from various "imagined communities"—the one to which they are said to belong but from which they are spatially cut off and the one that is at the center of their daily lives but with which they are not expected to identify. It is an identity shot through with "splintered fragments of desire, scattered packages of awareness, crumbs of contradictory wishes pulling this way and that . . ." (Shayegan 1992:150).

Deterritorialization gives rise to identities that are essentially modern, informed by acute historical consciousness and pervaded by attempts at reconciling time and space. Yet, the world in which these identities develop is anything but a "deterritorialized" world: on the contrary, Appadurai's "transnational cultural flows" are taking place in a world of bounded states more ordered and regulated than ever before. Although official efforts at controlling international labor migration, one of the main sources of deterritorialization, often seem unsuccessful, one can hardly deny that, except for a privileged minority, moving across borders, especially those between the Third World and the First World, is becoming more difficult by the day. Here, as in many areas of contemporary life, it is difficult for individual initiatives to escape the supervision and intervention of larger entities, the ultimate one being the state.

It is on the level of human experience that the criss-crossing of cultural life-worlds and the blending of time and space break up the standard pattern of boundaries and cast cultural certainties into a state of flux. It is in human subjectivities that deterritorialization causes "all that is solid [to] melt into air" (Marx, in Berman 1988). It is also in human subjectivities that air is tentatively given a new "solid" shape, for example, that of "imagined communities." An anthropology of deterritorialization is called for, one that looks into the complex dynamics between the growing "solidification" of the objective world and the increasing fluctuation of the subjective one.

Notes

1. In fact, the pattern was characteristic not only for Kuwait but also for the other small Gulf states of Qatar, Bahrain, and the United Arab Emirates, which exhibited similar features of labor importation from the same areas of the world, demographic imbalance, dominance, and exclusion.

2. One could also have recourse to the argument that, being Arabs, the Kuwaitis and the Middle Eastern expatriates share a common Islamic view of women's restricted participation in public life. If I am reluctant to use this argument it is because of the clear evidence that the extent to which Muslim societies submit to this precept varies widely: women in Egypt, Algeria, and Iraq, for instance, are well represented in the work force compared to women in Saudi Arabia or Oman. Obviously, more than religion and tradition is involved here, as is argued in Chapter 7 concerning the difference between Kuwaiti and *bidoon* women.

3. Nabil once used the word "absurd" to describe his feeling of belonging in Kuwait.

9

Postscript

The Iraqi invasion and its aftermath left the aspects covered by this study largely unchanged. For a short while, immediately after Kuwait's liberation in February 1991, the Kuwaitis were the largest ethnic group in the country;[1] the last time such a demographic structure obtained was in 1961. But already a year later, in 1992, the ethnic composition of the population had reverted to its pre-invasion state, with the number of expatriates slightly higher than that of the Kuwaitis (796,049 versus 602,000).[2] In 1995, the total population is 1.84 million as against 2.2 million in August 1990. According to the Ministry of Planning, the Kuwaitis now make up 37.2 percent, the non-Kuwaitis 56 percent, and the *bidoons* 6.8 percent of the population (Table 9.1). The initial relief which the Kuwaitis felt at being the majority in their own country was quickly swept away by the realization that the enormous tasks of tidying up and rebuilding Kuwait after the looting and wanton destruction by the occupying forces could simply not be carried out without the expatriates. The gates to labor migration were consequently flung wide open again.

TABLE 9.1   Population in Kuwait in 1995

Kuwaiti	682,000	(37.2%)
Arab expatriates	448,000	(24.5%)
Non-Arab expatriates	576,000	(31.5%)
Bidoon	124,000	(6.8%)
Total	1,840,000	

Source: Kuwait, Ministry of Planning, 1995.

TABLE 9.2   Labor Force in Kuwait in 1995

Kuwaiti	160,000	(16%)
Arab expatriates	282,000	(28.5%)
Non-Arab expatriates	524,000	(53%)
Bidoon	24,000	(3%)
Total	990,000	

Source: Kuwait, Ministry of Planning, 1995.

One thing has changed, though, and that is the ethnic composition of the non-Kuwaiti population. The expulsion of the Palestinians[3] created a vacuum that is being partly filled by another Arab national group, the Egyptians. But the most remarkable change is the switch away from Arab to Asian migrants, with the result that Asians today dominate the local labor market: 53 percent against the 47 percent made up by Kuwaitis, non-Kuwaiti Arabs, and *bidoons*[4] (Table 9.2). Kuwait has thus given up its distinctive preferential policy toward Arab manpower and has aligned itself with its Gulf neighbors. As in their case, Kuwait's Asian migrants today come overwhelmingly from India and the Philippines.

The structure of dominance articulated around the *kafala* and the politics of exclusion have also remained firmly in place. Kuwait emerged from the war with a weakened economy, which has a negative impact on the general wage level, especially for the workers in the private and domestic sectors. Far from decreasing, the Kuwaitis' perception of their own vulnerability, which lies at the root of their politics of dominance and exclusion, has been heightened by the Iraqi invasion. On the other hand, this traumatic event has considerably strengthened their national identity and brought the process of "heart-and-mind" nation-building very much forward. As a result, mechanisms such as national identification through the dress code have lost some of their significance, at least as far as the men's *dishdasha* is concerned. For the women, the situation does not seem to have changed; but then, the meaning of the *abaya* has never been entirely ethnic. Its moral message, however contested, is still the same.

Finally, the invasion brought out into the open, and in a dramatic way, the problem of the *bidoons*. Because their main function in Kuwait was to serve in the army, the *bidoons* were a prime target of the Iraqi occupiers. To survive, many stateless had to hide their identities, which led the

Kuwaitis to accuse the whole group of betrayal and collusion with the enemy. Many were expelled; a very few have found asylum in Western countries, others again were taken prisoner by the Iraqis or have defected. But, by and large, the majority have remained in Kuwait. Gradually, and seemingly for lack of alternatives, the Ministry of Defense is reinstating a number of them in the army. The plight of those who are not so fortunate, and, not least, the plight of the Kuwaiti widows of *bidoons* and their children, who inherit their fathers' stateless status and thus exist in a limbo, remain unresolved problems at the time of writing, five years after liberation. The *bidoons* epitomize the dilemmas of demography, national security, and national identity which confront not only Kuwait but all the Arabian Gulf states today. The Iraqi invasion of Kuwait has shown citizenship to be one of the most crucial problems these states urgently need to address. In Kuwait, the 1995 decision to grant suffrage to the sons of naturalized citizens is an encouraging sign, but, as the Kuwaitis themselves point out, there is still much to be done.

Notes

1. There were then 583,019 Kuwaitis in Kuwait (ASA 1993). There are no official figures for the non-Kuwaitis, but they were estimated to be less than half a million.

2. ASA 1993.

3. Around 20,000 have remained of the approximately 400,000 in Kuwait before the war.

4. Ministry of Planning, quoted in the *Arab Times*, March 25, 1995.

Bibliography

Abercrombie, N., S. Hill, and B. S. Turner. 1984. *The Dominant Ideology Thesis*. London: George Allen & Unwin.

Aberle, D. F. 1950. "The Functional Prerequisites of a Society." *Ethics* 60: 110–11.

Abu Hakima, A. M. 1982. *The Modern History of Kuwait 1750–1965*. Montreal.

Addleton, J. S. 1992. *Undermining the Centre. The Gulf Migration and Pakistan*. Karachi: Oxford University Press.

Al-Taher, I. 1995. *Kuwait—The Reality*. Pittsburgh: Dorrance Publishing Co.

Anderson, B. 1993. *Imagined Communities*. London: Verso.

Appadurai, A. 1991. "Global Ethnoscapes: Notes and Queries for a Transnational Anthropology," in R. Fox, ed., *Recapturing Anthropology*. Pp. 191–210. Santa Fe: School of American Research.

Appleyard, R. T., ed. 1989. *The Impact of International Migration on Developing Countries*. Paris: Organisation for Economic Cooperation and Development.

Arendt, H. 1958. *The Human Condition*. Chicago: University of Chicago Press.

Arnold, F., and N. Shah, eds. 1986. *Asian Labor Migration*. Boulder: Westview.

al Awadi, B. 1985. "The Legal Status of Women in Kuwait." Photocopy.

Bardawil, F. P. 1988. *Reflections of a Lebanese Businessman Living in the Gulf*. Beirut: Librairie du Liban.

Barth, F. 1984. "Problems in Conceptualizing Cultural Pluralism, With Illustrations from Sohar, Oman," in D. Maybury-Lewis, ed., *The Prospects for Plural Societies*. Pp.77–87. Washington D.C.: American Ethnological Society.

———. 1989. "The Analyses of Culture in Complex Societies." *Ethnos* 54: 120–42.

———. 1992. "Towards Greater Naturalism in Conceptualizing Societies," in A. Kuper, ed., *Conceptualizing Society*. Pp. 17–33. London: Routledge.

———. 1993. *Balinese Worlds*. Chicago: University of Chicago Press.

Barth, F., ed. 1969. *Ethnic Groups and Boundaries*. Oslo: Universitetsforlaget.

Baudrillard, J. 1976. *Le Système des Objets*. Paris: Gallimard.

Beaugé, G. 1985. "Le Rôle de l'Etat dans les Migrations de Travailleurs et la Diversification Economique des Pays de la Péninsule Arabe," in G. Beaugé, ed., "Les Migrations Internationales au Moyen-Orient," Special Issue, *Revue Tiers-Monde* 103: 597–620.

———. 1986. "La Kafala: Un Système de Gestion Transitoire de la Main-d'Oeuvre et du Capital dans les Pays du Golfe." *Revue Européenne des Migrations Internationales* 2 (1): 109–22.

Benedict, B. 1962. "Stratification in Plural Societies." *American Anthropologist* 64: 1235–46.

Berger, P. 1964. *The Human Shape of Work*. New York: Macmillan.

Berger, P., and T. Luckmann. 1981. *The Social Construction of Reality*. London: Penguin.

Berman, M. 1988. *All That is Solid Melts into Air*. New York: Penguin.

Bhabha, H. 1991. *Nation and Narration*. London: Routledge.

Birks, J. S., and C. A. Sinclair. 1980. *International Migration and Development in the Arab Region*. Geneva: International Labor Office.

Blauner, R. 1964. *Alienation and Freedom*. Chicago: University of Chicago Press.

Bonacich, E. 1972. "A Theory of Ethnic Antagonism: The Split Labor Market." *American Sociological Review* 5: 533–47.

Borofski, R., ed. 1993. *Assessing Cultural Anthropology*. New York: McGraw-Hill.

Bouhdiba, A. 1985. *Sexuality in Islam*. London: Routledge & Kegan Paul.

Bourdieu, P. 1977. *Outline of a Theory of Practice*. Cambridge: Cambridge University Press.

Braithwaite, L. 1960. "Social Stratification and Cultural Pluralism," in V. Rubin, ed., *Social and Cultural Pluralism in the Caribbean*. Pp. 816–36. *Annals of the New York Academy of Sciences*, vol. 83, art. 5: 761–916.

Brand, L. A. 1988. *Palestinians in the Arab World*. New York: Columbia University Press.

Bulloch, J. 1984. *The Gulf: A Portrait of Kuwait, Qatar, Bahrain and the UAE*. London: Century Publishing.

Burgat, F. 1995. *L'Islamisme en Face*. Paris: La Découverte.

Buttimer, A., and D. Seamon, eds. 1980. *The Human Experience of Space and Time*. London: Croom Helm.

Carré, O. 1993. *L'Islam Laïque ou le Retour à la Grande Tradition*. Paris: Armand Colin.

Castles, S., and G. Kosack. 1973. *Immigrant Workers and Class Structure in Western Europe*. London: Institute of Race Relations. Oxford University Press.

Chandadvarkar, A. G. 1980. "Use of Migrants Remittances in Labor-Exporting Countries." *Finance and Development* 17 (2): 36–9.

Clifford, J. 1986. "Introduction: Partial Truths," in J. Clifford and G. E. Marcus, eds., *Writing Culture*. Pp. 1–26. Berkeley: University of California Press.

_____. 1988. *The Predicament of Culture*. Cambridge: Harvard University Press.

Cohen, A. 1974. *Urban Ethnicity*. ASA Monographs, No.12. London: Tavistock.

_____. 1974. *Two-dimensional Man*. Berkeley: University of California Press.

Cole, J. R., and N. R. Keddie, eds. 1986. *Shi`ism and Social Protest*. New Haven: Yale University Press.

Colson, E. 1984. "The Reordering of Experience: Anthropological Involvement with Time." *Journal of Anthropological Research* 40 (1): 1–13.

Committee for the Support of the Stateless. 1991. Photocopy ms. distributed in Kuwait in April, after the liberation of Kuwait.

Crystal, J. 1990. *Oil and Politics in the Gulf: Rulers and Merchants in Kuwait and Qatar.* Cambridge: Cambridge University Press.

_____. 1992. *Kuwait. The Transformation of an Oil State.* Boulder: Westview.

Darwiche, F. 1986. *The Gulf Stock Exchange Crack.* London: Croom Helm.

Deliège, R. 1992. "Replication and Consensus: Untouchability, Caste and Ideology in India." *Man* 27 (1): 155–73.

Devons, E., and M. Gluckman. 1964. "Introduction," in M. Gluckman, ed., *Closed Systems and Open Minds: The Limits of Naivety in Social Anthropology.* Pp. 13–19. Edinburgh: Oliver & Boyd.

Dib, G. 1978. "Migration and Naturalization Laws in Egypt, Lebanon, Syria, Jordan, Kuwait, and the United Arab Emirates." *Population Bulletin* (ECWA). Part I: 15 (1978): 33–62. Part II: 15 (1979): 3–18.

Dickson, H. R. P. 1951. *The Arab of the Desert.* London: George Allen & Unwin.

Dickson, V. 1978. *Forty Years in Kuwait.* London: George Allen & Unwin.

Durkheim, E. 1985 [1893]. "The Division of Labour in Society," in *Readings from Emile Durkheim.* Chichester: Ellis Horwood.

Eades, J., ed. 1987. *Migrants, Workers, and the Social Order.* ASA Monographs, No. 26. London: Tavistock.

Eelens, F., T. Schampers, and J. D. Speckmann, eds. 1992. *Labour Migration to the Middle East. From Sri Lanka to the Gulf.* London: Kegan Paul International.

Epstein, A. L. 1978. *Ethos and Identity.* London: Tavistock.

Eriksen, T. H. 1991. "The Cultural Contexts of Ethnic Differences." *Man* 26: 127–44.

_____. 1992. *Us and Them in Modern Societies.* Oslo: Universitetsforlaget.

Esman, M. J., and I. Rabinovitch, eds. 1988. *Ethnicity, Pluralism and the State in the Middle East.* Ithaca: Cornell University Press.

al Essa, S. Y. 1981. *The Manpower Problem in Kuwait.* London: Kegan Paul.

Fabian, J. 1983. *Time and the Other.* New York: Columbia University Press.

Featherstone, M., ed. 1992. *Global Culture.* London: Sage Publications.

Field, M. 1984. *The Merchants.* London: John Murray.

Foster, R. J. 1991. "Making National Cultures in the Global Ecumene." *Annual Review of Anthropology* 20: 235–60.

Frank, A. G. 1967. *Capitalism and Underdevelopment in Latin America.* New York: Monthly Review Press.

Furnivall, J. S. 1942. "The Political Economy of the Tropical Far East." *Asian Affairs* 29: 195–210.

_____. 1976 [1944]. *Netherlands India. A Study of Plural Economy.* Amsterdam: B. M. Israel BV.

_____. 1948. *Colonial Policy and Practice*. Cambridge: Cambridge University Press.

Gaitskell, D., and E. Unterhalter. 1989. "Mothers of the Nation: A Comparative Analysis of Nation, Race and Motherhood in Afrikaaner Nationalism and the African National Congress," in N. Yuval-Davis and F. Anthias, eds., *Woman–Nation-State*. Pp. 58–78. Basingstoke: Macmillan.

Garfinkel, H. 1967. *Studies in Ethnomethodology*. Englewood Cliff, New Jersey: Prentice-Hall.

Gaventa, J. 1980. *Power and Powerlessness*. Oxford: Clarendon Press.

Geertz, C. 1973. "The Integrative Revolution: Primordial Sentiments and Civil Politics in New States," in C. Geertz, ed., *The Interpretation of Culture*. Pp. 255–310. New York: Basic Books.

Gellner, E. 1981. *Muslim Society*. Cambridge University Press.

Gerner, D. 1985. "Petro-Dollar Recycling: Imports, Arms, Investment and Aid." *Arab Studies Quarterly* 7 (1): 1–26.

Ghabra, S. 1987. *Palestinians in Kuwait*. Boulder: Westview.

Giddens, A. 1979. *Central Problems in Social Theory*. London: Macmillan.

_____. 1984. *The Constitution of Society*. Cambridge: Polity Press.

_____. 1991. *Modernity and Self-Identity*. Cambridge: Polity Press.

Glasser, R. 1970. *Leisure—Penalty or Prize?* London: Macmillan.

Go, S., and L. Postrado. 1986. "Filipino Overseas Contract Workers: Their Families and Communities," in F. Arnold and N. Shah, eds., *Asian Labor Migration*. Pp.125–44. Boulder: Westview.

Goffman, E. 1959. *The Presentation of Self in Everyday Life*. London: Penguin Books.

Goody, J. 1992. "Culture and Its Boundaries: A European View." *Social Anthropology*, vol. 1, 1A August 1992: 9–32.

Gramsci, A. 1971. *Selections from the Prison Notebooks*. London: Lawrence & Wishart.

Gupta, A., and J. Ferguson. 1992. "Beyond 'Culture': Space, Identity and the Politics of Difference." *Cultural Anthropology* 7 (1): 6–23.

Gunatilleke, G., ed. 1986. *Migration of Asian Workers to the Arab World*. Tokyo: The United Nations University Press.

al Haddad, M. 1981. *The Effects of Detribalization and Sedentarization on the Socio-economic Structure of the Tribes of the Arabian Peninsula*. Unpublished dissertation, University of Kansas.

_____. 1985. "Ethnic Groups and Ethnic Stratification in Kuwait City," in Aidan Southall, Peter J. M. Nas, and Ghaus Ansari, eds., *City and Society*. Pp. 105–26. Leiden: Institute of Cultural and Social Studies.

Hannertz, U. 1992a. "The Global Ecumene as a Network of Networks," in Adam Kuper, ed., *Conceptualizing Society*. Pp. 34–58. London: Routledge.

_____. 1992b. *Cultural Complexity: Studies in the Social Organization of Meaning*. New York: Columbia University Press.

Hansen, K. T. 1989. *Distant Companions*. Ithaca: Cornell University Press.

_____. Forthcoming. "Part of the household inventory: Men servants in Zambia."

Hattox, R. S. 1985. *Coffee and Coffeehouses*. Seattle: University of Washington Press.

van Hear, N. 1992. *Migrant Workers in the Gulf*. London: Minority Rights Group International.

Heikal, M. 1992. *Illusions of Triumph*. London: Harper Collins Publishers.

Hitti, P. 1970. *History of the Arabs*. London: The Macmillan Press.

Hobsbawm, E., and T. Ranger, eds. 1992. *The Invention of Tradition*. Cambridge: Cambridge University Press.

Hourani, A. 1991. *A History of the Arab People*. London: Faber and Faber.

Ibn Khaldun. 1967. *The Muqaddimah*. London: Routledge & Kegan Paul.

Inalcik, H., and D. Quatært, eds. 1994. *An Economic and Social History of the Ottoman Empire, 1300–1914*. Cambridge: Cambridge University Press.

International Labor Office. 1990. *Rapport du Directeur Général: Travailleurs Migrants Touchés par la Crise du Golfe*. Geneva: ILO.

_____. 1991. *Rapport Informel sur les Travailleurs Migrants Touchés par la Crise du Golfe*. Geneva: ILO.

Ingold, T., ed. 1990. *The Concept of Society is Theoretically Obsolete*. Manchester: Group for Debates in Anthropological Theory.

Ismael, J. 1982. *Kuwait. Social Change in Historical Perspective*. New York: Syracuse University Press.

Izzard, M. 1979. *The Gulf. Arabia's Western Approaches*. London: John Murray.

Jenkins, R. 1986. "Social Anthropological Models of Inter-Ethnic Relations," in J. Rex, and D. Mason, eds., *Theories of Race and Race Relations*. Pp. 170–86. Cambridge: Cambridge University Press.

Joseph, S. 1993. "Gender and Civil Society. An Interview with Suad Joseph." *Middle East Report* 183: 22–6.

Joukhadar, A. 1980. "Les Étrangers au Koweit." *Population* 1: 57–82.

Kanafani, G. 1978. *Men in the Sun and Other Palestinian Stories*. London: Heinemann Educational Press.

Kandiyoti, D. 1989. "Women and the Turkish State: Political Actors or Symbolic Pawns?" in N. Yuval-Davis, and F. Anthias, eds., *Woman–Nation–State*. Pp. 126–49. Basingstoke: Macmillan.

_____. 1991. "Identity and Its Discontents: Women and the Nation." *Millenium* 20 (3): 429–44.

Kassim, A. F. 1986. "Joint Venturing in Kuwait. Company Law Explained." *Arab Law Quarterly* 1: 432–5.

Kearney, M. 1986. "From the Invisible Hand to Invisible Feet: Anthropological Studies of Migration and Development." *American Review of Anthropology* 15: 331–61.

Khaled, L. 1973. *My People Shall Live*. London: Hodder and Stoughton.

Khouja, M. W., and P. G. Sadler. 1979. *The Economy of Kuwait*. London: Macmillan.

Khoury, P. S., and J. Kostiner, eds. 1991. *Tribes and State Formation in the Middle East*. Berkeley: University of California Press.

Korale, R. B. M. 1986. "Migration for Employment in the Middle East: Its Demographic and Socioeconomic Effects on Sri Lanka," in F. Arnold and N. Shah, eds., *Asian Labor Migration*. Pp. 194–212. Boulder: Westview.

Kuper, L. 1969. "Ethnic and Racial Pluralism: Some Aspects of Polarization and Depluralization," in L. Kuper, and M. G. Smith, eds., *Pluralism in Africa*. Berkeley: University of California Press.

Kuper, L., and M. G. Smith, eds. 1969. *Pluralism in Africa*. Berkeley: University of California Press.

Lawyers Committee for Human Rights. 1992. *Building the Rule of Law. Human Rights in Kuwait after Occupation*. New York.

Leach, E. R. 1954. *Political Systems in Highland Burma*. London: Bell.

LeBaron B. R. 1951. "The Pearl Fisheries in the Persian Gulf." *The Middle East Journal* 5: 161–80.

Lévi-Strauss, C. 1966. *The Savage Mind*. London: Weidenfeld and Nicolson.

Lienhardt, P. 1993. *Disorientations: A Society in Flux: Kuwait in the 1950s*. Reading: Ithaca Press.

Longuenesse, E. 1985. "Les Migrants dans la Structure Sociale des Pays du Golfe," in A. Bourgey et al., eds., *Migrations et Changements Sociaux dans l'Orient Arabe*. Pp. 169–213. Beirut: Centre d'Etudes et de Recherches sur le Moyen Orient Contemporain (CERMOC).

Lorimer, J. G. 1970 [1915]. *Gazetteer of the Persian Gulf, Oman and Central Arabia*. Westmead: Gregg.

Lukes, S. 1974. *Power. A Radical View*. London: Macmillan.

Malinowski, B. 1922. *Argonauts of the Western Pacific*. London: Routledge & Kegan Paul.

Malkki, L. 1992. "National Geographic: The Rooting of Peoples and the Territorialization of National Identity Among Scholars and Refugees." *Cultural Anthropology* 7 (1): 24–43.

Marx, K. 1977. *Capital*. Moscow: Progress Publishers.

Mernissi, F. 1983. *Beyond the Veil: Male–Female Dynamics in Modern Muslim Society*. London: Saqi Books.

Middle East Watch. 1992. *Punishing the Victim. Rape and Mistreatment of Asian Maids in Kuwait*. New York.

Miliband, R. 1969. *The State in Capitalist Society*. London: Weidenfeld and Nicolson.

Mitchell, J. C. 1956. *The Kalela Dance*. Manchester: Manchester University Press.

_____. 1974. "Perception of Ethnicity and Ethnic Behaviour: An Empirical Exploration," in A. Cohen, ed., *Urban Ethnicity*. Pp. 1–36. ASA Monographs 12. London: Tavistock.

Moffat, M. 1979. *An Untouchable Community in South India*. Princeton: Princeton University Press.

Momen, M. 1985. *An Introduction to Shi`i Islam*. New Haven: Yale University Press.

Moore, S. F. 1993. "The Ethnography of the Present and the Analysis of Process," in R. Borofski, ed., *Assessing Cultural Anthropology*. New York: McGraw-Hill.

Morris, H. S. 1956. "Indians in East Africa: A Study of Plural Society." *British Journal of Sociology* 7 (3): 194–211.

_____. 1967. "Some Aspects of the Concept of Plural Society." *Man* 2 (2): 169–84.

al Moosa, A. R. 1986. "Stability of the Foreign Labour Force in Kuwait." *The Arab Gulf Journal* 6 (1): 53–6.

_____. 1987. "Factors Affecting Residency of Immigrant Workers in Kuwait." *The Arab Journal of Social Sciences* 2 (2): 283–306.

al Moosa, A. R., and K. McLachlan. 1985. *Immigrant Labour in Kuwait*. London: Croom Helm.

al Mughni, H. 1993. *Women in Kuwait. The Politics of Gender*. London: Saqi Books.

Nagi, M. 1982. "Labor Migration and Development in the Middle East: Problems and Policies." *International Review of Modern Sociology* 12: 185–210.

Nancy, M. 1985. "Du Liban vers le Golfe: deux cas de migration villageoise," in A. Bourgey et al., eds., *Migration et Changements Sociaux dans l'Orient Arabe*. Pp. 85–189. Beirut: CERMOC.

al-Naqeeb, K. 1990. *Society and State in the Gulf and Arab Peninsula*. London: Routledge.

Nath, K. 1982. "Education and Employment Among Kuwaiti Women," in L. Beck, and N. Keddie, eds., *Women in the Muslim World*. Pp. 172–88. Cambridge: Harvard University Press.

Ortner, S. 1984. "Theory in Anthropology Since the Sixties." *Society for the Comparative Study of Society and History* 26 (1): 126–65.

Pant, G. 1987. "Indo-Gulf Economic Relations: A Profile." *International Studies* 24(3): 177–207.

Parker, S. 1983. *Leisure and Work*. London: Allen & Unwin.

Parsons, T. 1967. *The Social System*. London: Routledge & Kegan Paul.

Ramazani, N. 1988. "Islamic Fundamentalism and the Women of Kuwait." *Middle East Insight*, Jan./Feb.: 21–5.

Rex, J., and D. Mason, eds. 1986. *Theories of Race and Ethnic Relations*. Cambridge: Cambridge University Press.

Roseberry, W. 1992. *Anthropologies and Histories*. New Brunswick: Rutgers University Press.

Rihani, A. 1983 [1930]. *Around the Coasts of Arabia*. New York: Caravan Books.

Robertson, R. 1992. *Globalization*. London: Sage Publications.

Rosaldo, R. 1988. "Ideology, Place, and People Without Culture." *Cultural Anthropology* 3 (1): 77–87.

Roy, O. 1994. *The Failure of Political Islam*. London: I. B. Tauris.

Rubin, V., ed. 1960. "Social and Cultural Pluralism in the Caribbean." *Annals of the New York Academy of Sciences*, vol. 83 (5): 761–916.

Rumaihi, M. 1986. *Beyond Oil*. London: Saqi Books.

Russell, S. S. 1986. "Remittances From International Migration: A Review in Perspective." *World Development* 14 (6): 677–96.

_____. 1989a. "Politics and Ideology in Migration Policy Formulation: The Case of Kuwait." *International Migration Review* 23 (1): 24–47.

_____. 1989b. "Migration and Political Integration in the Arab World," in G. Luciani, ed., *The Arab State*. Pp. 373–93. London: Routledge.

_____. 1992. "International Migration and Political Turmoil in the Middle East." *Population and Development Review* 18 (4): 719–27.

_____. 1995. "International Migration Policies and the Status of Female Migrants." Proceedings of the United Nations Expert Group Meeting on International Migration Policies and the Status of Female Migrants. San Miniato, Italy, 28–31 March 1990.

Russell, S. S., and M. A. Al-Ramadhan. 1994. "Kuwait's Migration Policy Since the Gulf Crisis." *International Journal of Middle East Studies* 26: 569–87.

Rutz, H. J., ed. 1992. *The Politics of Time*. American Ethnological Society Monograph Series, No.4. Washington: American Anthropological Association.

Sahlins, M. 1985. *Islands of History*. Chicago: University of Chicago Press.

SanMiguel, V. 1978. *Pastor in Kuwait*. Kuwait: Bishop's House.

Sanad, J., and M. Tessler. 1988. "The Economic Orientations of Kuwaiti Women." *International Journal of Middle East Studies* 21: 443–68.

Sassen-Koob, S. 1981. "Towards a Conceptualization of Immigrant Labor." *Social Problems* 29 (1): 65–85.

Sayad, A. 1991. *L'Immigration ou les Paradoxes de l'Altérité*. Bruxelles: De Boek Wesmael.

Scott, J. C. 1985. *Weapons of the Weak: Everyday Forms of Peasant Resistance*. New Haven: Yale University Press.

Seccombe, I. J. 1985. "International Labor Migration in the Middle East: A Review of Literature and Research. 1974–84." *International Migration Review* 19 (2): 335–52.

_____. 1986. "Duty Shaikhs, Subcontractors, and Recruiting Agents: The Impact of the International Oil Industry on Recruitment and Employment in the Persian/Arabian Gulf, 1900–1950." *Orient* 27: 252–79, 339–40.

Shah, N. M. 1983. "Pakistani Workers in the Middle East: Volume, Trends and Consequences." *International Migration Review* 17 (3): 410–23.

_____. 1986. "Foreign Workers in Kuwait: Implications for the Kuwaiti Labor Force." *International Migration Review* 20 (4): 815–32.

Shah, N., and S. Al Qudsi. 1989. "The Changing Characteristics of Migrant Workers in Kuwait." *International Journal of Middle East Studies* 21: 31–55.

_____. 1990. "Female Work Roles in a Traditional Oil Economy: Kuwait." *Research in Human Capital and Development* 6: 213–46.

Shah, N., S. Al Qudsi, and M. A. Shah. 1991. "Asian Women Workers in Kuwait." *International Migration Review* 25(3): 464–86.

Shayegan, D. 1992. *Cultural Schizophrenia: Islamic Societies Confronting the West*. London: Saqi Books.

al Shaykh, H. 1989. *Women of Sand and Myrrh*. London: Quartet Books.

Sherbiny, N. A. 1984. "Expatriate Labor Flows to the Arab Oil Countries in the 1980s." *The Middle East Journal* 38 (4): 643–67.

Simmel, G. 1971. *Selected Writings*. Edited by Donald N. Levine. Chicago: University of Chicago Press.

Simpson, G. E., and J. M. Yinger. 1986. *Racial and Cultural Minorities*. New York: Plenum Press.

Smith, A. 1986. *State and Nation in the Third World*. Brighton: Wheatsheaf Books.

_____. 1991. *National Identity*. London: Penguin Books.

_____. 1993. *Theories of Nationalism*. New York: Holmes & Meier.

Smith, M. G. 1960. "Social and Cultural Pluralism," in V. Rubin, ed., *Social and Cultural Pluralism in the Caribbean*. Pp. 763–85. *Annals of the New York Academy of Sciences*, vol. 83 (5).

_____. 1967. *The Plural Society in the British West Indies*. Berkeley: University of California Press.

_____. 1969a. "Institutional and Political Conditions of Pluralism," in L. Kuper, and M. G. Smith, eds., *Pluralism in Africa*. Pp. 27–65. Berkeley: University of California.

_____. 1969b. "Some Developments in the Analytical Framework of Pluralism," in L. Kuper and M. G. Smith, eds., *Pluralism in Africa*. Pp. 415–58. Berkeley: University of California.

Smith, R. T. 1961. "Review of *Social and Cultural Pluralism in the Caribbean*." *American Anthropologist* 63: 155–7.

Stahl, C. W., and F. Arnold. 1986. "Overseas Workers' Remittances in Asian Development." *International Migration Review* 20 (4): 899–925.

Stoler, A. L. 1989. "Making Empire Respectable: The Politics of Race and Sexual Morality." *American Ethnologist* 16 (4): 634–60.

Strauss, C., and N. Quinn. 1993. "A Cognitive/Cultural Anthropology," in R. Borofski, ed., *Assessing Cultural Anthropology*. Pp. 284–98. New York: McGraw-Hill.

Tajfel, H., ed. 1978. *Differentiation Between Social Groups*. London: Academic Press.

Tambs-Lyche, H. 1991. "Om Etniske Stereotypiers Oppbyggning og Form." *Norsk Antropologisk Tidsskrift* 2: 141–50.

Tétrault, M. A., and H. Al Mughni. 1995. "Modernization and Its Discontents: State and Gender in Kuwait." *The Middle East Journal* 49 (3): 403–17.

Tibi, B. 1990. "The Simultaneity of the Unsimultaneous: Old Tribes and Nation-States in the Modern Middle East," in P. S. Khoury, and J. Kostiner, eds., *Tribes and State Formation in the Middle East*. Pp. 127–52. Berkeley: University of California Press.

Tilly, C. 1984. *Big Structures, Large Processes, Huge Comparisons*. New York: Russell Sage Publications.

Turner, B. S. 1990. "Outline of a Theory of Citizenship." *Sociology* 24 (2): 189–217.

Villiers, A. 1940. *Sons of Sindbad*. London: Hodder & Stoughton.

Walby, S. 1989. *Theorizing Patriarchy*. Oxford: Blackwell.

_____. 1992. "Woman and Nation." *International Journal of Comparative Sociology* 33 (1–2): 81–100.

Wikan, U. 1982. *Behind the Veil in Arabia*. Baltimore: Johns Hopkins University Press.

Wallerstein, I. 1988. "Should We Unthink the Nineteenth-Century Social Sciences?" *International Social Science Journal* 118: 527–31.

Watts, M. 1992. "Space for Everything." *Cultural Anthropology* 7 (1): 115–29.

Wilson, F. D. 1985. "Migration and Occupational Mobility." *International Migration Review* 19 (2): 278–92.

Wolf, E. 1982. *Europe and the People Without History*. Berkeley: University of California Press.

_____. 1988. "Inventing Society." *American Ethnologist* 15 (4): 752–61.

Wright, E. O. 1987. *Classes*. London: Verso.

Wright, R. 1986. *Sacred Rage*. New York: Simon & Schuster.

Wuthnow, R., J. D. Hunter, A. Bergesen, and E. Kurzweil. 1984. *Cultural Analysis*. London: Routledge & Kegan Paul.

Yuval-Davis, N., and F. Anthias, eds. 1989. *Woman–Nation-State*. Basingstoke: Macmillan.

Zubaida, S. 1989. *Islam, the People and the State*. London: I. B. Tauris.

Kuwaiti legal documents (official translations):
Aliens' Residence Law, No. 17 of 1959 and All Implementing & Amending Laws and Regulations with Latest Amendements.
Law of Commercial Companies. 1960.

New Private Sector Labour Law, No. 38 of 1964 With Amendments up to 1989.
Rent Law. Law Decree, No. 35 of 1978 Governing Real Estate Lease and Rent.

Statistical documents published by the Kuwaiti Ministry of Planning:
Annual Statistical Abstract. 1987, 1988, 1989, 1993.
Social Statistics. 1986, 1987, 1988, 1989.
Research Studies on Population (RSP). 1987:
No. 1: "Major Demographic Features of the Population of Kuwait."
No. 2: "Recent Changes in the Growth, Composition, and Sectoral Distribution
    of the Labour Force in Kuwait: 1975–1985."
No. 3: "The Changing Pattern of Migration in Kuwait."
No. 5: "Migration and Non-National Labour in GCC Countries: An Analysis of
    Trends, Patterns of Employment and Problems."

Index

About the Book and Author

When Iraq invaded Kuwait in 1990, the sight of tens of thousands of non-Kuwaiti Arabs, Indians, East Asians, and Westerners fleeing or trapped under occupation made the outside world suddenly aware of a singular fact of Kuwaiti society—that Kuwaitis are an absolute minority in their own country. Basing her analysis on extensive fieldwork and archival research, the author examines the social dimension of labor migration to Kuwait since independence in 1961, exploring how the presence of over one million foreign workers has influenced the way Kuwaitis organize their lives and perceive themselves. In particular, Longva looks at the relations between two sharply differentiated social categories and the politics of exclusion that have allowed Kuwaitis to protect their rights and privileges as citizens against infringement by the huge influx of expatriates. Longva examines the little-studied system of kafala, or sponsorship, under which all foreign workers enter and reside in the country, showing how it has become the most critical source of power for native Kuwaitis vis-à-vis immigrants. She also addresses aspects of ethnicity and class, describes the life of expatriates, and looks at developments in gender relations and the role of women in building the national identity in the context of migration and modernization.

Anh Nga Longva is associate professor of social anthropology at the University of Bergen, Norway.